The MANUAL of COLOUR BREEDING

Parrakeets, Lovebirds, Cockatiels and other Parrots

Including
Universal Breeding Programmes

JIM HAYWARD

Published 1992 by The Aviculturist Publications
Carterton Breeding Aviaries
Brize Norton Road
Carterton Oxford
ENGLAND

© Copyright 1992 J. & P. Hayward
ISBN 0-9519098-0-0

DEDICATION & ACKNOWLEDGMENT
To the bird breeders and traders in Britain, Germany, Holland,
Belgium, Denmark, Sweden, Spain, Australia, Singapore, USA, India
and South Africa who have generously sent photographs, slides,
breeding results, descriptions and information over the many years
of preparation which have at last culminated in this manual.

CONTENTS

The Pairings and Universal Breeding Programmes can be modified for use with Colour Varieties of:
Budgerigars, Canaries, Zebra Finches, Bengalese, Gouldians, Parrot Finches, all other Grass Finches, Diamond Doves, Pigeons, Quail, Waterfowl, British Finches and Softbills, Game Birds, Bantams and larger Poultry.
Any avian species which has – or develops – a selection of Primary Colour Varieties.

THE BIRDS ON THE COVER
From top left:
Lutino Alexandrine Parrakeet, Roseino Roseate Cockatoo,
Cinnamon Pearl Pied White-faced Cockatiel,
Blue Masked Lovebird and Lavender Peach-faced Lovebird.

INTRODUCTION

THE WIDESPREAD culture of psittacine colour varieties is recent in comparison with the long established Budgerigar and Canary fancies. In the late nineteen-fifties the only varieties regularly available to British aviculturists seemed to be Blue Masked Lovebirds and 'Yellow' Red-rumped Parrakeets, and these were very expensive for the times. Through the 'sixties and 'seventies, specialist breeders all over the world had the forethought to use their skills in successfully building strains of both spectacular and subtle mutation colours in several species. This has lead to a wide and growing selection of varieties being available to the enthusiast of the nineteen-nineties. When the first examples of these rarities came onto the open market their prices were astronomic, but now - in some cases - they are so widely bred as to be no more expensive than their wild-type counterparts.

It became obvious that many of the popular names given to these new varieties would be the root of much confusion as more and more new mutations burst forth, and were used to create combination and compound varieties. In order to clear away the incorrect terms and ambiguities that had been created, a system of naming which provided a logical framework for the future and replaced the existing muddle with clarity and conciseness was desperately needed.

Throughout the 'eighties the writer promoted the use of a basic naming system which would fit the bill, and - for the greater part - this has been accepted in Britain. No ingenious alternatives which would lead to improvement have been presented throughout the intervening years, therefore the original concept has been refined and expanded to allow for use with the latest colour mutations in several psittacine genera - so creating a Universal Naming System.

Now when breeders of Lovebirds, Cockatiels, Indian Ringnecks, Grass Parrakeets and Rosellas are in conversation they might speak simply of: a 'Dilute', instead of: a 'Golden Cherry', a 'Silver', a 'Buttercup', a 'Yellow' or a 'Pastel' - names which are all used to describe the same type of pigment effect in the species mentioned. Grass Parrakeet breeders will be clearly understood by others if a 'White-breasted' Splendid is properly described as a 'Blue', and those Splendids previously incorrectly described as 'Blue' are correctly referred to as 'Marine'. Ground colours in combination with Ino can now be clearly signified as Albino, Ivorino, Creamino, Lutino or Roseino, and Grey can be distinguished from the Dark Factor so that Greygreen is not confused with Olive Green.

This manual has been written primarily to provide pairings and breeding programmes which will be easy for the beginner as well as the experienced breeder to apply to the particular species which they choose to keep. Explanations of genetic theory have been presented in more than one way, to help the beginner fully understand the subject; but even if it takes some time to assimilate this information, the pairings and programmes can be used straightaway - as long as the instructions which accompany them are carried out carefully. Sections 4, 5, 6, and 7 should provide sufficient initial information for the breeder to make full use of the programmes in section 8.

This manual differs from publications that merely provide lists of pairings and expectations; instead, it gives clear suggestions and instructions for programmes which lead to definite goals, and these season by season Universal Breeding Programmes can be entered at the stage at which the necessary birds are held. In conjunction with the provision of Inheritance Codes, the Universal Naming System and Universal Breeding Programmes contained in this book provide a sound working base from which colour breeding can be launched into the 21st century.

1

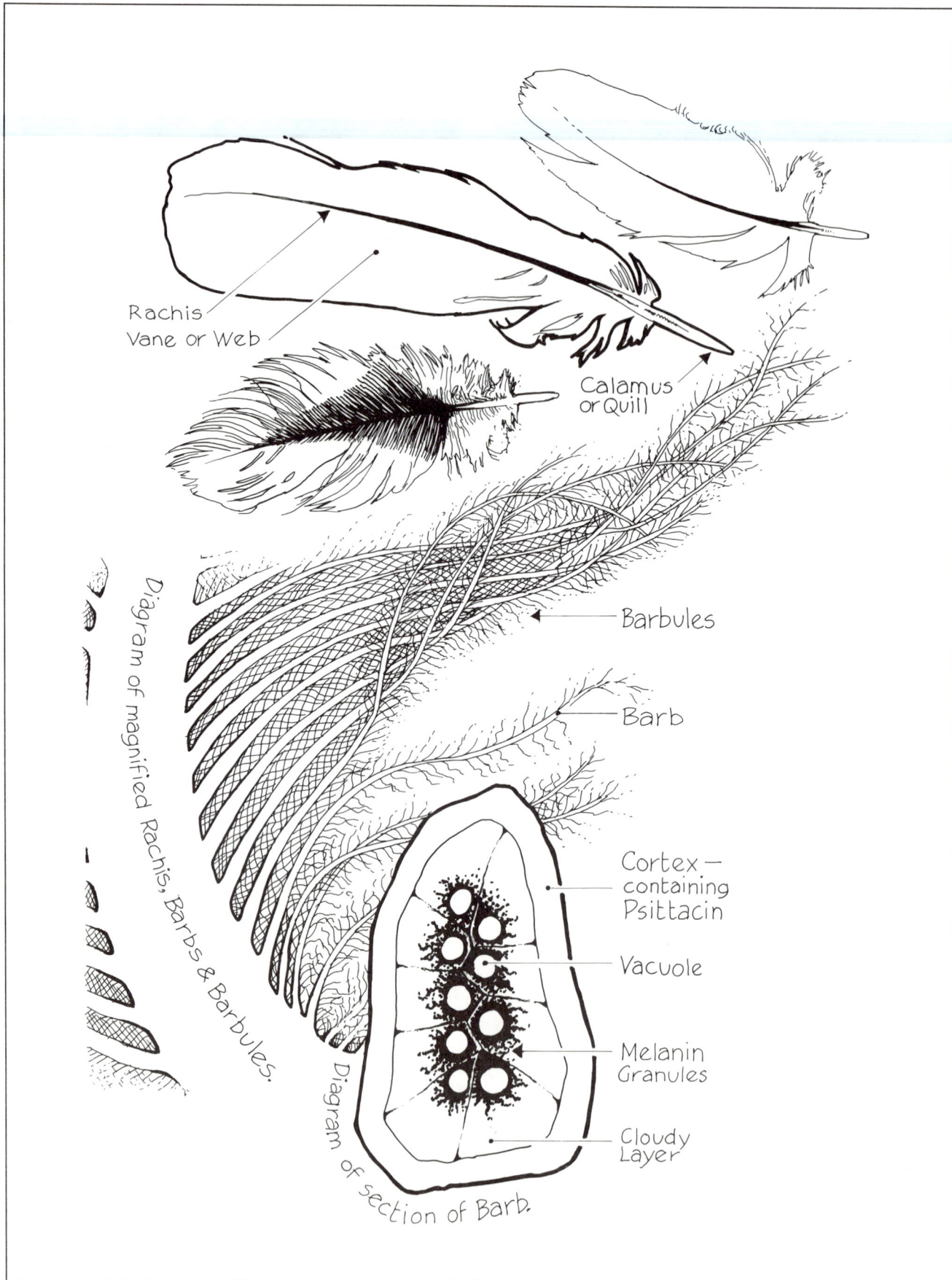

Rachis

Vane or Web

Calamus
or Quill

Diagram of magnified Rachis, Barbs & Barbules.

Barbules

Barb

Diagram of section of Barb.

Cortex —
containing
Psittacin

Vacuole

Melanin
Granules

Cloudy
Layer

Diagram 1: The Feather

1

COLOUR IN PARROTS

THE CREATION OF COLOUR IN PARROTS

COLOUR IN the plumage of the most brilliantly clothed of the parrots seems so solid, it is hard to believe that blues - and in consequence greens - are the result of what amounts to an optical illusion, and that no actual pigment of a blue or green colour is involved. The feather consists of a central shaft with the vane flaring out from opposite sides; the vane is made up of two rows of *barbs* and these are held together - in most cases - by tiny hooked *barbules*. It is the barbs which provide the greater part of the colour in a bird's plumage, with a minor contribution coming from the barbules.

The inner core of each barb is known as the *medulla* and the outer layer known as the *cortex*. Between the most inner part of the medulla and the cortex is sandwiched a spongy area of translucent protein based material which is honeycombed with microscopic air bubbles *(some say intertwined cylindrical shapes)* - this is known as the *cloudy layer*. Because of their varying purposes, feather barbs which come off feathers from different parts of the bird's body differ in thickness and shape, and their medulli are constructed of cells of various formations which are arranged in suitable configurations. Each cell within the medulla has a hollow sphere, or air bubble - a *vacuole*. This cellular construction provides strength and rigidity where needed, but still makes the whole structure light and buoyant. The various components of the feather differ between adult and immature birds in thickness.

The plumage, skin, nails, bills and eyes of birds are coloured in ways that have been evolved as the best camouflage within a given habitat, the best attraction for a mate, as a warning of danger, protection from the elements and so on. Parrots have at least two separate types of pigments in their feathers (blacks and browns, and reds and yellows) which, when combined with an optical effect, are capable of producing every colour in the rainbow - as far as many species are concerned. Anyone who is familiar with the many genera of psittacine birds will know of the vast array of colours and feather textures they are capable of displaying - but they may also be endowed with strange hues that we humans will never be able to even imagine.

According to the biologists at London University, Queen Mary College and University College Dublin (1988), we are all colour blind in comparison with birds and even some fish. Their research has found that, while humans are receptive to three channels of colour - red, green and blue - birds are also sensitive to ultra violet light, which gives them *four* colour channels. So, plumage which looks dull to us could be of a flashing brilliance to the prospective mates of the birds themselves.

Melanin Pigment

The vacuoles in each cell of the medulla are drawn towards the central core of the barb, and around these cluster granules of black and brown pigment. These pigments are known collectively as *melanin* and are to be found in many other creatures apart from birds, the human race included. In black feathers, melanin is situated not only in the medulla but also in part of the cortex; in green, blue, purple and maroon feathers, the melanin is generally confined much more to the medulla; in white, yellow, pink and light red feathers, melanin is either totally absent or present only in a negligible amount.

Melanin is a protein which is manufactured by the bird's specialized epidermal cells *(melanocytes)* from *tyrosine* - an essential amino acid - via several stages of a biochemical process involving a number of separate enzymes. The manufacture of melanin can be halted at any one of these various stages if the necessary enzymes are not all present - this may result in a change in number and size of the granules and a difference in plumage colour. If the amino acid *lysine* is absent from the diet, the process cannot even be initiated; this means that feathers will be lacking in blacks and browns and drastically different from their normal colour. Once lysine is again introduced by offering a full and varied diet, the new feathers grown after the moult will have regained their usual shade.

Birds affected in this way develop what seem to be Pied characteristics, with a showing of yellow and white feathers, and this persuades their owners that a new variety has erupted. A restoration to normality after the amino acid imbalance has been corrected rules out this possibility.

Just one of the most likely purposes of melanin could be related to the assimilation of calcium. Vitamin D is produced in a creature as a direct result of sunlight playing on its skin, fur, or feathers, and this vitamin is essential in the absorption of calcium into the creature's system. Too much vitamin D means that too much calcium will be absorbed and this could lead to calcification of kidneys and joints. In humans, it has been proved that a white man produces a great deal more vitamin D than a black man when exposed for an equal amount of time to the ultra violet light in the sun's rays. A black skin is plentiful in melanin pigment and would be beneficial in the sunny tropical areas of the world as a block against too much vitamin D, whereas a white skin is helpful in colder gloomier regions as an aid towards maximising the amount of vitamin D produced.

It is known that parrots are subject to the same process, and there are few species without a large supply of melanin carried in their plumage. This does nothing to explain those few species with a majority of melanin free plumage. It may simply mean that some lead a more secretive life amidst dense foliage where they are sheltered a great deal from the glare of the sun, but this still does not explain away such birds as the Australian 'white' cockatoos being apparently unprotected from possible calcification in their more open habitat.

Races of the same species of psittacine are often differentiated by the amount of melanin in their plumage; those from cloudier coastal areas may have lighter, brighter colours, while those whose habitat is inland and consequently more arid and sunny, may have a darker and glossier covering of feathers. In birds with highly iridescent plumage - like tropical starlings - the barbules lack 'hooks' and each is turned on its axis so that it becomes reflective and creates a metallic sheen; however, flight feathers lack this feature, otherwise they would be useless for their purpose - the barbs could not hold the web together.

According to the experts, where psittacines are concerned, only one type of melanin pigment exists; the differing shades from black to pale brown being caused by the melanin granules becoming smaller and fewer. Even so, canary experts have found that three different types of melanin exist in this species and name them as *phaeomelanin brown*, *eumelanin brown* and *eumelanin black* - these terms are also used to describe pigment in other finches. It still may be proved in the future that a similarly more extensive range of melanin types exists in psittacines.

Carotenoid Pigment

In many species of birds, the red and yellow colours are provided by carotenoid pigment contained in the vegetable matter in their diet; the brilliant hues of finches and weavers are obtained in this way and the pigment accumulates or is assimilated into the cortex of the feather barbs. Carotenoid pigment is oil soluble and gives colour to such diverse things as carrots, tomatoes, egg yolk, starfishes and prawns. There are exceptions to this method of attaining red and yellow colour. For example, in some cases melanin itself can present a dull yellow colour. The crimson flight feathers of Touracos contain a unique copper containing pigment known as *turacin* which can be extracted by soaking the feathers in a solution of water and alkali. The Great Indian Hornbill 'paints' the white feathers in its wings yellow by rubbing its bill on the preen gland at the base of its tail and then wiping the oil onto its plumage; the bird's preen gland produces an oil rich in carotenoid pigment.

For their rich colour, Flamingoes and Scarlet Ibis depend on a diet which includes small crustaceans such as shrimps, but they also take in amounts of green algae as they feed, and this too contains carotenoid pigment. In aviculture, so as to prevent their beautiful plumage from fading, they have to be colour fed with ground shrimp, muscles, cockles and/or carrot oil. Therefore, carotenoid colour of this type is not manufactured in the bird's system like melanin; but it is able to undergo mild chemical change. The yellow carotenoid in a Canary's feathers is known by breeders as *lipochrome* and can be turned red-orange by feeding the bird red pepper (paprika) or other colour foods just before the moult.

Psittacin Pigment
The yellow and red colour of psittacine birds – also seated in the cortex – is not of the same nature as these previously mentioned carotenoids. As far as is known, its chemical make-up and origin still remain to be discovered. Unlike finches, parrots cannot be colour fed with vegetable carotenoid, but it has been reported that South American Indians feed pet parrots with some kind of fish oil which changes any yellow plumage to orange or red. When such birds moult the colour does not disappear, but is reproduced in the new feathers without the need for a second dose of fish oil. This suggests that irreversible damage or change is caused to the source of the process of yellow pigment production. Also, by rubbing the liquid from the skin of certain frogs or toads into the holes left after quills have been drawn, Amerindians are said to be able to bring about a permanent change of green plumage to yellow or orange.

Tyndall Scattering
As has been said, blue pigment is non existent in a parrot's plumage, and the blue colour we see is caused by *Tyndall scattering.* The Tyndall effect can be seen in the blue of the sky (which is caused through the scattering of light by particles in the atmosphere), in bubbles and droplets of water. 'White' light is made up of all colours of the rainbow and can be split into its component colours by optical systems; a demonstration can be easily made by using a prism which separates them into their various wave lengths. Long wave length light is red, and short wave length light is blue. Blue is reflected when the depth and structure of the cloudy layer within the feather barb is ideal for returning short wave light from the white light passing through. When blue is reflected through yellow pigment, then green colour is created. If the cloudy layer is narrow, or made narrower and becomes devoid of air bubbles through mutation, then blue can be lost and replaced by grey; grey reflected through yellow creates greygreen.

In birds such as the canary and its closest relatives there is no Tyndall effect, only *structural colour;* a greenish effect is created by *apposition;* melanin rich barbules alternate with barbules lacking melanin but containing yellow pigment to create the illusion of a greenish colour. Blue-grey is created by melanin rich barbules alternating with barbules lacking both melanin and yellow pigment.

In psittacines, short wave length light (blue) bounces back through the cloudy layer off the melanin granules within the medulla, and is modified in its tone by the varying density of the melanin. In addition, it is modified by the pigment held in the cortex – through which it has to pass and re-pass.

Three Colour Components
So – there are three basic components contained within a parrot's feathering which ultimately determine the colours we see. Firstly the content of pigment within the medulla, secondly the structure of the cloudy layer, and thirdly the content of pigment within the cortex. All of these things can be altered to a very

great extent, and this has an important influence on the range of colour within a bird's plumage. Age can cause alteration, saturation with water can negate the Tyndall effect, and the fine powder made by the down feather can bring about a slightly paler tone and make plumage matt instead of glossy. In species which produce a lot of powder down – like the white cockatoos – this might also act as a 'sun block' to offset harmful calcification, as well as acting as a lubricant to prevent wear on feathers as they rub across each other during flight.

Yellow and Buff

The general fraying, wear and tear of feathers as the bird approaches the moult causes a loss in colour and condition; many parrots show signs of a slight bleaching or withdrawal of normally brilliant colour just before they moult. Canary breeders are familiar with another modifying factor on colour to do with the construction of the feather; *yellow* or *buff* type feathering brings about a concentration of colour in the former and a toning down of colour in the latter. *Yellow* feathering is harder, coarser and more stringy with less underdown, while *buff* feathering is thicker and more luxuriant in its texture with a heavy underdown. These differing types of feather are found in other cage and aviary birds beside canaries, and there seems no reason why they should not be found in psittacines.

Brilliance

Parrots with an overall glossy plumage can be selectively bred to maintain, or even slightly increase, this harder feather. Birds with iridescent patches of feathering are possible subjects for enhancement in these areas. For example, the facial areas of Turquoisine or Splendid Grass Parrakeets, which at night in torchlight appear almost luminous.

However, the most dramatic alterations to be brought about in a parrot's plumage are through *mutation* and this is a most fascinating and popular aspect of breeding psittacine birds.

Sexual Dimorphism – Monomorphism

In some species of psittacine bird, the identification of the sexes is made easy by outstanding differences in plumage colour and pattern – and in the colour of eyes and bills. These species can be further segregated into two main groups; in the first, sexual differences are obvious even in the fledglings (e.g. Red-rumped Parrakeet), and in the second, sexual differences are not made obvious until the young attain adult plumage – which may be in their second, third or even fourth year (e.g. Cockatiel, Indian Ringneck Parrakeet, Roseate Cockatoo). Both these groups are described as *Sexually Dimorphic*.

Though other parrot species may show slight differences in head, bill and body size, or in marginally brighter plumage between cocks and hens, otherwise they have no immediately recognizable differences – these are all described as being *Sexually Monomorphic* (e.g. Rosella, Quaker Parrakeet, Peach-faced Lovebird).

2

MUTATED COLOUR

MUTATION

WE CAN think of a *mutation* as a spontaneous change in the form, size or nature of a living thing, whether animal or vegetable. Environmental change may cause gradual subtle alteration to living organisms as they struggle to adapt to new conditions in order to survive, and these evolving specimens must be more successful because the alteration to their being has been instigated by necessity. If change is beneficial, a new sub-species may be founded, leading to the fading of the old form and the development of an entirely new species. However, an apparently rapid and aimless spontaneous change may work to the detriment of the species - especially in the wild state - making it less able to survive, in which case it will be quickly extinguished.

Colour mutants or varieties, have always been of particular interest and given great pleasure to many aviculturists, but there is often argument within and without bird keeping over the possibility of these varieties swamping out the natural wild forms. I do not believe this danger exists. It is forgotten that many years of painstaking work goes into the establishing of these psittacine colour mutants - they have to be cultivated.

There are very few Dominant mutations of psittacines and even these are lessened in their effect when paired to visually normal birds; continuance of this practice would see them eventually disappear. If left to their own devices, and not paired selectively, colour variants must - over several generations - revert to the wild type. First the Recessive forms would be swamped, then the Sex-linkeds and finally the Dominants. In the wild, the forces of nature would bring about a reversion to wild forms even more quickly. In aviculture a surfeit of certain Dominant varieties can be easily rectified by avoiding the inclusion of affected specimens in a breeding programme - their very nature makes sure that differences are visual, at least to some degree (i.e. normal birds cannot be split for a Dominant variety). However, it must not be forgotten that completely pure bred wild type specimens which carry no *hidden* factors for mutated colour are invaluable to breeders in various ways, including helping establish rare *new* mutations.

As far as can be seen, the establishment of colour varieties can only do good for a species by ensuring its popularity and continued breeding by aviculturists. As an example we can look at the Peach-faced Lovebird which is popular and widely bred all over the world as a direct result of the occurrence of mutant varieties. When I began breeding Peach-faceds they were still being imported, nowadays they are so numerous that it is unthinkable that they would ever again need to be brought in from their natural habitat in Africa. The same goes for many other species, including Indian Ringneck Parrakeets, Masked Lovebirds, Cockatiels, Red-rumpeds, Splendids, Turquoisines, so on and so on.

Mutants or Hybrids?
A great danger lies in the confusion between *mutants* and *hybrids* - especially where novice bird keepers are concerned. I am often asked if a hybrid lovebird or parrakeet will be split for one or the other of the parent species which have

contributed towards its appearance, as if pairing the hybrid with the correct partner would present the breeder with some young which were entirely pure bred. This could not be so, it would take many generations of back-pairing to eliminate totally the visual characteristics of one of the original parent species – and even then *throwbacks* would probably arise.

Many psittacine breeders automatically assume that hybrids are infertile and pose no danger to existing aviary stocks, but this is not true. Unchecked hybridization between closely related species and sub-species *does* lead to the loss of scarce races when vigourous crossbreds are let loose into unsuspecting breeders' stocks. As gardeners well know, hybrid vigour exists in the plant world – it is equally as potent in birds. For example, the detrimental effect of indiscriminate cross breeding can be seen in Grass Parrakeets, the larger Broadtails, Lovebirds, Lories and even Cockatoos and Macaws. The hybrids between the Scarlet Macaw *(Ara macao)* and the Blue and Gold Macaw *(Ara ararauna)* are even given the false status of a true species by being named *Catalina Macaws* – which is misleading and irresponsible.

Under strictly controlled conditions, carried out by knowledgeable and responsible individuals, hybridization can be employed as a last resort to save at least *some* characteristics of an endangered species. At the other end of the scale, as a general rule, attempts to instil a colour variety of one common species into another are more questionable. Irresponsible or novice breeders often sell off such hybrids before these long term projects are satisfactorily completed. The necessary destruction of birds surplus to the project would be unacceptable to most breeders.

It is necessary to look outside the family of parrots to find two examples of hybridization which are an unassailable *credit* to aviculture, these being the Bengalese Finch and the Red-factor Canary. The Bengalese is noted for its prolific nature, use as a foster parent and smart appearance; its origins are lost in antiquity but it is generally thought to be the result of an amalgam of several closely related Mannikins *(Lonchura)*. The Red-factor Canary has instigated a completely new culture amongst bird keepers; its glowing red pigmentation was instilled into the canary through hybrids with the South American Black-hooded Red Siskin *(Carduelis cucullatus)* – how much more of a credit this would have been if pure stocks of the now endangered Black-hooded Red Siskin had been built up at the same time.

True Mutation

Because it causes no adulteration when paired to one of its own kind, the mutant example which has occurred within its own species does not present the dangers of the hybrid. Colour varieties can be exhibited as pure mutant forms, combinations of two, or compounds of several mutations. It is important to realise that these mutants are not the result of hybridization between various related species – an idea grasped mistakenly by beginners as well as more experienced breeders – but have initially come about as aberrations or 'sports' within a true species. It must be impressed upon all breeders that cross breeding one species with another does not create mutations, but hybrids which can ultimately prove disastrous to the survival within aviculture of the species concerned. If hybridization were to be encouraged and continue unchecked, our aviaries would be full of worthless mongrels while the pure species would fall into decline and disappear.

Though mutation may cause physical differences (such as crests, curled feathers, elongation of the body, etc. as with Canaries), in psittacine birds we are at present concerned only with differences in colour and pattern.

Origins of Colour Varieties

The beginnings of a mutant colour variety may lie within a chemical change on a single gene, on a single chromosome at the creation of a sex cell of either a cock or a hen. Where Dominant varieties are concerned, the individual which results from the fruition of the mutant containing sex cell will show some visual difference in its appearance. This may not be so with Sex-linked varieties, and definitely not so with Recessive varieties in which the mutation will remain hidden but may be inherited by the individual's progeny. The hidden factor can be carried on down innumerable generations, until the carrier - referred to by breeders as split - finally meets a partner whose own genetic constitution will help lead to the mutant variety surfacing in a visual form in one or more of the pair's progeny.

Numerous reasons for changes in genes are suggested. Some say that continual inbreeding (pairing of closely related birds) will bring about mutation, but their appearance in this instance is most likely caused through the sequence outlined above - inbreeding brings about a quicker mutual introduction of birds carrying the same mutant genes. Others say that the process is caused by nature itself; bursts of harmful radiation during sunspot activity, gamma rays, X-rays, and even cosmic rays from outer space. The breakdown of the ozone layer and chemical contamination are also thought to bring about gene damage, as are nuclear waste, leaks from nuclear power stations and nuclear accidents of various types. Being close to these hazards may cause death, but being in the peripheral areas could cause either severe or minor gene damage - or mutation. As well as being a cause of cancer, elements in photo-chemical smog are also said to induce mutation.

After the Chernobyl disaster, the following years saw a spate of mutations in wild creatures in Britain, including White Foxes and Albino Hedgehogs. Australia has always been a prodigious source of colour mutations, but an inordinate number has arisen amongst the psittacines of that country in recent years, both in the wild and within aviculture. These include Pied Black Cockatoos (*Calyptorhynchus magnificus*), Dilute and Black (*Melanistic*) Eastern Rosellas, Pied Mealy Rosellas (*Platycercus adscitus palliceps*), Blue Stanleys, Lutino, Dilute and Cinnamon Pennants, Lutino and Cinnamon Adelaides, Lutino, Dilute and Cinnamon Red-vented Blue-bonnets (*Psephotus haematogaster haematorrhous*), Blue and Lutino Red-rumpeds, Golden Yellow Hooded Parrakeets (*Psephotus chrysopterygius dissimilis*), Blue and Lutino Twenty-eights, Lutino Swainson's Lorikeets (*Trichoglossus haematodus moluccanus*), Greygreen Scaly-breasted Lorikeets, and Dilute and White-faced Roseate Cockatoos. Colour aberrations have not only been springing up amongst native species; Australian breeders of foreign parrakeets and lovebirds have also had their fair share - the most interesting being a strain of Cinnamon Black-headed Conures (*Nandayus nenday*) with red-brown heads. Whether the cause of these mutations is natural or man made remains to be discovered.

There are more deliberate ways of causing mutation. Gamma irradiation has been used mostly to sterilize pre-packed medical and surgical equipment, and proposed more recently (and controversially in Britain) as a preservative of food. It has also been used in horticulture to create new colour varieties in garden flowers such as chrysanthemums; seeds are passed through a sealed irradiation chamber and given a measured dose of gamma rays. It is quite possible that attempts at treating eggs of psittacines in this way have been made in Europe.

The chemical colchicine has been used as a treatment for gout in humans, but is said to also have been used experimentally to create mutants, which it does by increasing the number of chromosomes. This substance is a poisonous alkaloid derived from the dried seeds and bulbs of plants of the genus Colchicum (e.g. the Autumn 'Crocus'). These unnatural methods would be regarded by most psittacine breeders as abhorrent or at least unethical - but a few might attempt to use them. There is also the likelihood that laboratories specializing in 'genetic engineering' will take advantage of the commercial possibilities of creating fantastic new coloured aviary bred parrots in the not too distant future.

Visual Effects of Mutation

When, through mutation, one or more of the colours in a psittacine's plumage is missing, a striking difference can be created in the appearance of the affected bird. Some kind of comparison can be made with the way that colour is built up in a parrot and the process of colour printing. In order to build up a full range of rainbow colours in a lithographic print, only four inks are needed - yellow, magenta, cyan and black. When all these colours are applied and overlaid in varying densities via their respective plates to a sheet of white paper, a picture represented by the full range of the colour spectrum can be produced.

The 'printer's inks' in the plumage of psittacine birds are *psittacin* (which gives yellow, orange and red and is responsible for pinks and creams), *melanin* (which gives blacks and browns and is responsible for greys and fawns) and the *Tyndall effect* working on the *cloudy layer* which gives blue colour and, in combination with psittacin yellow, is responsible for green. Yellow and red pigment is generally referred to as carotenoid, but - because of controversy over its nature in parrots - has become known as psittacin.

Creation of Colour by Omission of Pigment

From the following we can see that mutant colour is not created by the addition of new pigment but by the subtraction and alteration of existing pigment and changes to the feather material structure:

1. Psittacin yellow combined with melanin and the Tyndall effect creates *green* plumage.
2. Psittacin red combined with melanin and the Tyndall effect gives *muddy red* (e.g. Lovebirds) to *purple* and *mauve* plumage (e.g. Lories) at its very best.
3. The total lack of psittacin yellow or red, leaving just melanin and the Tyndall effect, creates *blue*.
4. Psittacin yellow combined with melanin, but with the Tyndall effect negated, gives *olive* or *greygreen*.
5. Psittacin red combined with melanin, but with the Tyndall effect negated, gives *brown* to *muddy green*.
6. The total lack of psittacin yellow and red, and the negation of the Tyndall effect, leaving just melanin, produces *grey*.
7. The retention of psittacin yellow and the lack of melanin leaves *yellow,* but with a faint green sheen in some areas. If the Tyndall effect is also negated the effect is of *matt yellow.*
8. The complete lack of psittacin and melanin but retention of the Tyndall effect gives *white,* but with a faint blue sheen in some areas. If the Tyndall effect is also negated the effect is of a *matt white.*
9. The retention of psittacin red, the lack of melanin but retention of the Tyndall effect leaves pure *red.*
10. The lack of psittacin yellow, compaction of melanin and partial modification of the Tyndall effect produces *ultramarine* to *violet.*
11. Where melanin black is at its most dense concentration - whether or not psittacin and the Tyndall effect are absent - the result can only be *black.*
12. Where melanin brown is at its most dense concentration - whether or not psittacin and the Tyndall effect are absent - the result can only be *brown.*

Of course there is a sliding scale existing between the total effects outlined above. The *Marine* variety is one example and, with its partial loss of psittacin, stands roughly half way on the descent from green to blue. Examples of the *Blue* variety can be seen in Indian Ringneck Parrakeets, Maskeds and Fischer's Lovebirds, Quaker Parrakeets, Pennant's Rosellas, Splendid Grass Parrakeets, Princess of Wales and Red-rumped Parrakeets; while Marines exist in Indian Ringnecks, Peach-faced Lovebirds, Splendids and Red-rumpeds.

The *Dilute* variety exists in several forms and many species, and stands half way on either the green to yellow or blue to white scale. It is important to remember that the presence or absence of psittacin affects *ground colour* while the presence or absence of melanin affects the contrasting *melanin overlay.*

Psittacine species such as the Cockatiel which, in their natural wild type, are unable to make use of the Tyndall phenomenon and reflect blue colour, can still differ in their ground colour. The White-faced Cockatiel is the equivalent of the

Blue variety in Budgerigars, Indian Ringnecks and Masked Lovebirds. There can also be an equivalent of Marine, in which ground colour is partially reduced; in Cockatiels this is further demonstrated by an equal reduction of psittacin red in the cheek patches. Dilute and Lutino Cockatiels demonstrate modification of the melanin overlay, in the first case by a partial amount and in the second case by a complete loss of melanin.

Grey varieties of birds which can normally show areas of green plumage, such as Grey Budgerigars and Grey Ringnecks, cannot be considered to be on a par with Normal Cockatiels because when the Grey factor is combined with their natural wild type deep yellow ground colour, it is the Greygreen variety which is shown. To create a similar Cockatiel type grey plumage, the ground colour of these two species would need to be reduced to cream, (i.e. Yellow-faced in Budgerigars, and Marine in Ringnecks), and this effect then combined with the Grey factor.

We have seen that mutations can occur which negate the Tyndall effect in psittacines, but could the ability to make use of the Tyndall effect be acquired through mutation so that species like the Cockatiel and Roseate Cockatoo could then display blue and green in their plumage? In 1990 I received a photograph which gave indication that this remote possibility should not be dismissed out of hand. The picture showed a mutant example of Duivenbode's Lory *(Chalcopsitta duivenbodei)*, a species which is noted for its unusual brown-bronze plumage – a result of melanin pigment, a deep golden yellow ground colour and a presumable lack of the type of feather structure which enables the Tyndall effect to come into play. Instead of being brown-bronze this bird had extensive areas of emerald green feathering, so it could be assumed that a mutation had taken place. In Cockatiels, so far, there are only examples which show a barely visible tinge of greenish grey.

Ground Colour

As far as psittacines seem to be concerned, reds and yellows – psittacin yellow and psittacin red – are the same type of ground colour pigment. Effects on these two colours, when present on the same specimen, are usually made in equilibrium; if one is diluted or lacking then so is the other. But there are two cases where the rule is broken. Firstly, the *Tangerine (Orange-faced)* variety in the Peach-faced Lovebird reduces the red and pink of the lovebird's face and forehead to pale orange, without seeming to effect the yellow ground on the rest of the bird.

Secondly, *Pied* varieties (which totally obliterate melanin in patches of varying size) cause a shrinking of areas of pink and red in Peach-faceds. However, the Pied effect in Australian and Asiatic Parrakeets has shown to be even more detrimental by totally destroying the ability to produce psittacin red and replacing it with psittacin yellow in pied areas – e.g. Pied Red-rumpeds, Pied Eastern Rosellas, Pied Splendids, Pied Crimson-wingeds *(Aprosmictus erythropterus)* and Pied Indian Ringnecks. The long term prospects for Pieds in such species should be carefully considered and the advisability of their propagation closely questioned.

Red Suffusion

Reports of complete or partial *red suffusion* are increasing and can be seen commonly in Peach-faced Lovebirds. It is most striking in this species when it occurs with either Lutino, Dilute or Pied specimens (paradoxically, this kind of red colour *can* spread in Pied Peach-faceds). When red suffusion appears on otherwise green plumage in parrakeets and lovebirds, the resulting colour is muddy red. However, it is interesting to note that the most deep and rich violet-purple colours in Lories and Lorikeets are created by natural psittacin red combined with melanin pigment and the action of the Tyndall effect.

Red colour can appear on any yellow ground specimen, and might be described as the alteration of psittacin yellow to psittacin red, or the spread of psittacin red to the detriment of psittacin yellow – the opposite to the Tangerine variety of the Peach-faced Lovebird. In the past I have bred such birds to the second generation. Others believe that the characteristic is not inheritable in this lovebird and that the change from yellow ground to red ground is due to a dietary deficiency or is indicative of serious liver and kidney disease.

Originating in America, an interesting theory on red suffusion of this type claims the cause to be blood parasites *(Protozoa)* and not mutation. It is suggested that the parasites take up red pigmentation from haemoglobin; their presence in the bloodstream at the time of the moult – when new feathers are formed – can result in feather material being stained red by the dead pigmented protozoa. Furthermore, where blood parasites are carried in the circulatory system of nesting hens, the Protozoa can be passed on to the bird's progeny – thereby giving an impression of an inherited tendency towards red suffusion.

Apart from Peach-faced Lovebirds, a few other remarkable specimens have been seen to exhibit this red suffusion and these include a hen Lutino Indian Ringneck and a hen Dilute ('Yellow') Red-rumped Parrakeet – the first originating from my own aviaries and the second from an Israeli breeder. In Australia there are red suffused Princess of Wales Parrakeets. The effect seems to be possible only in species in which red or pink normally exists in at least a small proportion of the plumage.

In the Splendid Grass Parrakeet, cocks in which the scarlet breast patch spreads to cover the whole lower abdomen have been known for years and are now established. Likewise, hens have the same red colour superimposed over their normally yellow lower abdomens. This is not regarded as a mutation but as an existing trait which has been increased gradually by selective breeding.

The same type of effect is also established in the Turquoisine Grass Parrakeet, but here the origin is more obscure. In some it is believed to have been introduced through hybridization with the Splendid, while other examples are said to be the descendants of a practically unrecorded rare wild strain in which the yellow of the upper breast and lower abdomen of the normal type are replaced by orange-red.

Melanin Modification

Ino
The *Ino* variety causes a total elimination of melanin pigment and is established in many aviary species including Indian Ringnecks, Peach-faceds, Maskeds, Cockatiels, Elegants, Budgerigars, Red-rumpeds and Princess of Wales Parrakeets. The Ino form of Green (or Normal) strips away melanin so that only pure ground colour remains. This results in birds being coloured yellow, cream and white, with any red, orange or pink areas of plumage being clarified and made more vivid – this is the *Lutino*. When Ino is combined with Marine, the normal yellow ground colour of Green (or Normal) is reduced to cream, cream is made paler, and pinks and reds are reduced to apricot or salmon pink – this is the *Creamino*. Ino combined with Blue creates a bird with completely white plumage – the *Albino*. Ino also removes melanin from eyes, in most cases leaving them pink and red, or ruby; feet, nails and bills become flesh coloured in most species, but species which have naturally red bills retain this colour – unless Ino is combined with Blue. *Psittacula* parrakeets are examples of an exception in which the bills retain their red colour even when in the Albino or Blue form.

The Ino is a useful tool for discovering the depth and type of ground colour present in a particular strain of birds, and of demonstrating the true effect of ground colour modifiers when melanin is stripped away in combination varieties. With the aid of Ino, the existence of pure Blue varieties can be proved or disproved without doubt.

Dilute
The *Dilute* varieties are so called because they dilute melanin pigment. Within a single species there can be several types which show considerable differences in

their grades of effect on melanin. These varieties are widespread throughout avicultural subjects and include Dilute ('Silver') Cockatiels, Dilute ('Yellow') Turquoisines, Dilute ('Pastel') Rosellas, Dilute ('Yellow') King Parrots, Dilute ('Golden Cherry') Peach-faceds, and so on. In some examples, green areas are reduced to lime or almost pure yellow, and blue areas are either lightened slightly or almost reduced to pure white. Dilute varieties can be combined with ground colour modifiers to create subtle shades of pale blue and silver grey in those species which normally show predominantly green plumage.

The possibility of more than one type of melanin pigment in psittacines has been mentioned previously. The strongest indication of this can be seen in one of the latest Dilute colour mutations of the Pennant's Rosella, in which the melanin content of black feathers on the back and wings is lacking, almost reducing them to white, but substantially retained in areas such as cheek patches, wings and lateral tail feathers - giving a strong blue colour. With crimson plumage lightened, the overall effect is a most striking red, white and blue Rosella.

Another type of Dilute variety in the Indian Ringneck Parrakeet - *the Clearhead* - also shows a maximum reduction of melanin in the head (of the cock) with a minimum reduction in the rest of the plumage; perhaps this too could indicate the presence of two types of melanin.

Cinnamon

The *Cinnamon* variety eliminates melanin black by replacing it with melanin brown. Apart from pure ground colour, all areas of plumage are lightened, and blacks are changed to brown or fawn. The eyes are usually plum to brown, and bills, nails and skin are also slightly paler. Other Cinnamon type varieties - generally with a lighter base of melanin brown - are named in Europe as *Fallow* or *Isabel (Isabelle, Isabella)* which often leads to confusion, as there seems to be no specific criteria upon which they are named.

There are Cinnamon Cockatiels, Splendids, Elegants, Bourke's, Budgerigars, Peach-faceds, etc.; as with Dilute, Cinnamon is frequently used in combination and compound varieties.

Pied

The various *Pied* varieties cause patchy elimination of melanin pigment, so that a strongly contrasting variegated effect is achieved when ground colour is revealed. In some patches of feathering affected by variegation, the melanin is not fully eradicated and this can leave yellow plumage tinged with lime, and white plumage tinged with blue or grey. Feet, nails and bills may also be patched with flesh colour in some species, but eyes usually retain their normal colour.

It should *not* be expected that the depth or delineation of ground colour will be affected, but, as has been pointed out, Pied varieties can shrink or totally eliminate psittacin red. As well as being an undesirable trait in species which normally have some red or apricot plumage in the Green and Marine series, difficulty in sexing normally dimorphic species is another unwelcome side effect - e.g. Pied Red-rumpeds. Also, some slightly pied Cockatiel cocks are known to retain hen-like plumage features into maturity, such as grey patches on the face and striations on flight and tail feathers.

Rare strains of Pieds have existed in which there has been a 'time lapse' for the variegated effect to show itself - usually not until the birds have attained adult plumage. It is common for pied areas to spread with each passing season, rather like the slow invasion of a disease.

Alteration or Negation of the Tyndall Effect

Mutations that alter the feather barb structure instead of the pigment content are rarer; these include *Grey*, the *Dark Factor* and - as far as is known - the *Violet Factor*. The latter is said to cause flatter and wider barbs with no great alteration to the cloudy layer. Apart from a compaction of melanin granules in violet barbs, none alter the melanin or psittacin level.

Being cumulative, the *Dark Factor* is recognized in two depths; the lesser of these – Dark (Single Dark Factor) – causes the reflected blue light off the melanin granules to give darker greens and darker blues; the greater – Olive in the Green series and Slate in the Marine and Blue series (Double Dark Factor) – causes the elimination of the reflection of blue, so that green is altered to olive (brown-green) and blue is altered to slate (grey-blue). As far as is known, apart from the Budgerigar, this variety has only been established in the Turquoisine Grass Parrakeet, Peach-faced Lovebird, Masked Lovebird and the Lineolated Parrakeet.

As previously mentioned, the *Grey* variety has been established in the Indian Ringneck Parrakeet as well as the Budgerigar. It has also been bred in the Plum-headed Parrakeet *(Psittacula cyanocephala cyanocephala)*, fixed in the Scaly-breasted Lorikeet and – through hybridization – introduced into the Musk *(Glossopsitta concinna)*, Varied *(Psitteuteles versicolor)* and Swainson's Lorikeets. However, in these five latter species it can so far be only expressed as Greygreen because there is no established Blue variety with which to eliminate yellow ground colour. The Grey variety can be distinguished from the Dark Factor by the lack of specimens of an intermediate shade in the former.

The presence of the *Violet Factor* can be shown visually in combination with most colour varieties, but the typical violet colour is seen at its best when combined with the Blue variety and a Single Dark Factor. It has been a popular variety with Budgerigar breeders for decades but – as far as is known – has only been established in one other psittacine, the Peach-faced Lovebird. Though there is no Blue Peach-faced in existence, the Violet factor in combination with the Marine produces quite good coloured birds. The combination with the Dark Factor seems to have hit some snags and to have shown few benefits so far – further experimentation seems to be required.

Other Colour Effects

So far, the most commonly known types of visual effects caused by three groups of primary mutant factors have been covered, but other types of modifying factors exist, and more and more are likely to occur as the years pass. Some cause *rearrangement* or *limited displacement* of pigment in set areas of plumage, or even in each individual feather in a set area of plumage.

For example, in the back feathers of the *Pearl* Cockatiel melanin pigment has been removed from the centre areas of the feather vane each side of the quill, drawn inwards along the centre line, and outwards to its edges. By combining this variety with the Ino it has further been demonstrated that the Pearl Variety causes the underlying psittacin yellow to undergo the very *opposite* of this process. There is a mutation of the Turquoisine Grass Parrakeet in which the plumage undergos a similar change to the Pearl Cockatiel, but has been mistakenly named as 'Pied', it too is best described as *Pearl*.

The strawberry pink of the *Rosa* Bourke's Grass Parrakeet is caused by enhanced ground colour and almost complete elimination of melanin from specific areas. It is often compared with the *Opaline* variety of the Budgerigar because of its clear 'saddle', but the Opaline still owes its body and mantle colour to melanin pigment and the Tyndall effect. The Rosa shows most affinity with the *American Clearbody* Budgerigar which retains dark markings on the wings but lacks most of the melanin throughout its body feathering, revealing the ground colour.

Known of and illustrated in Gould's time – when it was thought to be a distinct species and named the Fiery Parrakeet *(Platycercus ignitus)* – the *Ruby* is a rare mutation of the Eastern Rosella in which the red of the head and breast spreads over most of the body. But the most unusual and recently established mutation of the Eastern Rosella is predominantly black, presumably due to an increase in melanin production. This is the only truly melanistic *mutant* variety so far reported in psittacine birds, though it has a direct parallel with the *naturally* occurring melanistic phase of Stella's Lorikeet *(Charmosyna papou stellae)*. Could this also be a mutant, but one which has established itself in the wild alongside its original predominantly red wild form?

14

Mutant Colour Forms in the Wild

Are other mutant forms of psittacine evolving and establishing themselves in the wild state? Individual 'sports' can and do crop up in any species, but the only parrot which comes to mind where a colour variety seems to have spread through a whole race is the 'Tres Maria' Amazon. The Yellow-fronted Amazon (*Amazona ochrocephala ochrocephala*) occupies a distribution area covering the greater part of the South American continent lying north of the Amazon river, and has a stable pattern of colouration itself, but its sub-species - which spread through the narrow isthmus of Central America - develop an increased propensity towards variegation as they spill into the southern part of Mexico.

The increase of yellow patches of plumage as birds mature is a classic feature of Pied varieties, as also is the loss of melanin pigment from bills and feet - and these characteristics are prominent in the most northerly races of this Amazon. The Mexican Double Yellow-headed Amazon (*A.o.oratrix*) shows variegation to a marked degree, but the 'Tres Maria' (*A.o.tresmariae*) shows even greater yellow variegation and gives further credence to the theory of mutant genes for Pied increasing as the species has spread and evolved.

The nominate species, with its vast region of distribution and equally vast 'gene pool', is less prone to the development of mutations and maintains the status quo with its original wild type genes predominating. However, the 'Tres Maria' has boxed itself in on the tiny islands which are its home, and this must have lead to a greater occurrence of inbreeding and a consequent multiplication and concentration of the mutant genes for piedness. If evolution should proceed on the same course, it could transpire that a totally pure yellow Amazon Parrot will be the final result of this trend.

Half-siders and Variegated Ground Colour

When the National Exhibition of Cage Birds was held at Olympia in London in the nineteen fifties, I remember being enthralled by the exhibits in the numerous classes for Budgerigar colour varieties. All the new mutations of the day were there, clustered together in a few classes, and these included the first Cresteds, 'Feather Dusters' and even some birds with feathered leggings - like Belgian Bantams. Amongst these exotic and even weird looking mutants were a handful of ordinary looking Budgerigars which at first glance seemed completely out of place. But then, a Light Green turned on the perch and was changed to a Skyblue, a Grey pivoted and was suddenly Greygreen, and a Lutino was now transformed into an Albino! The lighting system was not to blame and they had not been cunningly dyed, these were birds I was hoping to see - the *Half-siders*.

In those days it was suggested that Half-siders were the result of a mutated gene, but could not be inherited. Even so, it seems that there are strains of Budgerigars which have a greater ability than most to produce these rare aberrations. At the present time the most acceptable theory regarding the origin of Half-siders suggests that a chromosome is 'lost' from one half of the egg cell at its first division, and that subsequent divisions follow the pattern of the normal cell on one side of the body and the incomplete cell on the other.

It is usual for a 'split' to be able to show the visual results of this 'accident' which occurs during the multiplication of cells. For example; the normal cells on one side of a Light Green split Blue would develop into a bird which would be visually green with a yellow mask, but if the appropriate chromosome were missing from cells on the other side - so that blue colour held sway - the other half of the bird would be skyblue with a white mask. If the 'victim' were to be a pure bred Light Green or Skyblue, not carrying any hidden factors, then the 'accident' could have no visual effect.

As well as Half-siders made up of Light Green and Skyblue, Grey and Greygreen, and Lutino and Albino, there have been examples of Dark Green and Cobalt, Dark Green and Skyblue, and even Dilute Skyblue and Dilute Cobalt; Yellow-faced varieties have also been involved, but there does seem to be a limit to the colour varieties which can be subject to Half-siding. This might be because the 'lost'

15

chromosomes which rule the inheritance of colour also carry genes vital to, or capable of controlling, other processes essential to the development of the embryo - and of course if this were so the embryo would die at an early stage in its growth.

There are also *Three-quarter birds;* in their case the important chromosome has been lost during the *second* division of cells. The division of cells may continue for a number of sequences before the rare mishap occurs, and this may lead to just a single patch of different colour. Its size will depend upon the stage of development at which the alteration came about - such birds are described as *Mosaics.*

As far as I can discover, the only other species of psittacine bird to have produced Half-siders is the Eclectus Parrot *(Eclectus roratus),* and these are even more remarkable. The Eclectus is noted for its marked sexual dimorphism; the cock is predominantly vivid green with red on its sides and under its wings, while the hen is coloured in various shades of violet, mauve and crimson with a touch of yellow in some sub-species. There are no established colour varieties in this parrot, and so its Half-sider is split longitudinally between the cock's plumage on one side, and the hen's on the other! One such bird illustrated in an American book on Eclectus Parrots shows the hen's plumage to be on the left hand side; as a hen parrot has only one ovary which is also located on the left side, it has been amusingly speculated whether there would be a testis on the right side making it a hermaphrodite - a bird which could not only lay eggs but also fertilize them!

In 1990 I was sent two photographs as examples of Half-siders, a Budgerigar and a Masked Lovebird, both of which were produced by breeders in Britain. Their colour was not sharply defined longitudinally but patched in a seemingly haphazard fashion - much more like a type of Pied or Variegated variety rather than a Half-sider. It is strange that two different species with the same pigment abnormalities should turn up at about the same time, and a coincidence that the same thing should have also happened in Australia.

I have photographs dating from 1987 of Australian bred examples of both Masked and Peach-faced Lovebirds which appear to be the same type of colour aberrant as the British birds. It is hoped that these are not 'accidents' like Half-siders but of a new inheritable variety which causes Pied ground colour.

The established Pied varieties in psittacine birds all bring about a lack of melanin pigment in affected areas, which causes great contrasts in plumage colour; green is changed to yellow, and blue to white. A Pied variety which instead of eradicating melanin pigment acts on *psittacin* pigment would change yellow to *white* and green to *blue* - and this is exactly the effect seen in the Budgerigar and Masked Lovebirds as mentioned. No Blue variety exists in the Peach-faced Lovebird, but in these birds green plumage is patched with *marine.* In all cases the colours are patchworked in a jigsaw fashion.

It is perfectly feasible that *psittacin* Pieds should become established as a converse of *melanin* Pieds. If ground colour variegation is established as an inheritable characteristic, what name can it be given? It should be short, uncomplicated, and give no strong indication as to colour - so that it can be used universally within combination and compound varieties. Previously used names for melanin Pieds must be avoided, therefore the term Pied must itself be ruled out, as well as Variegated, Marked, Ticked, Harlequin, Checked and Chequered - but 'Jigsaw', 'Patched' or even 'Jazz,' might be suitable.

So we see that colour varieties are continually evolving with new developments likely to occur at any time; enthusiastic breeders maintain a constant watch on the possibilities which these can present. As mentioned previously, colour mutants are our present concern, but other mutations are likely. In Budgerigars there have been *Long-flights* (elongated body, head and mask, long tail and flights), *Feathered-legs,* and *Cresteds* (Tufted, Half and Full-circular - almost as well developed as in Canaries). So far, the only other psittacine to show such features is the Peach-faced Lovebird with a single *Feather-foot* reported (USA) and *Cresteds* showing slight feather disruption at the back of the head (Australia).

16

3

RELEVANT GENETIC THEORY

CELL, CHROMOSOME & GENE

THE MATERIAL which makes up the composition of both animals and plants is of cellular construction and – for the greater part – each *cell* contains a *nucleus* (the control base) which itself can contain 'plans' for the construction, characteristics and maintenance of the entire organism – the 'plans' are known as *chromosomes*. The chromosomes are strings of 'detailed instructions' which are split up into smaller adjoining units known as *genes*. Each 'set of plans' can also be regarded as a legacy which is passed onto the heirs of the animal or plant at fertilization, with individual donations being contributed from paternal and maternal sides. By its invigorating action, this continual exchange and re-combination of traits helps to ensure the success and survival of the species within its existing environment.

Every living thing has a specific number of pairs of chromosomes per nucleus *(the diploid number);* for example a human being is said to have a diploid number of twenty-three and an onion eight! A Budgerigar – and probably other psittacines – has thirteen pairs of macro chromosomes and an even greater number of smaller chromosomes. The sizes and shapes of the chromosomes vary, but each one finds its own matching partner to which it clings – mutually attracted chromosomes are described as *homologous*.

Autosomes

Mutated genes can occur on the *autosomes;* 'autosome' is used to identify those chromosomes other than the special pair which decides the sex of the new individual. Colour varieties which arise because of a mutated gene on any of the autosomes are described as either *Autosomal Recessives* or *Autosomal Dominants*, with the latter type being further segregated into *Autosomal Complete Dominant* or *Autosomal Incomplete Dominant* types.

For an *Autosomal Recessive* variety to express itself in a visual form, the mutant gene must be present on both autosomes of the pair; the gene is described as *homozygous* for that variety – true breeding. If it is present on only one of the autosomes, the gene is unable to express itself visually but can be inherited by the progeny of the affected individual; the gene is described as *heterozygous* for that variety – not true breeding.

For an Autosomal *Complete* Dominant to be expressed in a visual form the gene need be present on only one of the pair of autosomes, but to be fully potent in its ability to pass on its legacy, it must be present on both autosomes of the pair. Autosomal *Incomplete* Dominants are only partially expressed visually where the gene is present on only one of the autosomes. To be expressed fully in both its visual effect and inheritable form, the gene must be carried on both autosomes of the pair.

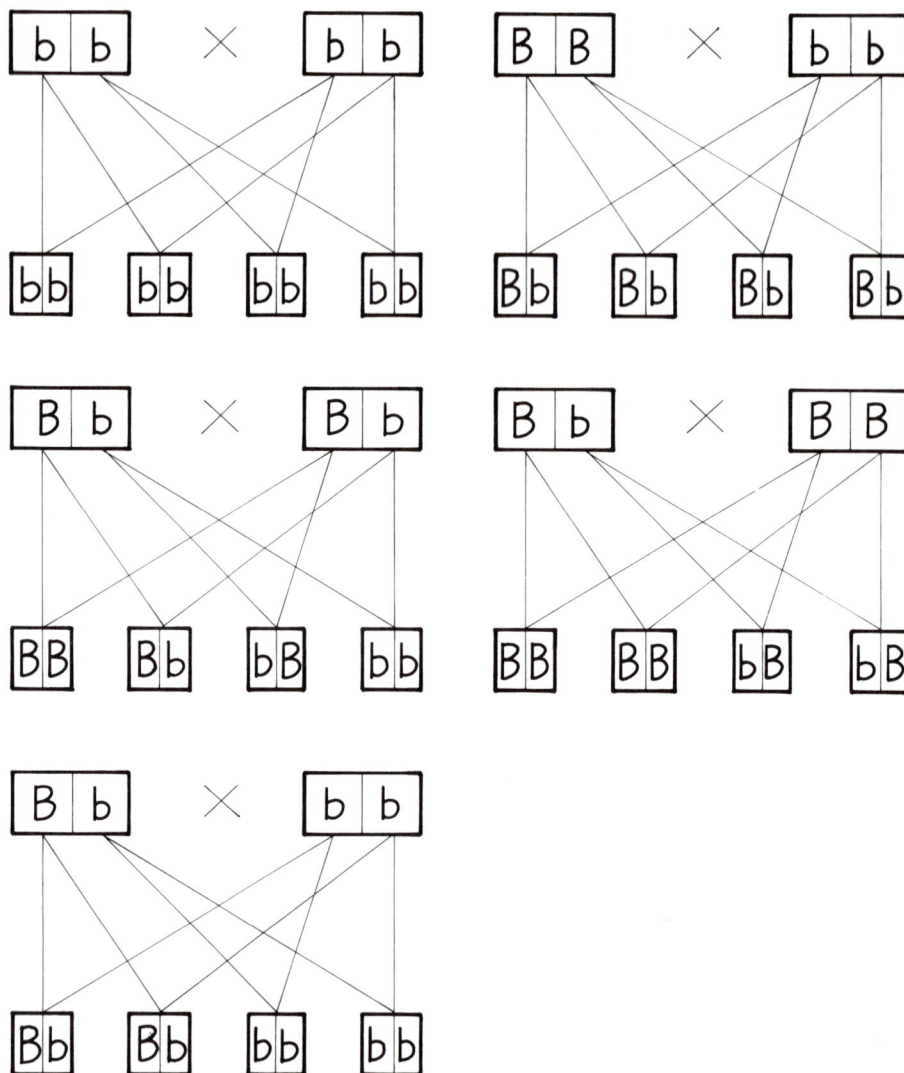

Diagram 2: Autosomal Recessive Inheritance (Example: Blue)

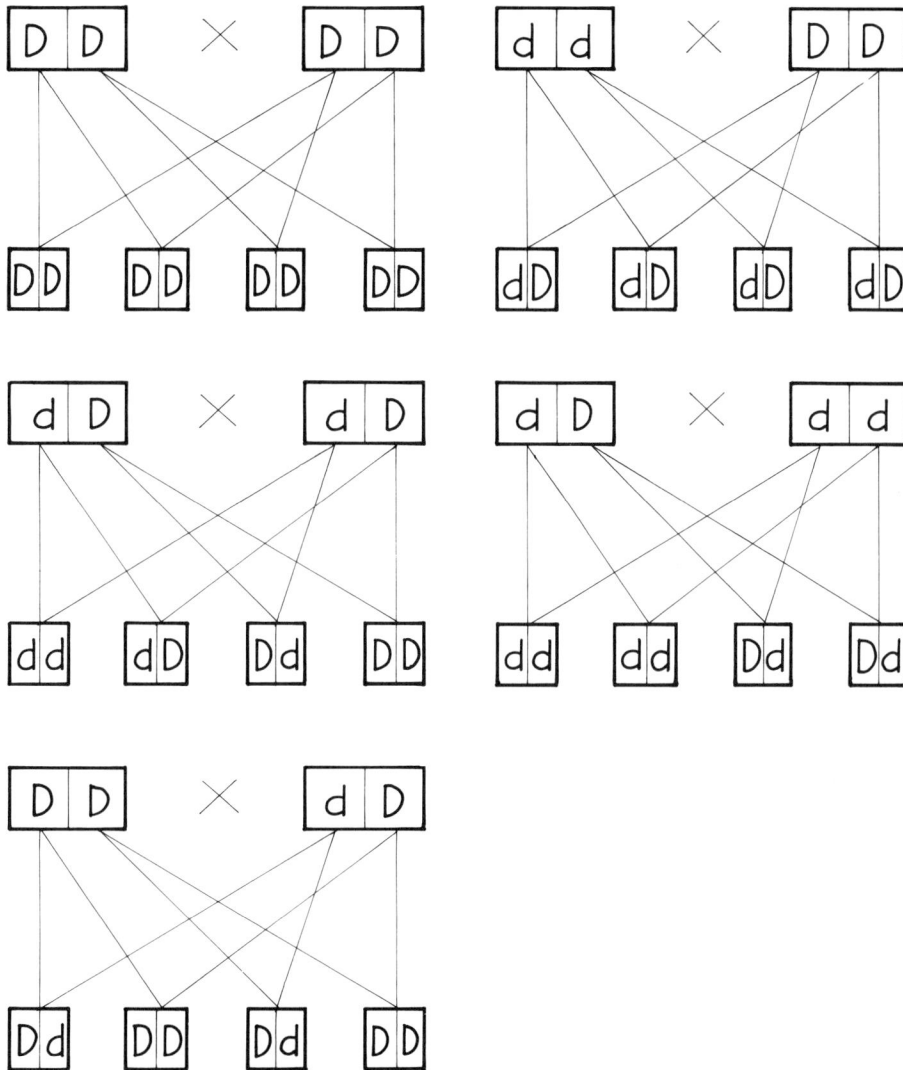

dd = Green
DD = Olive Green
dD = Dark Green
Dd = Dark Green
D = Dark
d = non-Dark

Diagram 3: Autosomal Dominant Inheritance (Example: Dark Factor)

Some geneticists show the transfer of genes from parents to young by use of *the Roman Square* (or other derivatives) in which one parent's genes for its colour varieties are arranged horizontally at the top while the other parent's are set vertically on the left side. The simple example below shows a breeding pair of Greens split Blue – (*Bb*) and (*Bb*) – and the three possible genetic types of young which these parents can produce – (**BB, Bb, bB, and bb**) – which are: one Green, two Greens split Blue and one Blue.

	B	*b*
B	**BB**	**Bb**
b	**bB**	**bb**

Other writers on genetics use the more illustrative method as shown in *Diagrams 2, 3, 5, 6, 7, 8, 10, 11, 12, 14, 15, 16, 17, 18* and *19.* Elsewhere in this manual, the matings and colour expectations are set out in the simplest and most easily understood fashion possible, so they may be used even without study of this section on genetics.

Creation of Gametes (Sex Cells) by Meiosis

The *gametes (sex cells)* originate from a division of cells *(meiosis)* within the testes of the cock and the ovary of the hen. The paired chromosomes within the dividing cell separate, and one from each pair make up *two sets of single chromosomes* – one set *(the haploid number, the ge-nome)* going into each of the two resulting cells. Normal biological regulation prevents both individuals of a pair of chromosomes ending up in the same cell, but there is no predetermination with regard to which cell each will go.

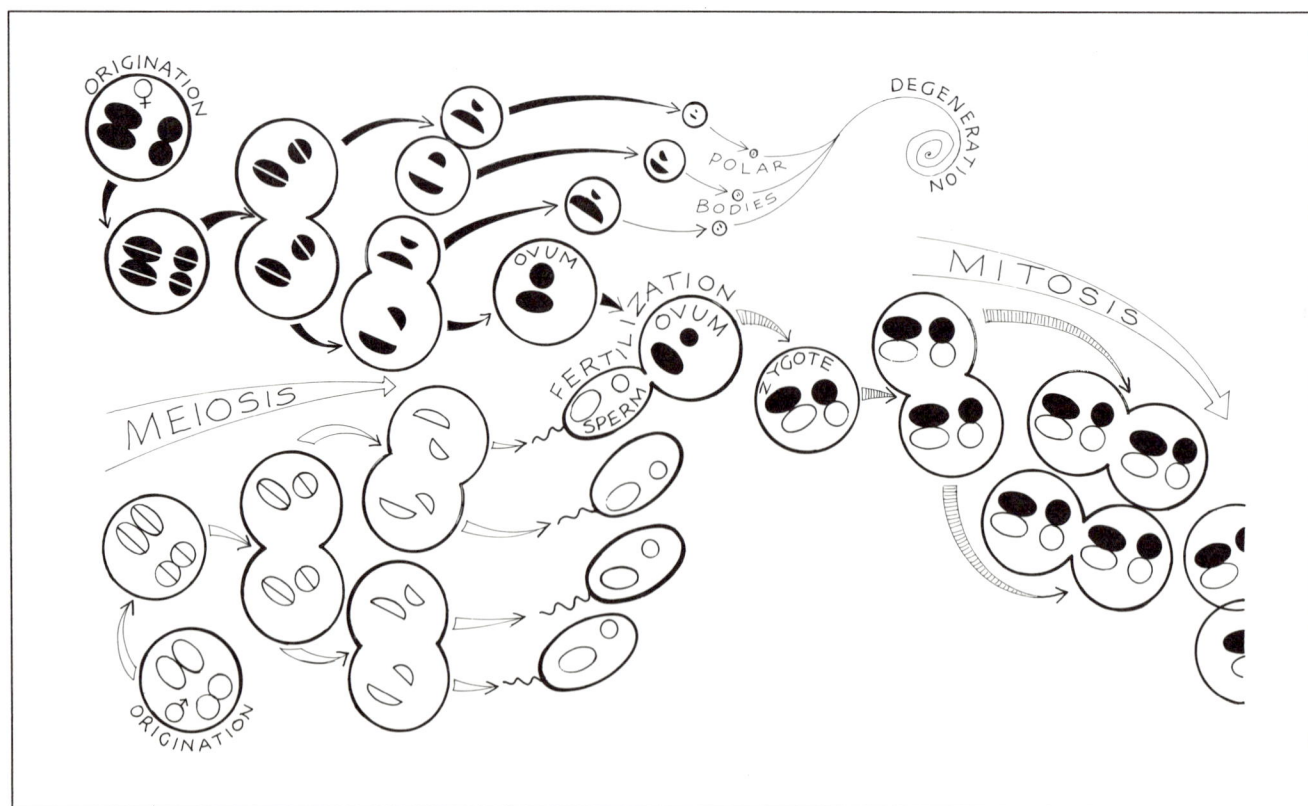

Diagram 4: Meiosis – Fertilization – Mitosis

The two new cells divide again, but this time - so as to once more provide a set of single chromosomes for each cell - the chromosomes split down their length and are then described as *chromatids*.

Now there are four new gametes each with a full set of chromatids; each of the four gametes from the cock goes towards forming a *sperm*, but of the four produced from the hen only one results in an *ovum (egg cell)* and the others *(polar bodies)* degenerate and fade away.

At fertilization, one of the cock's sex cells (with its full set of single chromosomes) combines with that of the hen and a new cell is created - the first cell of the new individual, the *zygote*. The zygote contains a complete set of single chromosomes from each parent, and each chromosome finds its homologous partner from amongst the opposite set so that - once again - a complete set of paired chromosomes is present.

The zygote continues to divide - now described as *mitosis* - but this time each new cell has its full compliment of paired chromosomes. By the time the egg is laid the zygote has divided countless times, and the mass of cells can be seen as a tiny speck on the surface of the yolk. Once the egg has been ejected from the hen's cloaca, it must be incubated so as to provide the warmth that will encourage embryonic growth.

The Sex Chromosomes

In each set of paired chromosomes, one pair decides the sex of the new individual. Both of the cock's sex chromosomes are designated as XX - a matching pair - but the hen has only one X chromosome which pairs with a smaller chromosome designated as Y. Some geneticists tell us that the Y chromosome carries *no* genes, while others just refer to its inability to carry a full compliment of genes to match those on the X chromosome.

Each zygote receives one sex chromosome from its father - which must be X - and one from its mother, which can be X or Y. If the zygote receives another X chromosome from its mother, it must develop into a cock, but if it receives Y, it must become a hen - XY. From this we can see that the hen's sex chromosome contribution decides the gender of the embryo; in mammals the opposite is true - females are XX and males are XY.

Some writers refer to the pairs of sex chromosome as ZZ and ZW; ZZ equals XX *(male)* and ZW equals XY *(female)*.

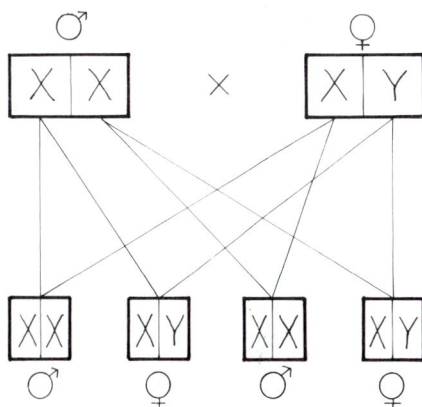

Diagram 5: Inheritance of Sex Chromosomes

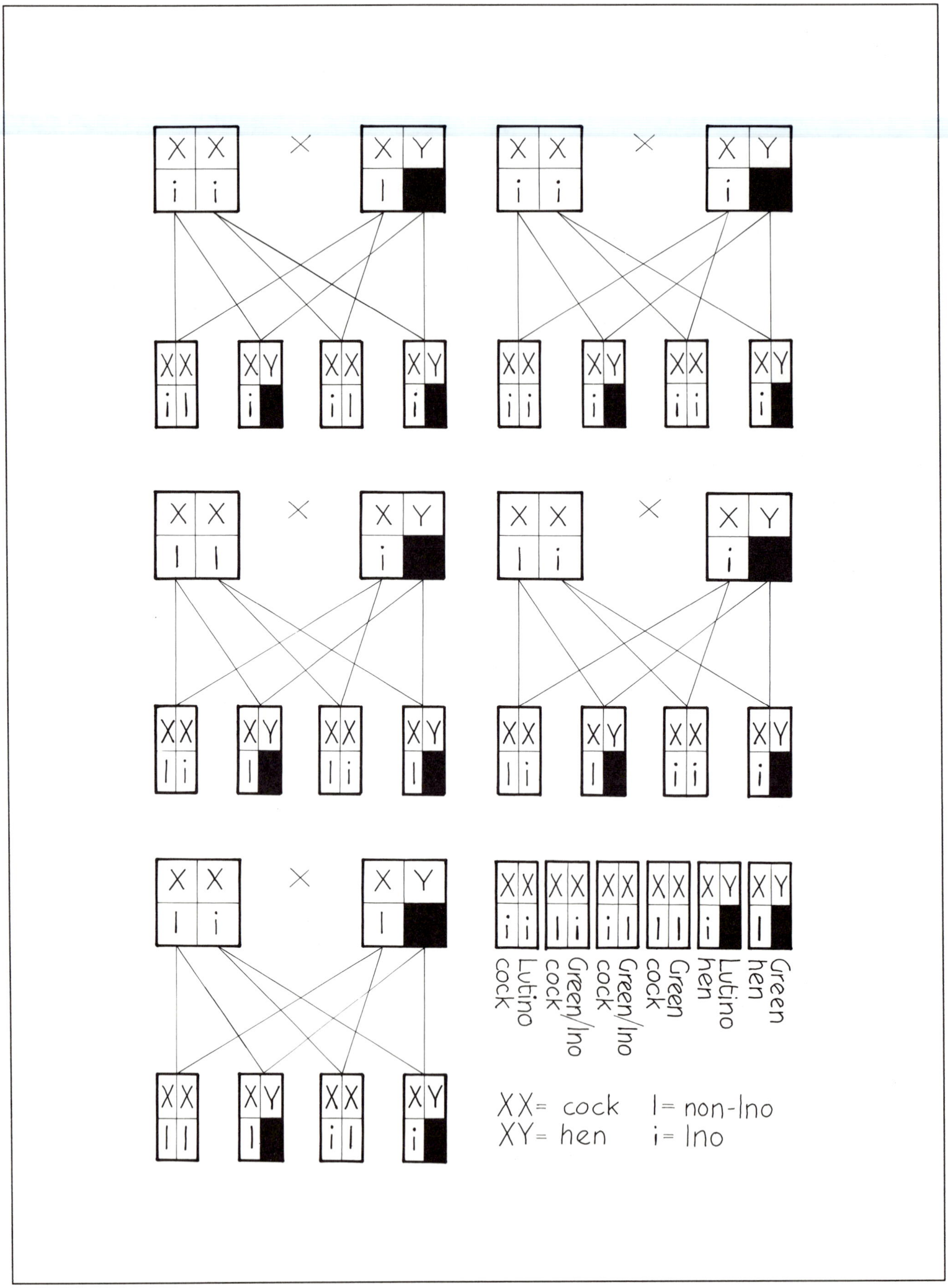

Diagram 6: Sex-linked Recessive Inheritance (Example: Ino)

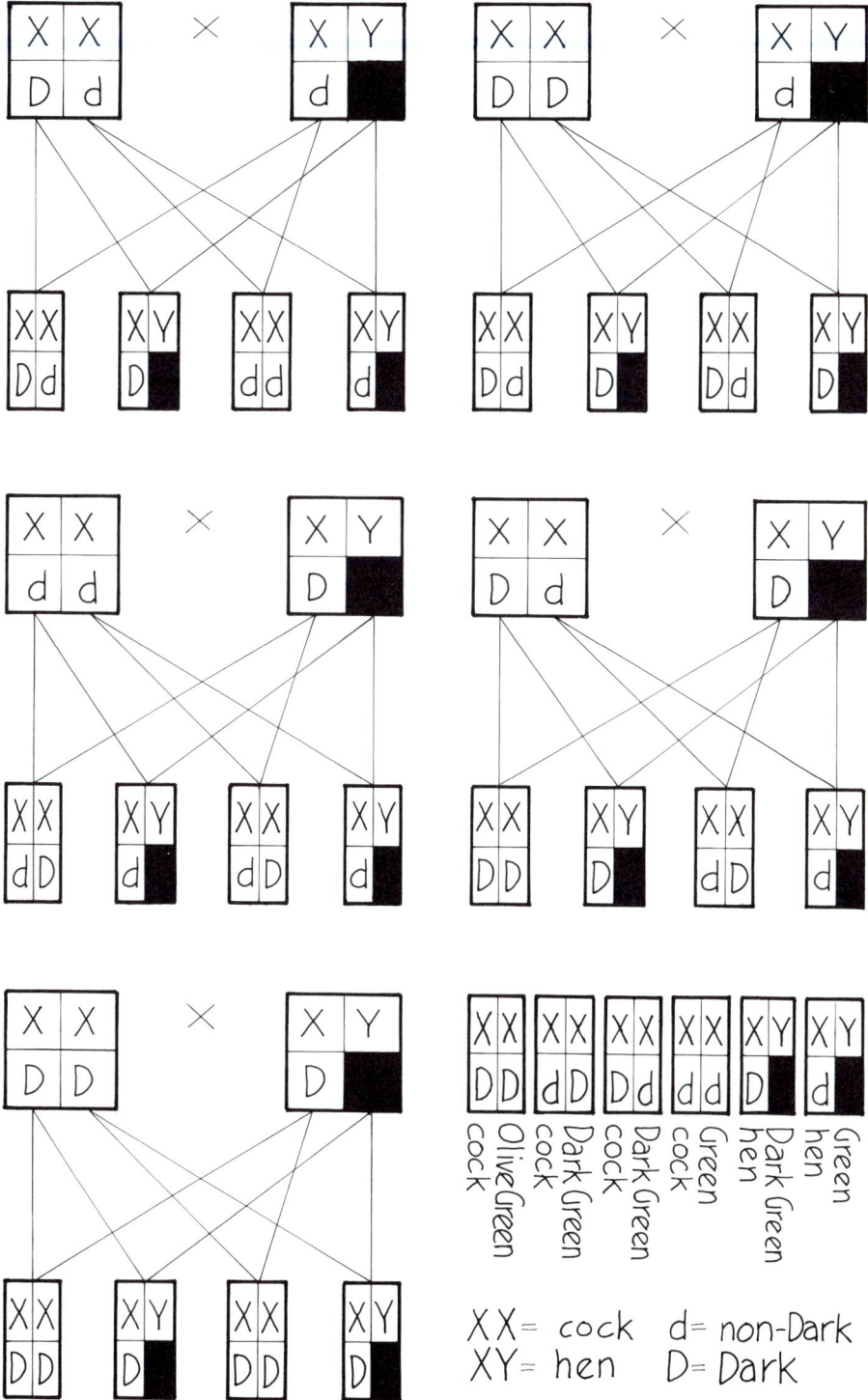

Diagram 7: Sex-linked Dominant Inheritance (Hypothetical Example: Dark Factor)

Sex Linkage

As well as the possibility of genes which govern colour being present on the autosomes (chromosomes which have no determination over the sex of the individual), they may also be present on the sex chromosomes. As previously mentioned, colour genes cannot be carried on the hen's Y chromosome, but only on her single X chromosome; they can of course be carried on both of the cock's X chromosomes. Therefore, such colour genes are directly dependent on the sex chromosomes for their inheritance and are described as *Sex-linked*.

Sex-linked Recessive Inheritance

If the same mutant colour gene is present on both of the cock's X chromosomes, he will be visually of that colour variety *(homozygous for the variety)*, but if the mutant gene is only on one of his X chromosomes, he will not show it in his appearance, but will still be able to pass on the gene to his progeny – he is *split (heterozygous)*.

The hen is handicapped in this respect, because she has only one X chromosome to carry the mutant colour gene. However, if the mutant gene is present on just her single X chromosome she will show its effect in her appearance, because there is no 'anti-mutant colour gene' (normal gene or non-mutant allelomorph) on her Y chromosome to prevent its expression. She is able to pass on the gene to her male progeny because they must receive her X chromosome, but unable to pass the gene on to her female progeny because they can only receive her ineffectual Y chromosome. She is also unable to be split for the mutant colour gene, and is either visually *of* the mutant colour variety or totally *devoid* of it.

If an X chromosome which carries the mutant colour gene is passed from father to daughter, the daughter *must* be visually of that colour; but for any of his sons to show the mutant colour visually, they must receive an X chromosome carrying the mutant gene from *both* their parents. If the sons receive an X chromosome carrying the mutant gene from their father, but have a normal mother who can only pass on an X chromosome carrying a 'non-mutant colour' gene, then they can *only* be split for the mutant colour. That is: to be visually of the Sex-linked Recessive mutant colour the young cocks *must* come from a mother who shows that same colour in *her* appearance.

Sex-linked Dominant Inheritance

Though at present there are no *Sex-linked Dominant* varieties in psittacine birds – which makes it safe to refer to Sex-linked Recessives as simply 'Sex-linked' – this may not always be so, some geneticists believe that Sex-linked Dominants could appear.

When Recessive mutant genes arise on the autosomes (Autosomal Recessives) the well known Recessive pattern of inheritance follows its course; when a Recessive gene arises on the sex-chromosomes, the new variety is tied to the mechanism governing the inheritance of the male (XX) and female (XY) and is fully described as Sex-linked Recessive.

All known Dominant mutant genes arise on the autosomes (Autosomal Dominants) and – as has been described – can be further separated into types which have differing systems of expression (Complete and Incomplete). It is feasible that, in the future, mutant varieties of both these types could arise on the sex-chromosomes.

Let us imagine that a Grey variety exists as a Sex-linked Complete Dominant, with (S) equal to Single Factor and (D) equal to Double Factor. If the pattern of inheritance of a Complete Dominant were superimposed over the inheritance of the sex-chromosomes, the following theoretical pattern should apply:

(S)Greygreen cock x Green hen

24

Continued from previous page.

(S)Greygreen cocks & hens, & Green cocks & hens.

(D)Greygreen cock x Green hen

all (S)Greygreen cocks & hens.

These first two sets of pairings and expectations are exactly the same as would be anticipated for an Autosomal Complete Dominant variety, *but* when the hen carries a factor for Grey on her single X chromosome, the theoretical results become far more interesting:

Green cock x (S)Greygreen hen

*(S)Greygreen cocks, & *Green hens.

(S)Greygreen cock x (S)Greygreen hen

(S)Greygreen cocks & hens, (D)Greygreen cocks & *Green hens.

(D)Greygreen cock x (S)Greygreen hen

(D)Greygreen cocks, & (S)Greygreen hens.

*Note: * Sexable by colour.*

Though all the Greygreens (Single and Double Factor) will have the same appearance, there will be no Double Factor hens because of the Y chromosome's inability to carry genes for colour.

Now, let us imagine this time that a Dark Factor variety exists as a Sex-linked Dominant. If the pattern of inheritance of an Incomplete Dominant were superimposed over the inheritance of the sex-chromosomes the following theoretical pattern should apply:

Dark Green cock x Green hen

Dark Green cocks & hens, & Green cocks & hens.

```
┌─────────────────────────────────────────────────────────────────────┐
│              Olive Green cock x Green hen                             │
└─────────────────────────────────────────────────────────────────────┘
                                    ▮
┌─────────────────────────────────────────────────────────────────────┐
│              all Dark Green cocks & hens.                            │
└─────────────────────────────────────────────────────────────────────┘
```

Again, the first two pairings are exactly as would be expected for an Autosomal Complete Dominant variety, but when the hen carries a factor for Dark on her X chromosome the theoretical results should provide even more sexable youngsters:

```
┌─────────────────────────────────────────────────────────────────────┐
│              Green cock x Dark Green hen                             │
└─────────────────────────────────────────────────────────────────────┘
                                    ▮
┌─────────────────────────────────────────────────────────────────────┐
│              *Dark Green cocks, & *Green hens.                       │
└─────────────────────────────────────────────────────────────────────┘
```

```
┌─────────────────────────────────────────────────────────────────────┐
│              Dark Green cock x Dark Green hen                        │
└─────────────────────────────────────────────────────────────────────┘
                                    ▮
┌─────────────────────────────────────────────────────────────────────┐
│   Dark Green cocks & hens, *Olive Green cocks, & *Green hens.        │
└─────────────────────────────────────────────────────────────────────┘
```

```
┌─────────────────────────────────────────────────────────────────────┐
│              Olive Green cock x Dark Green hen                       │
└─────────────────────────────────────────────────────────────────────┘
                                    ▮
┌─────────────────────────────────────────────────────────────────────┐
│         *Olive Green cocks, & *Dark Green hens.                     │
└─────────────────────────────────────────────────────────────────────┘
```

*Note: * Sexable by colour.*

Because the Dark Factor could only be carried on the hen's X chromosome, it has been assumed that hens could not be produced in Olive Green (Double Dark Factor). However, because the hen's Y chromosome cannot carry an *anti*-Dark gene (normal gene or non-Dark allelomorph) to partially counteract the action of the Dark gene, it could alternatively be assumed that the Single Dark gene would act as a Double Factor and cause full effect, so that a Dark Green hen would be represented visually as an Olive Green hen! When we remember that Sex-linked Recessive hens carry only one mutant sex-linked gene but are still visually of that variety, this interesting proposition does not seem so far fetched.

The Linkage Theory
Not to be confused with Sex-linkage, the operation of *Linkage* with regard to colour varieties has no dependence on the sex of the individual. Linkage refers to the inheritance of two - or even more genes - in association with each other, which occurs when they are located on the *same* chromosome. Where abnormal difficulty is experienced in combining certain varieties in a visual form, Linkage could be suspected.

The rules of inheritance laid out by Mendel (1822-1884) did not allow for the possibility - contained in later theory - that genes for certain characteristics might be situated on the same pair of chromosomes, and that this would prevent the combination of these genes from being achieved. The characteristics which

Mendel had studied in his botanical experiments were apparently carried on separate pairs of chromosomes, and therefore behaved independently of each other.

Because they were having problems in combining the two varieties, in the early days of colour breeding with Budgerigars, breeders came to believe that Blue and the Dark Factor were subject to this newer Linkage Theory. *(Note: Light Green and Skyblue carry no Dark Factor; Dark Green and Cobalt carry a Single Dark Factor; Olive and Mauve carry Double Dark Factor.)*

Example of Mendelian inheritance:
First Season:

```
                          Olive x Skyblue

                          all Dark Greens/Blue.
```

Second Season:

```
                    Dark Green/Blue x Skyblue

    25% each of Dark Greens/Blue, Light Greens/Blue, Cobalts and Skyblues.
```

Linkage Theory (Programme A):
First Season:

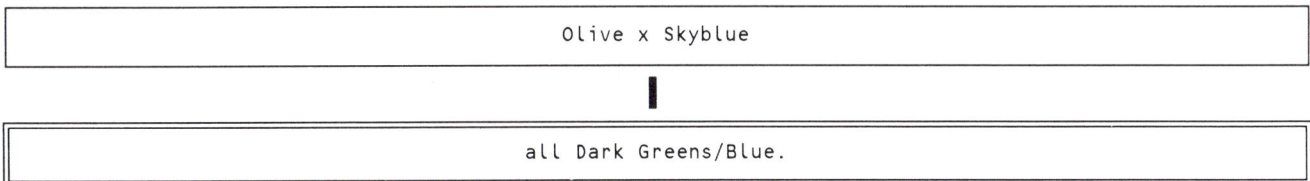

```
                          Olive x Skyblue

                          all Dark Greens/Blue.
```

Second Season:

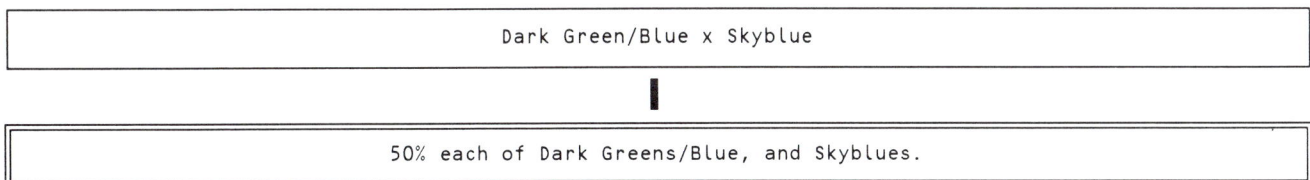

```
                    Dark Green/Blue x Skyblue

           50% each of Dark Greens/Blue, and Skyblues.
```

Linkage Theory (Programme B):
First Season:

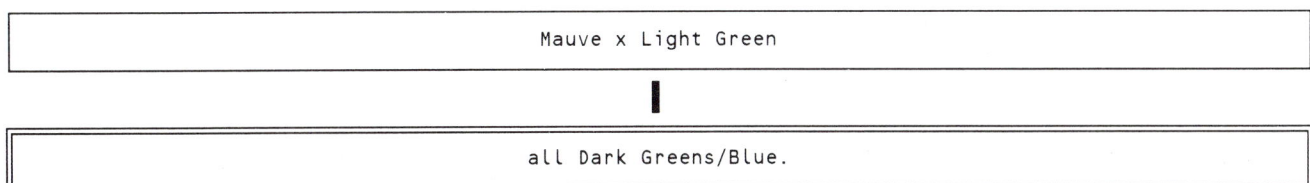

```
                        Mauve x Light Green

                          all Dark Greens/Blue.
```

Second Season:

Dark Green/Blue x Skyblue

▮

50% each of Light Greens/Blue, and Cobalts.

So, according to Linkage Theory, two very different sets of results should be obtained in the second season by using what appear to be identical birds. To differentiate the two types, they were described as *Type I* and *Type II;* Dark Green/Blue Type I originating from *Olive* x *Skyblue*, and Dark Green/Blue Type II originating from *Mauve* x *Light Green*. Otherwise; Dark Factor and *non*-Blue (Green) being located on the same chromosome in Type I birds, and Dark Factor and Blue located on the same chromosome in Type II birds.

Luckily for the development of the Dark Factor being fully introduced into the Blue Series Budgerigars, the Linkage Theory was found to be unreliable. A small percentage - 14% - of Cobalts and Light Greens/Blue appeared in nests from the second season pairing of Programme A, and an equal amount of Skyblues and Dark Greens/Blue appeared in nests from the second season pairing of Programme B. These discrepancies representing a flaw in the Linkage Theory had to be explained, because - if percentages were ignored - the expectations of young had now reverted to those quoted in old Mendelian Theory!

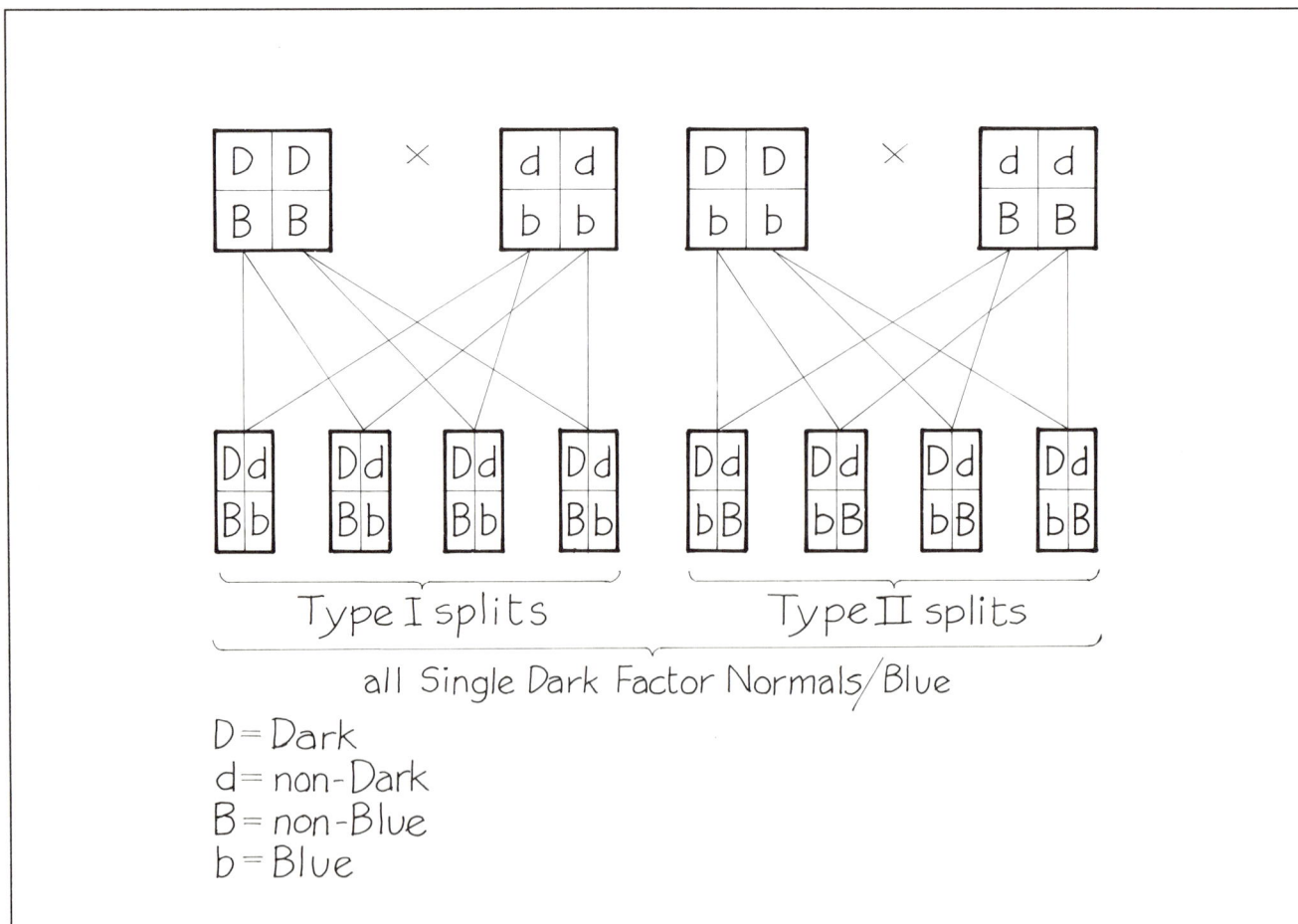

Diagram 8: Linkage Theory (Autosomal) - Origination of Type I & Type II Splits (Example: Blue & The Dark Factor)

28

The Crossover Theory (Re-combination of Linked Genes)

Geneticists had an imaginative but complicated biological explanation to these exceptions in the Linkage Theory; the *Crossover Theory*, which is said to work in the following way. During meiosis, we can imagine the wriggling chromatids twisting, turning and finally breaking into segments at the points at which the pairs of chromosomes are stuck together. The segments 'cross over' to fuse with the appropriate sections on the opposite chromosome of the pair, so that genes are swopped and form a linkage which is the opposite of that which previously existed. Crossover can occur at meiosis of all chromosomes, but is only made obvious when there are linked colour genes.

Some theorists indicate that this breaking and rejoining of chromatids is infrequent, while others give the impression that it happens continually at the formation of gametes. It is further noted that the frequency at which Crossover young appear gives away the exact position of the relevant genes on the chromosome. Where two genes are situated side by side, the chance of the chromatid breaking at the point which separates them is more remote than if they were located farther apart. If they were to be located at opposite ends of the chromatid, then in theory they would be able to cross over at each meiosis. The frequency at which Crossover is believed to occur for a given pair of characteristics is known as the *'Crossover Value'* and is expressed as a fraction or as a percentage; the lower the percentage of young produced, the closer the relevant genes are presumed to be to each other on the chromosome. The Crossover Value is established from averages of actual breeding results.

Sex-linked Recessive Crossover

By their nature, Sex-linked Recessive varieties can only be present on the X chromosomes, and therefore Crossover must take place for specimens to be finally produced which show visual combination of any Sex-linked varieties.

As with Dark Green/Blue Budgerigars, according to theory, there should be Type I and Type II birds in *all* psittacine *cocks* which are split for two Sex-linked Recessive varieties. For example, where Cockatiels are concerned, Normal cocks split Pearl and Ino which originate from a *Pearl Lutino cock or hen paired to a Normal* should be described as Type I. Whereas, Normal cocks split Pearl and Ino which originate from a *Pearl Normal cock paired to a Lutino hen*, or a *Lutino cock paired to a Pearl Normal hen*, should be described as Type II.

In other words, Type I cocks have inherited both Sex-linked genes from a single parent, but Type II cocks have inherited one Sex-linked gene from each parent.

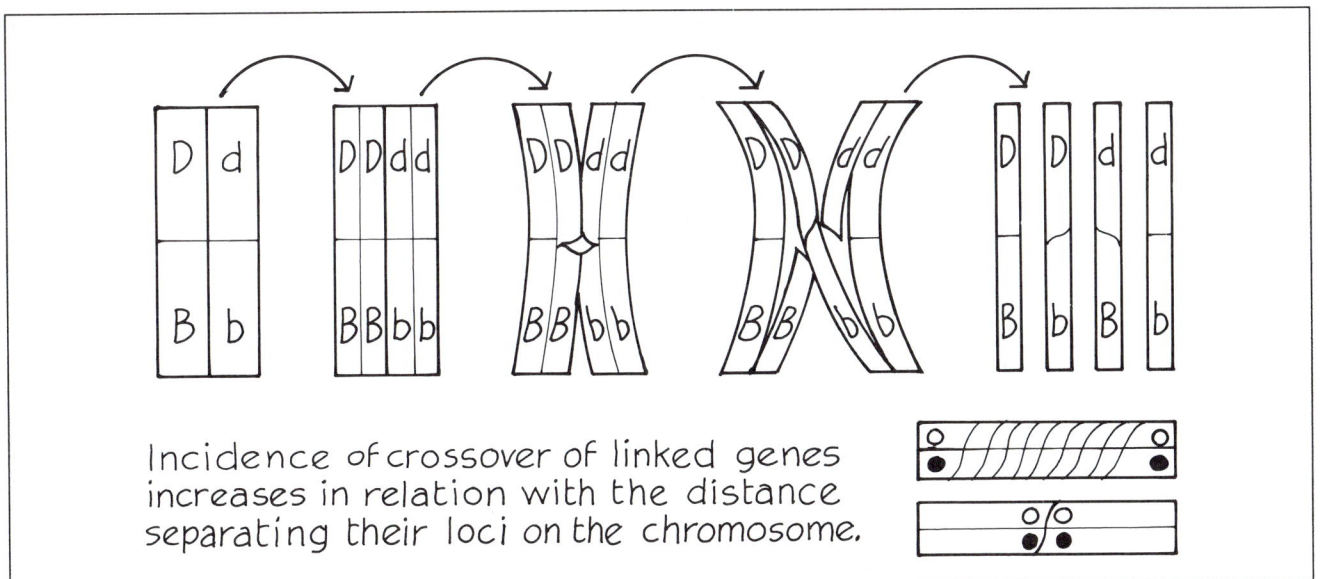

Incidence of crossover of linked genes increases in relation with the distance separating their loci on the chromosome.

Diagram 9: Crossover of Chromatids

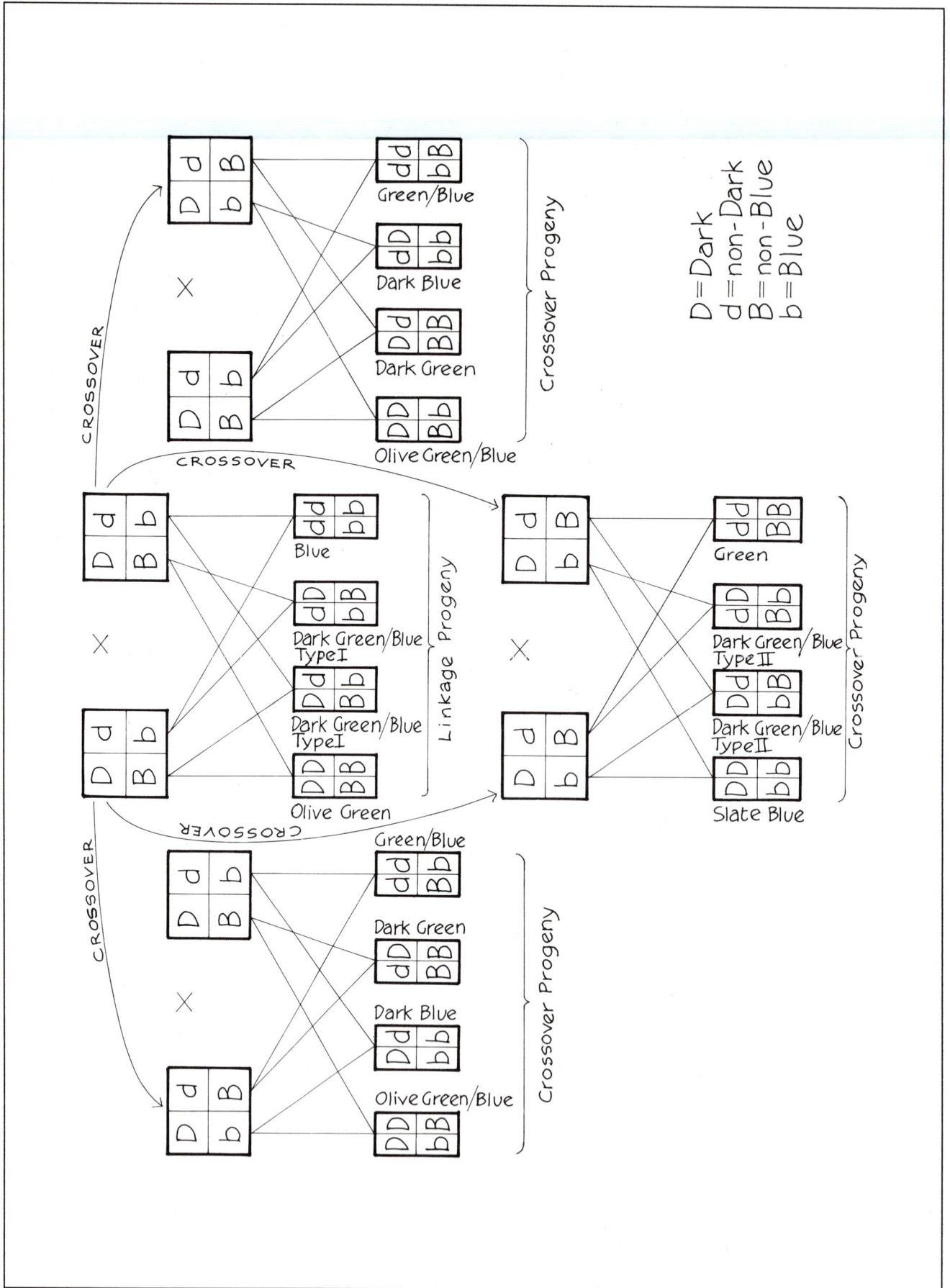

Diagram 10: Crossover applied to Linkage (Example: Blue & the Dark Factor)

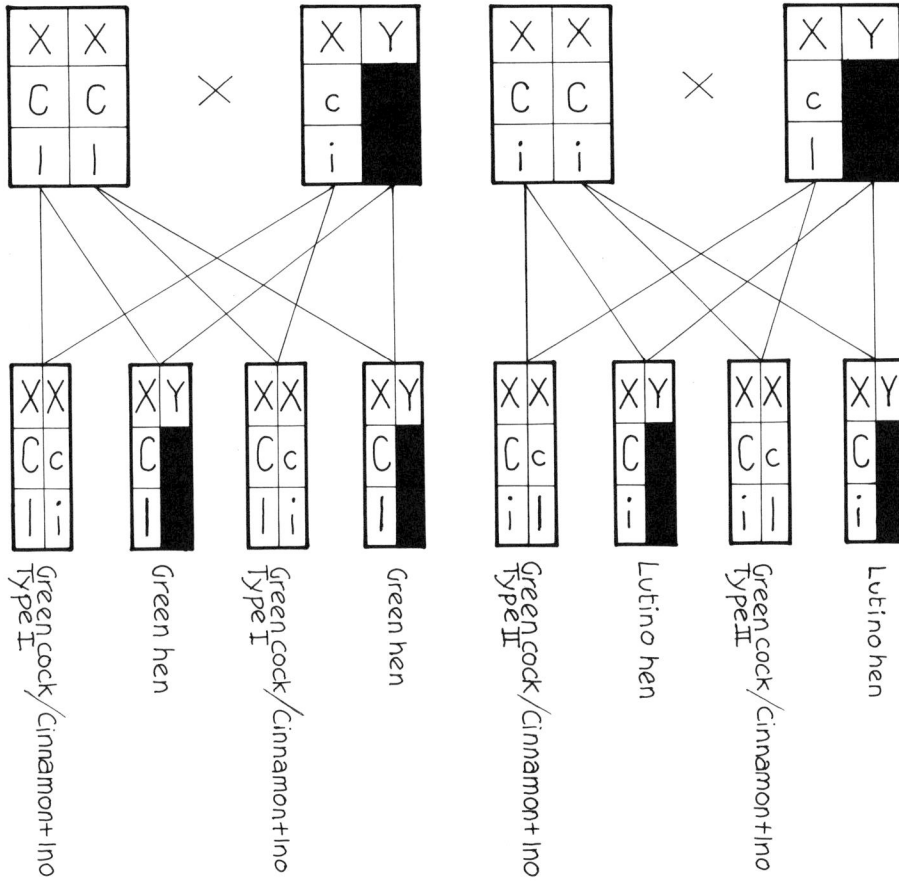

XX = cock   l = non-Ino
XY = hen   i = Ino
            C = non-Cinnamon
            c = Cinnamon

Note: *If instead of the above, the left hand breeding pair consisted of a Cinnamon Lutino cock x Green hen and the right hand pair consisted of a Cinnamon Green cock x Lutino hen, the Types (I or II) of the cocks produced would be unaltered but hens off the 'Type I' pairing would be changed to Cinnamon Lutino and hens off the 'Type II' pairing to Cinnamon Green.*

Diagram 11: Linkage Theory (Sex-linked Recessive) –
Origination of Type I & Type II Split Cocks (Example: Cinnamon & Ino)

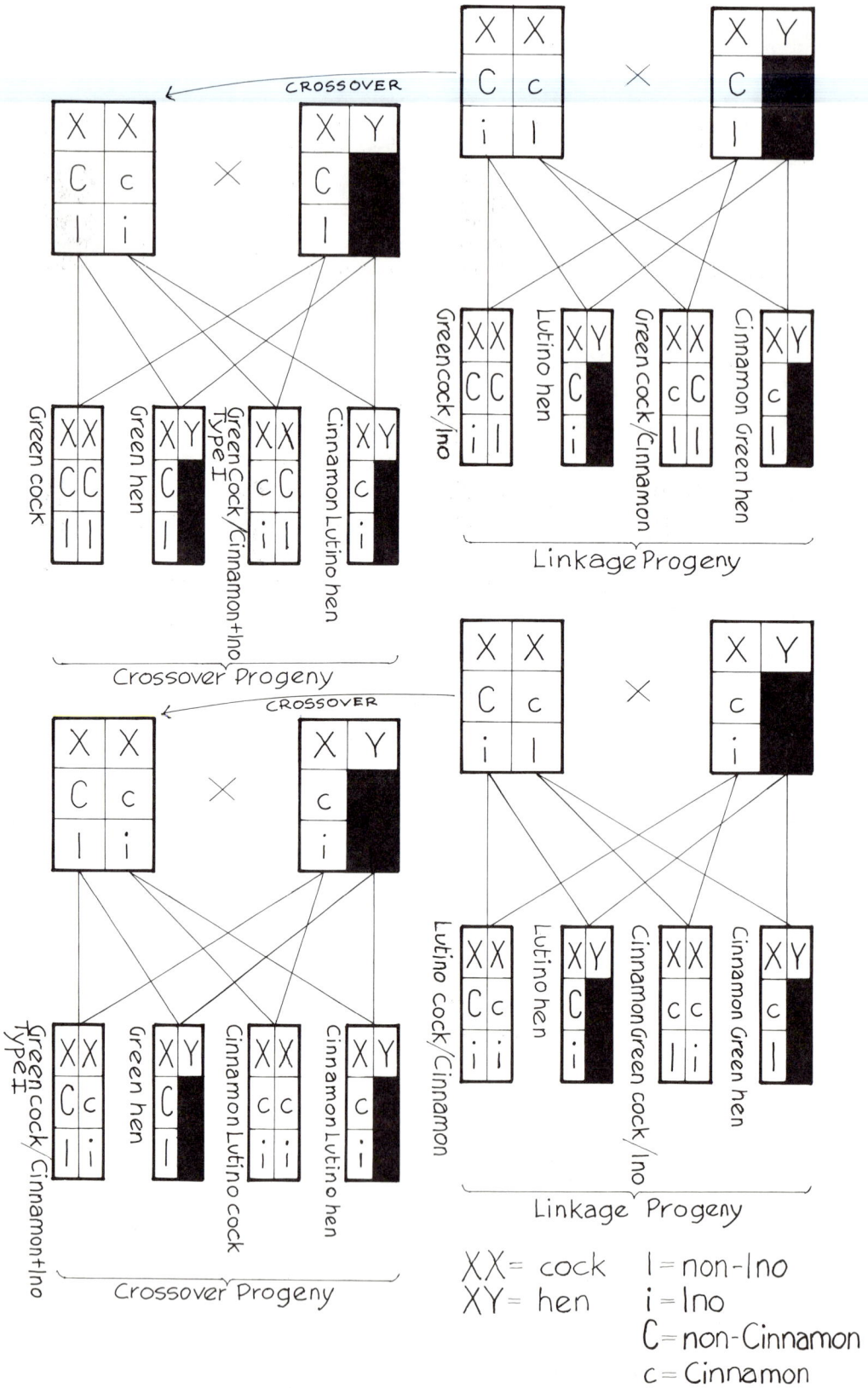

Diagram 12: Crossover applied to Linkage plus Sex-linkage
(Example: Cinnamon & Ino)

XX = cock   I = non-Ino
XY = hen   i = Ino
             C = non-Cinnamon
             c = Cinnamon

32

Phenotype and Genotype

When mutant colour varieties are described as being of the same *phenotype*, they are the same *visually;* when described as being of the same *genotype,* they are of the same *genetic constitution.* Two psittacines which share the same phenotype do not necessarily share the same genotype; for example a pure bred Green specimen of an Indian Ringneck is the same phenotype as a Green split Blue Ringneck, but it is not the same genotype.

There can be equivalent phenotypes and genotypes across species; a pure bred Lutino Indian Ringneck Parrakeet is the equivalent of a pure bred Lutino Peach-faced Lovebird; though a Lutino Elegant Grass Parrakeet may be the same phenotype as Lutinos in both Ringnecks and Peach-faceds, it is certainly not the same genotype - being Autosomal Recessive instead of Sex-linked Recessive, it differs in its mode of inheritance. If it is easily proved that mutants such as Ino can arise on either autosomes or X-chromosomes, then it cannot be taken for granted that the Dark Factor and the Blue Factor will always arise on the same pair of autosomes - as they have done in the Budgerigar.

In the nineteen eighties, lovebird breeders grasped the Crossover theory - applied to the Dark Factor and Blue Factor in Budgerigar culture - as an iron clad truth to be also applied to the combination of the Dark Factor and Marine Factor in Peach-faceds. No thought was given to the fact that these two mutant genes might *not* be on the same pair of autosomes, at the same *loci (gene locations)* or that the Marine is *not* a pure Blue variety, and might not even be an allele of a pure Blue Peach-faced when such a bird does finally emerge.

In any case, the Linkage Theory and the Crossover Theory must be placed in their proper perspectives; they provide only a measurement of the percentage of young of the sought after combination variety which can be expected to be produced. Where percentages are not included in expectations, for practical purposes these two theories need not be considered. If the breeder totally disregards Linkage and Crossover, it is still possible to predict expectations from specific pairings - provided the basic patterns of inheritance for Autosomal Recessives, Autosomal Dominants and Sex-linked Recessives are known.

Lethal Mutations

Where little headway is gained in establishing a primary mutant variety in a relatively free breeding species, the suspicion arises that the gene may be lethal - or in some aspect partially incapacitating to the individual which carries it. In *Lethal* mutations the gene which controls a colour difference may also be inhibiting or accelerating an unidentified but vital process necessary for the individual's continued well being.

The gene may not be potent enough to prevent life until present on both chromosomes of a pair, when it hinders or stops certain chemical processes and general physical development. In the Canary, the Crested - an Autosomal Dominant variety - represents a potentially harmful gene; a Crested should be paired to a Crest-bred (non-Crested), for when Crested is paired to Crested any resulting Double Factor young are likely to be hatched with the skull malformed or its top missing. Apparently, no lethal mutant genes have yet been discovered in parrots.

We can see that chromosomes are busy little objects and many weird occurrences are known. Instead of the usual Diploid (paired) chromosomes, Triploid chromosomes have been recorded - in organisms as diverse as plants and parrots. Likewise, during meiosis, the chromatid fragments can rejoin after inverting themselves; they may become attached to the end of a complete chromatid, or even cross over with a chromatid of another pair. In these presumably rare events, surviving specimens are said to be rendered partially or completely sterile.

Allelomorphs (Alleles)

Each gene is situated at a specific point *(locus)* on its chromosome, and each string of genes making up a chromosome is mirrored by its matching partner (apart from the hen's mismatched pair of sex-chromosomes). When an inheritable mutation alters a gene, it changes in its chemical composition and this modifies its normal purpose. The *'normal'* gene at the matching locus of the other chromosome of the pair is said to be an *allelomorph* (shortened to *allele*) of its opposite *mutant* gene.

It is said that lightning never strikes the same place twice, but this is not true where mutation of genes is concerned. At meiosis, within the testes or ovary of another individual of the same species, an identical gene on an identical chromosome may also change its composition and create a *second* mutation which gives a differing level of effect from the *first* mutation. Alternatively, in a single individual of an established strain of the first mutation, the mutant gene might mutate again, and also provide this differing level of effect.

Though infrequent, it does happen. This *second* mutant gene is an allele of its *'normal'* counterpart on the opposite chromosome, and also an allele of the *first* mutant gene which is at the equivalent locus on its own chromosome. The three genes, the 'normal' and both mutants, are *allelomorphic* towards each other.

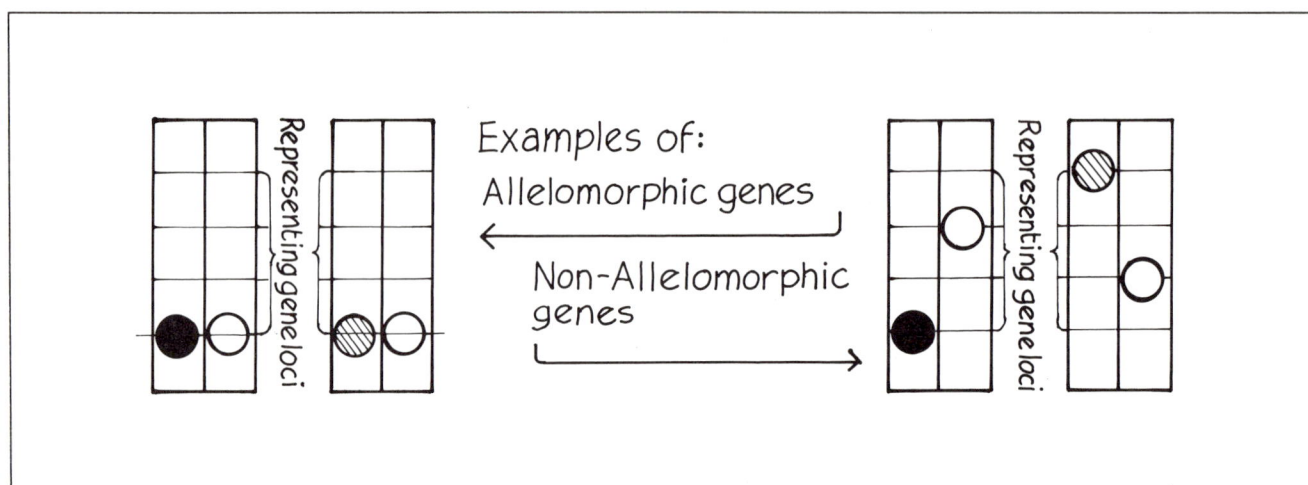

Diagram 13: Position of Allelomorphs on the Chromosomes

Each and every mutated gene – whether Autosomal Dominant, Autosomal Recessive or Sex-linked Recessive – has its counterpart 'normal' gene allele, and their interaction is covered by each variety's pattern of inheritance. The 'normal' gene might be thought of as an agent which is opposed against the mutant, trying to prevent its expression. It is also described as non-(variety), for example, non-Blue, non-Dark, non-Dilute, and so on. Where a second allelomorphic mutant gene replaces the counterpart 'normal' gene on the other chromosome of the pair, one of these two mutants acts out the function of the missing 'normal' gene in dealings with its opposite number.

When two *separate* pure bred Autosomal Recessive varieties are paired together and produce young which all share the same appearance of just *one* of the parents – with no normal wild type young ever appearing – the two varieties are most likely to be alleles. The variety which is visually represented in all the young takes the place of the 'normal' gene in its relationship towards the subordinate variety. For example, in the Splendid Grass Parrakeet, there exists a Marine variety and a Blue Variety which are presumed to be alleles; when these two are paired together their young are Marines split Blue. Other such examples include Marine and Blue Indian Ringneck Parrakeets, and Japanese and American Dilute Peach-faced Lovebirds. In the latter species the paler Japanese Dilute is subordinate to the darker American Dilute. *(See Diagrams 14 & 15).*

When two *separate* pure bred Autosomal Recessive varieties are paired together and produce young which are all *intermediate* in appearance between the two varieties – without ever producing normal wild type young – they can still be alleles. This time one variety has taken on the role of an Incomplete Dominant in its relationship with its allelomorphic subordinate. So far, the only psittacine species, other than the Budgerigar, to show this type of allelomorphism is the Peach-faced Lovebird; when a Marine is paired to a Lavender, the resulting young are of intermediate colour. *(See Diagrams 16 & 17).*

There are also examples of allelomorphism of Sex-linked Recessives in the Peach-faced Lovebird and the Indian Ringneck Parrakeet. In both species, the Sex-linked Dilute takes on the role of the Dominant towards the Lutino, but the involvement of sex-linkage makes the pattern of inheritance more complex than the previous examples of allele pairings. *(See Diagrams 18 & 19).*

Allelomorphism is disproved when all or some of the progeny from a pair made up of two examples of different pure breeding mutant varieties are normal in appearance. Varieties which are alleles of each other share two common features. Firstly, they cause the same type of visual effect because they are based on the same original 'normal' gene; they can only modify that gene's function by reducing its potency by degrees from maximum to nil; each mutant allele represents a fixed proportion of the function of the allelomorphic 'normal' gene on that same scale. Secondly, each mutant allele shares the same type of inheritance as its allelomorphic partners in relationship with their 'normal' gene allele.

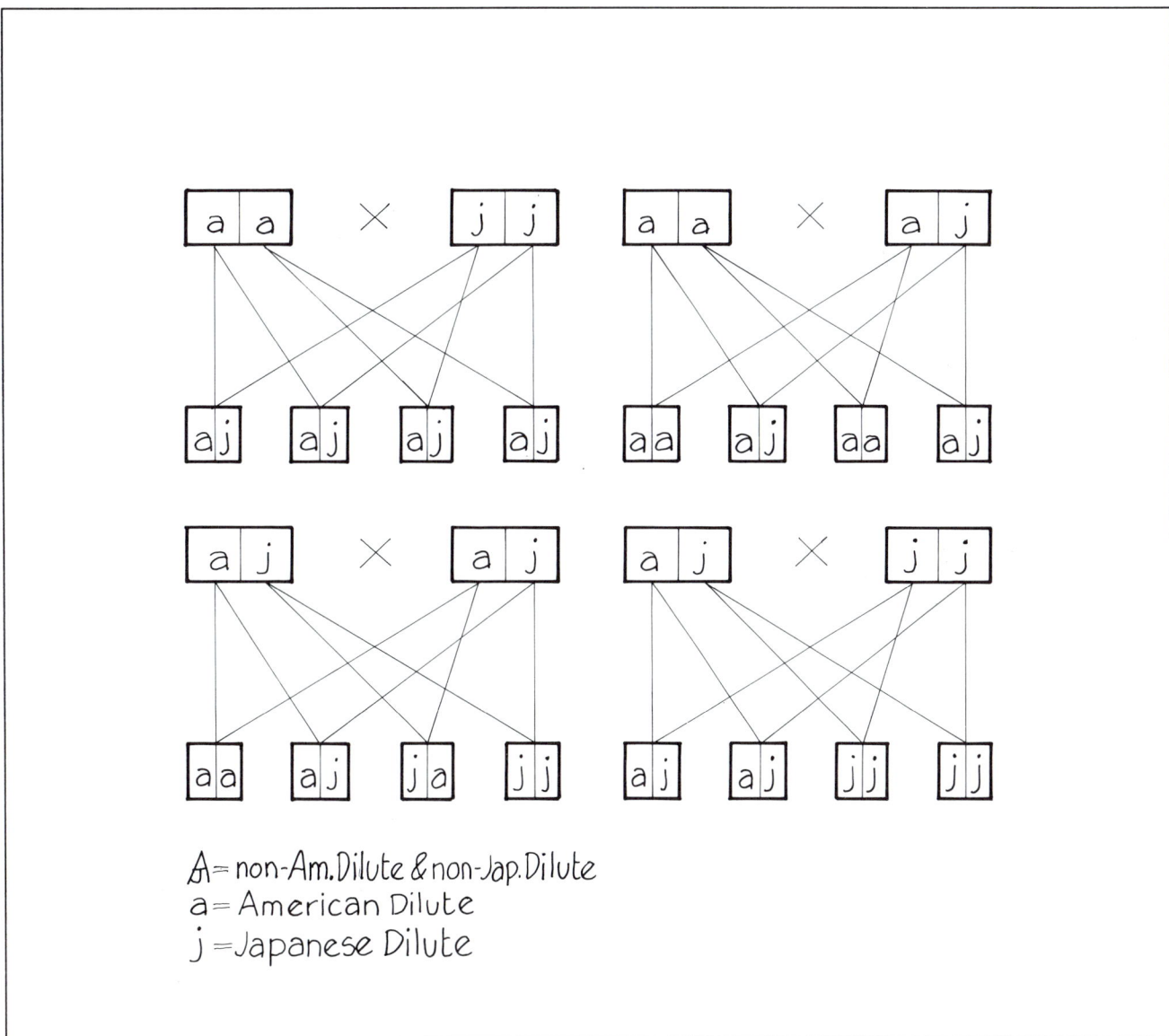

Diagram 14: Allelomorphism
(Example: American Dilute, Japanese Dilute & Wild Type Allelomorphs)

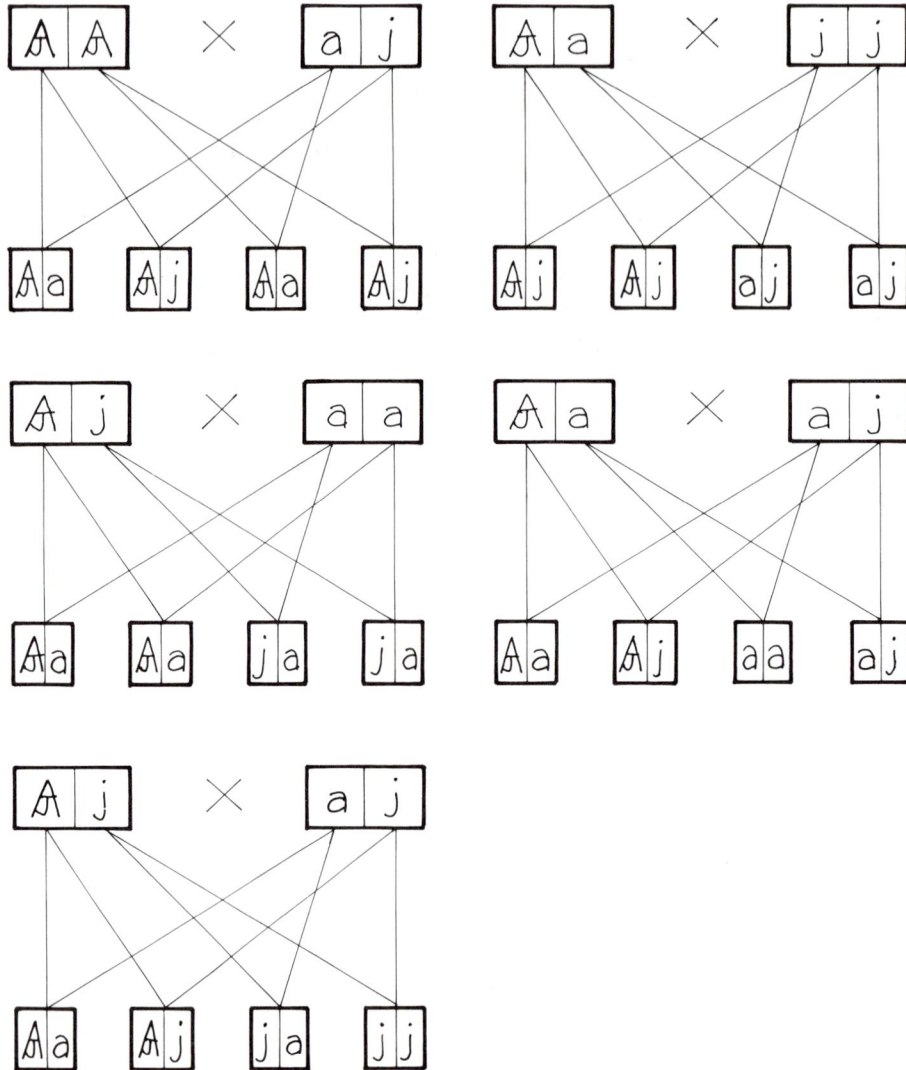

Diagram 15: Allelomorphism (Conclusion of Diagram 14)

36

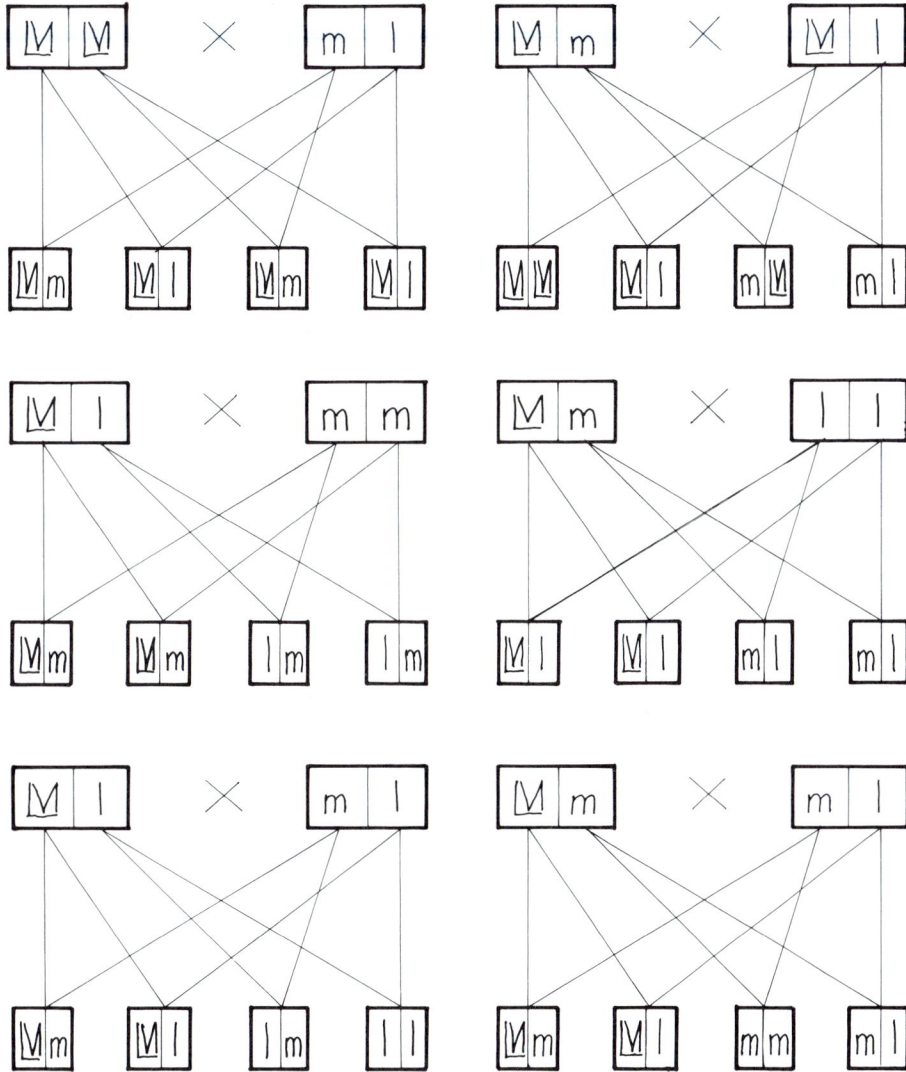

mm = Marine
l l = Lavender
m l = Marine-Lavender
l m = Marine-Lavender

M̲M̲ = Green
M̲m = Green/Marine
M̲l = Green/Lavender
m = Marine
l = Lavender
M̲ = non-Marine
& non-Lavender

Diagram 16: Allelomorphism –
One Mutant Gene (Autosomal Recessive in the General Structure)
Acting as Incomplete Dominant towards its Mutant Allele
(Example: Marine & Lavender)

37

m m	×	l l	

m l	m l	m l	m l

m l	×	m l	

m m	m l	l m	l l

m l	×	m m	

m m	m m	l m	l m

m l	×	l l	

m l	m l	l l	l l

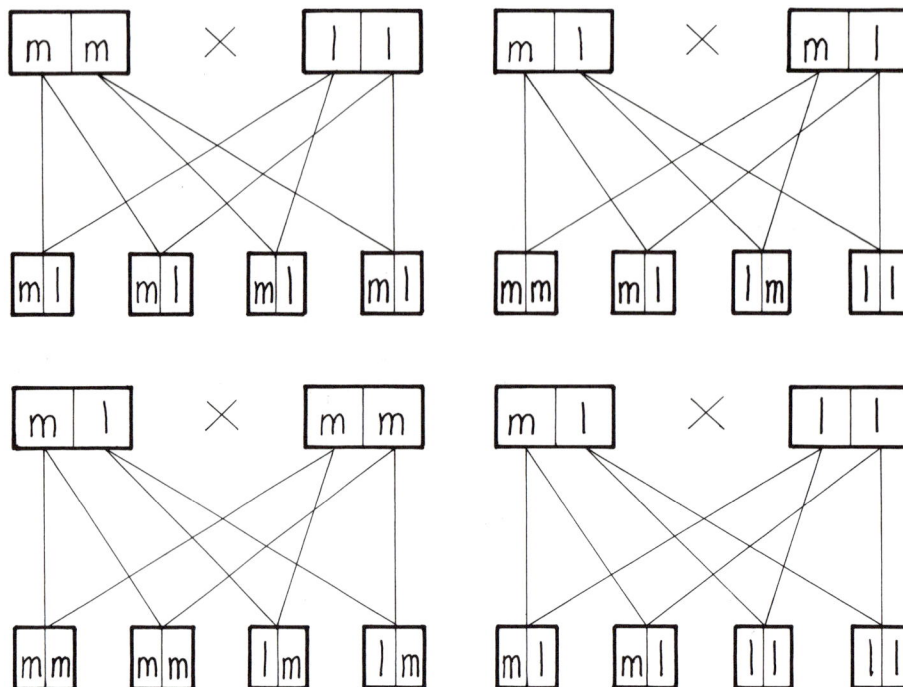

mm = Marine
l l = Lavender
m l = Marine-Lavender
l m = Marine-Lavender

MM = Green
Mm = Green/Marine
Ml = Green/Lavender
m = Marine
l = Lavender
M = non-Marine
& non-Lavender

Diagram 17: Allelomorphism (Conclusion of Diagram 16)

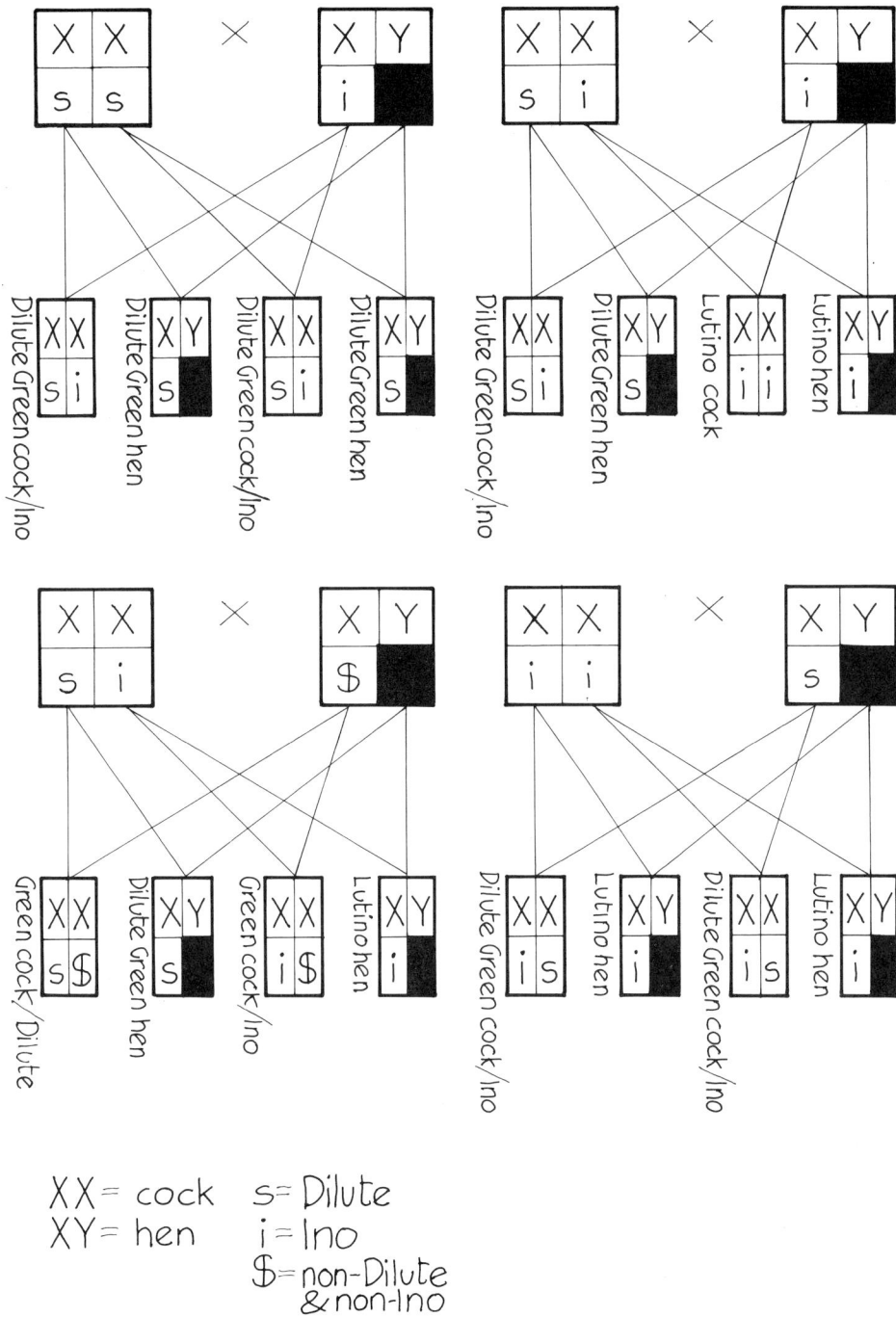

Diagram 18: Sex-linked Allelomorphism
(Example: Sex-linked Dilute & Sex-linked Ino)

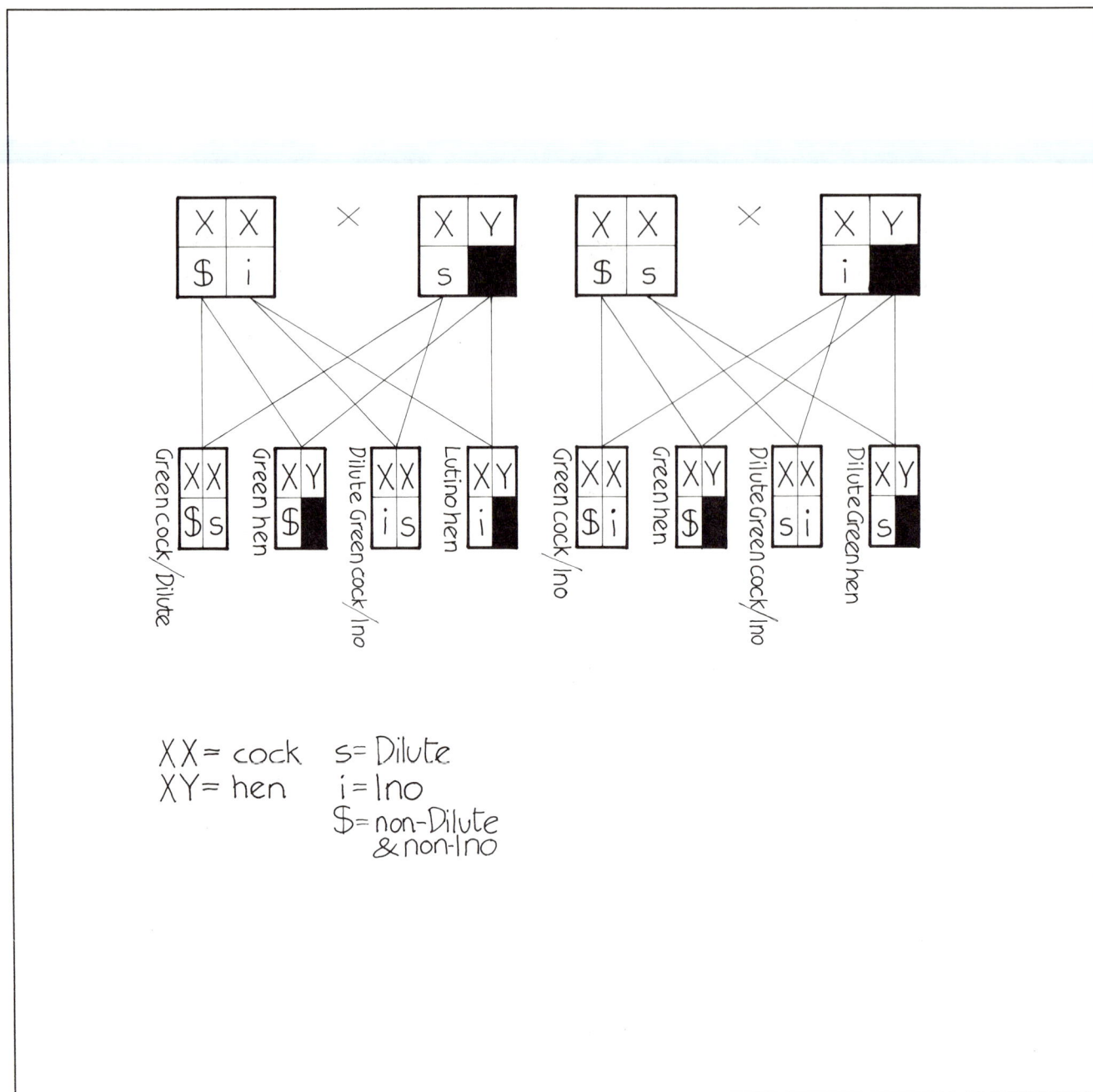

Diagram 19: Sex-linked Allelomorphism (Conclusion of Diagram 18)

Apart from the Marine and Lavender alleles in the Peach-faced Lovebird, and the Greywing and Clearwing alleles in the Budgerigar – in which the Dominant partner has not yet been identified – of those pairs of allelomorphic mutants known, the Dominant partner is the mutant variety which is able to carry out the function of the 'normal' allele to the greater degree.

Alleles cannot be combined to create a greater effect than the most effective of them can achieve, because only one or the other can occupy the allotted location point of the original 'normal' gene on each of the pair of chromosomes. They can only be a set of variations on a theme, and because of this the normal cross over of chromatid segments has no relevance.

Other than the Budgerigar, allelomorphs within psittacine species have so far only occurred in pairs, but it is quite possible that more than two alleles will develop from the same 'normal' gene or from an existing mutant gene in other psittacines. However, as will now be obvious, in the case of future multiple alleles, it will still only be possible for *two* of these genes to exist at one time on a pair of chromosomes; no more than two mutually allelomorphic genes can be carried by a single specimen – whether variety or non-variety.

The numerous emerging varieties in Rosellas, Red-rumped Parrakeets, Indian Ringneck Parrakeets, Grass Parrakeets, etc., may prove to have other allelomorphic forms in the future, and this will initially present some confusion to breeders until their inheritance patterns are fully explored and decided.

Comparisons with Marine (& Lavender) and the Yellow-face Varieties in the Budgerigar

With reference to the Peach-faced Lovebird: caution is advised in making indiscriminate crosses between Marine and Lavender, the resulting young are various shades of colour which range between the two types and this means that the two varieties in their pure form could become scarce. Some breeders believe that a minute proportion of specimens which are close to a true blue are produced off Marine-Lavender x Marine-Lavender, but no proof can be traced to support this hypothesis.

The inference – from Continental breeders especially – is that the Lavender *is* in fact the true Blue, but has been masked by being in combination with the Marine; if the Lavender could be isolated from the Marine, then the true Blue would become established. This is not logical, and no evidence has been found to prove that this has been achieved or that it is true.

Marine and Lavender are believed to be alleles, it is known that the first cross produces birds which are roughly intermediate in colour. See the previous notes on *Allelomorphs (Alleles)*.

Confusion may have been caused by lovebird breeders comparing Marine and Lavender with the Yellow-face varieties in Budgerigar culture, which also affect the amount of psittacin in the plumage. Yellow-face Blues in Budgerigar culture are worth looking at; they are regarded as Dominant mutations, even though their effect cannot be seen in the Green series and Greens split Yellow-face are accepted. There are two types of Yellow-face varieties recognized, designated as Yellow-face Mutant I and Yellow-face Mutant II.

Yellow-face I (Yellow-face Blue) is said to *decrease* the amount of yellow pigment (i.e. Single Factor = yellow face, Double Factor = white face), so there is a puzzle that it should be regarded as dominant to Green when it does not affect the colour of Green birds and can only be exhibited in the Blue series. According to this, it could be argued that Yellow-face I could not exist visually without the Blue mutant. This is not so with the Marine Peach-faced Lovebird, and was not so with the Marine variety in the Splendid Grass Parrakeet previous to the existence of *its* Blue, where for generations no pure Blues were bred from Marines. If Marines were the genetic equivalent of Yellow-face I, visual Blues would have been bred years ago in the Peach-faced, and years previous to the final emergence of Blue in the Splendid Grass Parrakeet.

Yellow-face II (Golden-face Blue) is said to exist in its own right and a Double factor *increases* instead of decreases the yellow pigment (i.e. Single Factor = yellow face, Double Factor = yellow face and spread of yellow suffusion, changing blue to green-blue).

There is no evidence to suggest that the two Yellow-face varieties are alleles, but type I is said to be an allele of Blue. The two mutants act as Incomplete Dominants on a sub-level to Green. Cross breeding with the two types leads to further complication!

A breeder of Quaker Parrakeets in the south of England has produced Marines and Blues from a pair of apparently normal pure Blue birds. Could this indicate a mutation Blue which increases yellow pigment when in Double Factor, like Yellow-face II? The same pair also produce red-eyed Pied Marine young with variegated areas of white and cream.

READER'S NOTES on SPECIES & VARIETIES KEPT

Species	Variety	Inheritance	Page No

4

PATTERNS OF INHERITANCE

PREDETERMINED PATTERNS

THE BASIC IDEA of predetermined patterns of inheritance must be grasped before the breeder can progress on to combining the various colour factors or varieties. Even so, there is no real need for us to be *too* concerned with complicated detail; just like a mechanical device or piece of electronic gadgetry, it is not necessary to fully understand each intricate working part in order to be able to make good use of the resulting tool or concept which it provides. Should the reader wish to study the science of genetics in minute detail, there are many specialist text books available which explain this complicated subject in great width and depth – but in most cases it will be noted that each author gives the matter an individualistic slant. For most breeders the main purpose of learning the patterns of inheritance is to find either the shortest way of producing the maximum number of a particular variety, ways of combining varieties, or ways of establishing new mutants.

Practice does not always run true to theory and where I have found this to be so, I shall adhere to the facts that have been discovered. Though extremely rare, *freak* expectations have happened, but they only serve to remind us that anomalies can and do present themselves. It may also be found that quite subtle or even obvious differences in breeding results can occur across a number of species in a variety which has the same effect on pigment and is apparently of the same genetic type throughout those species.

In this section – for the sake of simplicity and to aid the novice as much as possible – instead of using solely the scientific nomenclature of the geneticist, here, only those few terms which are widely used and accepted by bird breeders will be used in describing the modes of inheritance and methods of combining varieties. Depending on the predominant colour of the species concerned, the wild type will be described as Normal, Green, or – in the unique case of Bourke's Parrakeet – Brown.

Speaking very basically – though it has been shown there are further ways of precise definition – the existing colour varieties can be divided into three groups which are classed as Dominant, Recessive or Sex-linked.

Split
Though not indicating the presence of a particular variety (or varieties) visually, *split* refers to the ability of a bird which can produce young of that variety (or varieties), and (or) young which are themselves *split* for that variety (or varieties). Before finally pairing with a mate which will at last allow the mutant variety to erupt visually in their young, such birds may have inherited this ability from their parents, grand-parents or even from ancestors of countless previous generations.

In Britain, psittacine breeders speak of birds being split *for* a certain colour variety, but in America they speak of birds being split *to* that variety. The much older culture of the canary breeder describes split birds perhaps more descriptively as *carriers* or as *carrying* a particular variety, which does more to convey the image of a bird as a safe and secure vessel for hidden contents.

Varieties which are either Autosomal Recessive or Sex-linked Recessive may produce young which can be described as split, and for ease of use in tables of expectations, split is denoted by an oblique line – e.g. Green/Blue. Dominant varieties *cannot* be carried in a split form; hens *cannot* be split for a Sex-linked Recessive variety, but cocks *can;* both sexes *can* be split for an Autosomal Recessive variety.

Autosomal Dominant Inheritance

A bird of a Dominant variety, when paired to a bird of the wild type, will produce young – either some or all of which – will show the characteristics of their mutant parent to some degree in their outward appearance. These young will be able to pass on their visual differences to their own young in a greater or lesser amount. The sex of the parent showing the Dominant variety has no bearing on the colours of the resulting young.

Autosomal Incomplete Dominant Inheritance

Often a Dominant variety may be of a type which has a cumulative effect visually, so that both partners of a breeding pair must show at least some measure of the factor in their appearance if any of their young are to exhibit the full and undiluted visual effect of that variety. Here we see that the Dark Factor is the prime example of *Autosomal Incomplete Dominance*, and its pairings and expectations are the best illustrations of the workings of its type. The range of effect is Dark Green (partial effect) and Olive Green (full effect) – Green is of course 'no effect'.

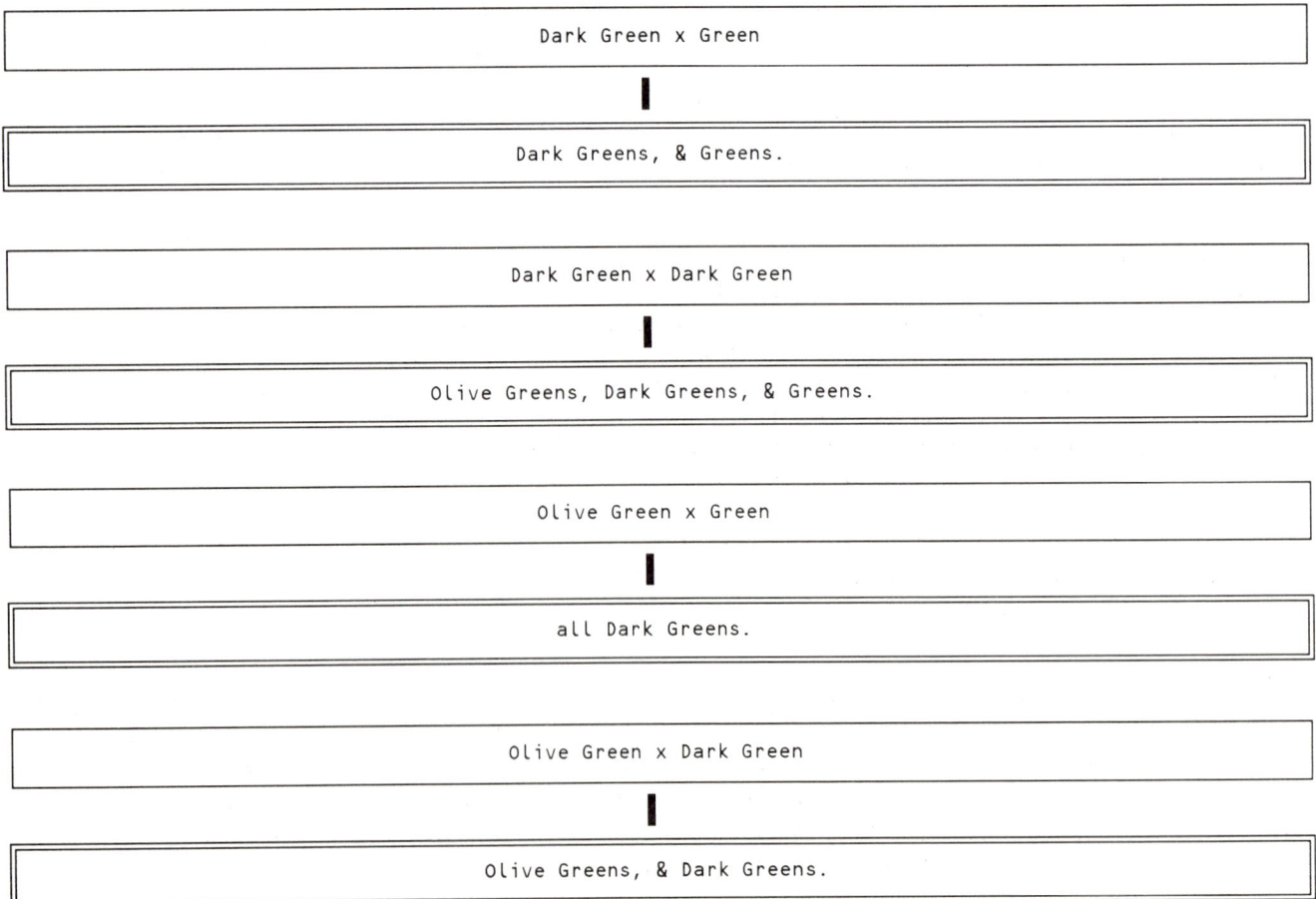

Dark Green x Green

Dark Greens, & Greens.

Dark Green x Dark Green

Olive Greens, Dark Greens, & Greens.

Olive Green x Green

all Dark Greens.

Olive Green x Dark Green

Olive Greens, & Dark Greens.

44

> Olive Green x Olive Green

> all Olive Greens.

Note: Olive Green is also referred to as Double Dark Factor Green and Dark Green as Single Dark Factor Green. 'Dark' and 'Slate' are used in the Blue, Marine and Lavender series.

The above illustrates very well how difficult it is for a new mutant to survive and increase in the wild state. Without the benefit of controlled breeding the effect of the mutation is gradually lessened until it disappears, unless the mutant or its progeny finally meet and pair with like individuals – a doubtful situation in the wild state.

Autosomal Complete Dominant Inheritance

Unlike Autosomal Incomplete Dominants, *Autosomal Complete Dominant* varieties should show no visual differences between Single and Double factor birds. In this case, Single and Double Factor are only a measure of the individual's ability to reproduce its variety within its progeny. For example, where a single specific Complete Dominant variety is concerned:

> Single Factor x Normal

> Single Factors, & Normals.

> Single Factor x Single Factor

> Double Factors, Single Factors, & Normals.

> Double Factor x Normal

> all Single Factors.

> Double Factor x Single Factor

> Double Factors, & Single Factors.

> Double Factor x Double Factor

> all Double Factors.

45

Autosomal Recessive Inheritance

For *Autosomal Recessive* characteristics to be displayed visually in the progeny of affected birds, the breeding pair must consist of either: two visual Recessives, a visual Recessive and a split, or two split Recessives. The sex of the visual or split Recessives has no bearing on the colour of their resulting young. For example, where a single Autosomal Recessive variety is concerned:

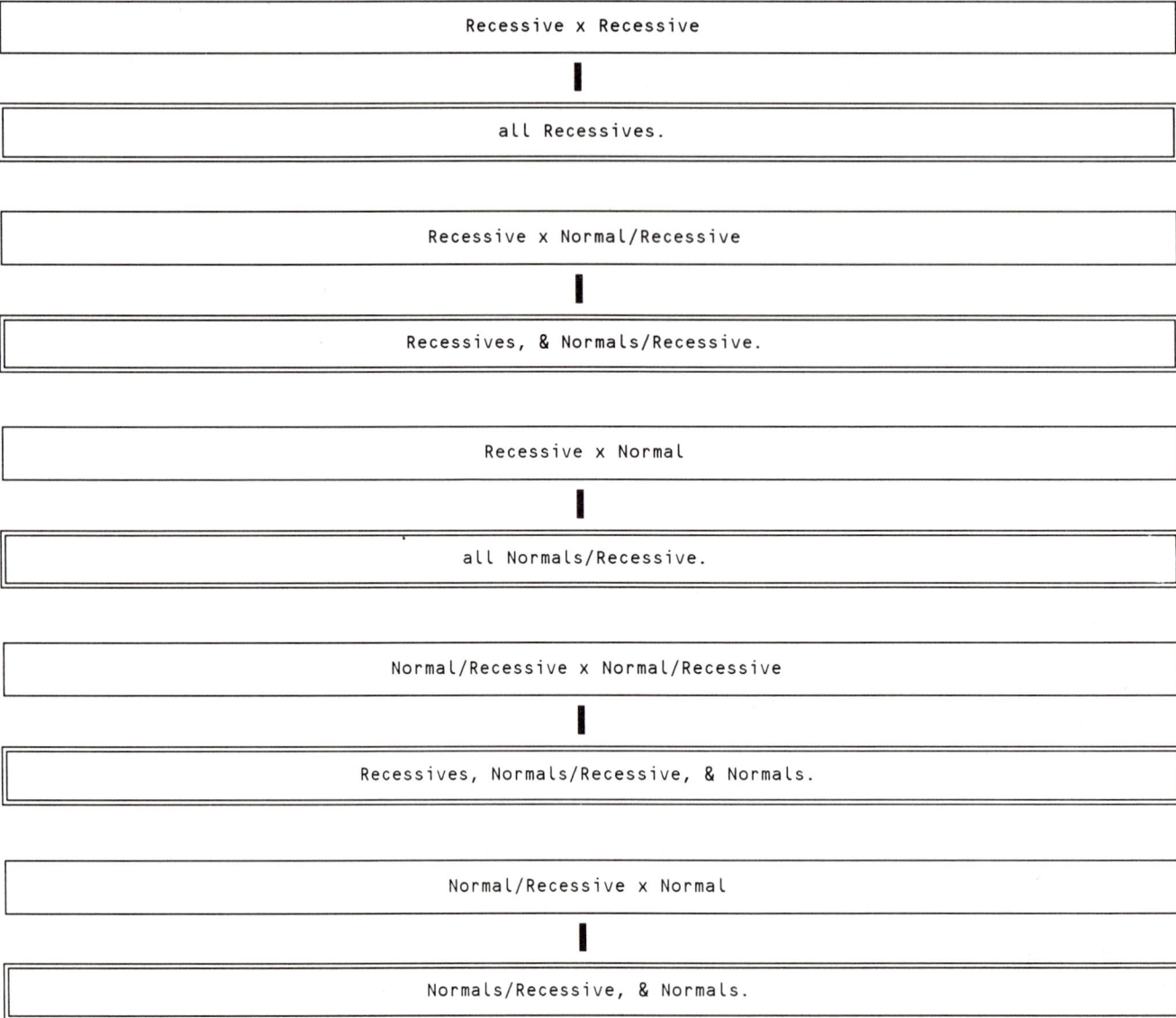

Recessive x Recessive

all Recessives.

Recessive x Normal/Recessive

Recessives, & Normals/Recessive.

Recessive x Normal

all Normals/Recessive.

Normal/Recessive x Normal/Recessive

Recessives, Normals/Recessive, & Normals.

Normal/Recessive x Normal

Normals/Recessive, & Normals.

By studying this list of pairings and expectations, it will be clearly seen that the last two pairings are the least desirable, and should be avoided where possible because they produce both Normals/Recessive and Normals. These birds will be impossible to tell apart by their appearance and so the breeder must resort to time consuming test matings in order to sift out any definite splits; hence the listing of 'possible' splits for this and that in bird sales advertisements. Obviously, 'possible' splits can also be split for nothing – and this fact is reflected in their comparatively cheap price!

Sex-linked Recessive Inheritance

The *Sex-linked Recessive* varieties are so named because the sex of the parent which exhibits or carries the mutant variety has a direct and all important control on which gender of young will inherit that variety. The cock has a much greater

46

ability to pass on the Sex-linked characteristics to its young than does the hen; *only cocks* can be split for a Sex-linked variety. For example, where a single specific Sex-linked Recessive variety is concerned:

```
Sex-linked cock x Sex-linked hen
```
I
```
all Sex-linked cocks & hens.
```

```
Sex-linked cock x Normal hen
```
I
```
Sex-linked hens, & Normal cocks/Sex-linked.
```

```
Normal cock/Sex-linked x Normal hen
```
I
```
Sex-linked hens, Normal cocks/Sex-linked, & Normal cocks & hens.
```

```
Normal cock/Sex-linked x Sex-linked hen
```
I
```
Sex-linked cocks & hens, Normal hens, & Normal cocks/Sex-linked.
```

```
Normal cock x Sex-linked hen
```
I
```
Normal hens, & Normal cocks/Sex-linked.
```

The above expectations show clearly why Sex-linked cocks are always most in demand; Sex-linked cocks paired to Normal hens produce young which — if they are of a red-eyed or plum-eyed variety — can all be sexed by their appearance immediately upon hatching, or — if dark-eyed — can be sexed while still growing their nestling feathers, even if they are a monomorphic species.

This beneficial arrangement has been of use in the past to poultry breeders when Sex-linked cockerels were run with non-Sex-linked pullets. In this way chicks were produced which did not incur the extra expense of employing poultry sexers.

Even so, many breeders overlook the fact that — apart from a breeding pair consisting of both partners of the same Sex-linked variety — it is the pairing of Normal cock split Sex-linked to Sex-linked hen which *produces* these more valuable Sex-linked cocks. Of course, in monomorphic species and species which do not show visual sexual differences in nestling and immature plumage, they cannot be sorted out immediately from the Sex-linked hens which appear in the same nest — but it is well worth waiting out this temporary inconvenience.

Dominance Can be Relative

We have seen that the wild type of the species (Normal, Green, etc.) is the watershed, the marker by which we judge and categorise the patterns of inheritance of the various psittacine varieties which have become established. However, in some rare instances – with Autosomal Recessives and Sex-linked Recessives – Dominance can be relative. There may be a 'pecking order' among closely allied mutant forms of a species (alleles). Where normally it would be expected that a first cross would cause a reversion to the wild type colour in the appearance of the young, this may not always be so – one variety can be subordinate to the other.

In the budgerigar, the Greywing shows Dominance over the Dilute, but both are Recessive to Green; i.e. Greywing Green x Dilute Green produces Greywing Greens split Dilute. In the Splendid Grass Parrakeet, the Marine shows Dominance over Blue, though both are Recessive to Green; i.e. Marine x Blue produces Marines split Blue. In the Peach-faced Lovebird, the Sex-linked Dilute shows Dominance over the Sex-linked Ino; i.e. Dilute Green cock x Lutino hen produces Dilute Green hens and Dilute Green cocks split Ino, when normally such a pairing would be expected to produce Dilute Green hens and Green cocks split Dilute and Ino.

Furthermore, it is possible but extremely rare for varieties to show what appears to be co-Dominance, so that paired together they produce young which show visual characteristics of both varieties or are mid-way in appearance. Each of these resulting young can pass on only *one* of these factors to each of their own progeny. For further explanation, see allelomorphs in the section on Relevant Genetics.

Planning Your Pairings

With a limited stock of birds, it is important to make the best use of the material to hand. By thoughtful planning the maximum production of certain varieties, combination and compound varieties can be achieved. The breeder may find it best to specialize in a single species, represented by a small selection of well chosen varieties which compliment each other and can be used to create other attractive colours. Trying to keep all the available varieties of the most developed species and making full use of the potential of their various qualities would be an impossible undertaking.

It is important to discover which pairings to avoid and which of the many possible combination and compound varieties are of no use from both a practical and aesthetic point of view.

Making the Patterns Work for You

It would be possible to found a number of strains of different colour varieties by obtaining a single specimen of a Compound Variety and, by first pairing it with a wild type bird, initiating a programme designed to separate the various component factors. However, if it is important to start off colour breeding the species of your choice with the least possible financial outlay, then the following suggestions will be useful.

The minimum requirement to start off with a specific Sex-linked Recessive variety would be a *split cock*, or better still two split cocks. Even if paired to non Sex-linked hens, these would produce a small amount of young Sex-linked hens. For example, with Indian Ringnecks, Alexandrines, Roseate Cockatoos, Cockatiels and Peach-faceds, two split Ino cocks could be paired for one season with two Green (Normal) hens; with good luck, each pair might produce at least one Lutino (Roseino for Roseate Cockatoos) hen which could be retained for breeding in the first possible season. At this time the original split Ino cocks could be taken from their Green (Normal) hens and mated with the other's daughter – so forming two unrelated pairs.

These pairs would produce Lutino cocks as well as Lutino hens, Green (Normal) hens, and more split Ino cocks. The third possible breeding season should then see a substantial number of useful birds with which to continue forming a sound strain.

First Season:

Green cock/Ino x Green hen

I

Lutino hens, Green cocks/Ino, & Green cocks & hens.

Second Season:

Green cock/Ino x Lutino hen

I

Lutino cocks & hens, Green hens, & Green cocks/Ino.

With this method the greatest outlay is time, but should a new mutation appear and specimens be at a premium, then this is an opportunity when it can be best employed. Strains of Autosomal Recessives varieties are not so easily formed, and the minimum requirement for production of visual Recessives is a breeding pair consisting of two splits. From a pair of splits a few visual Recessives will be thrown up, and these can be paired to unrelated splits the next possible breeding season – in a similar way as has been suggested for Sex-linked Recessives. Split paired to visual Recessive will produce a larger amount of young visual Recessive birds – and then the strain can be strengthened and enlarged.

First Season:

Normal/Recessive x Normal/Recessive

I

Recessives, Normals/Recessive, & Normals.

Second Season:

Normal/Recessive x Recessive

I

Recessives, & Normals/Recessive.

or:

Recessive x Recessive

I

all **Recessives**.

The minimum requirement for the production of psittacines displaying to some extent the features of an Autosomal Dominant variety is just one Dominant specimen – it has been previously explained that Dominant characteristics cannot be carried in a split form. If the breeder obtains two Dominant examples of a specific variety (of either sex) and pairs both with Normals, these must produce - depending on the variety - both Normals and Dominants, or all Single Factor Dominants. So in just the first season a young stock of unrelated birds can be conserved. In the next possible breeding season the Dominants can be paired together to concentrate the effect - where applicable - and to continue increasing their numbers.

First Season:

Double Factor Dominant x Normal

▌

all Single Factor Dominants.

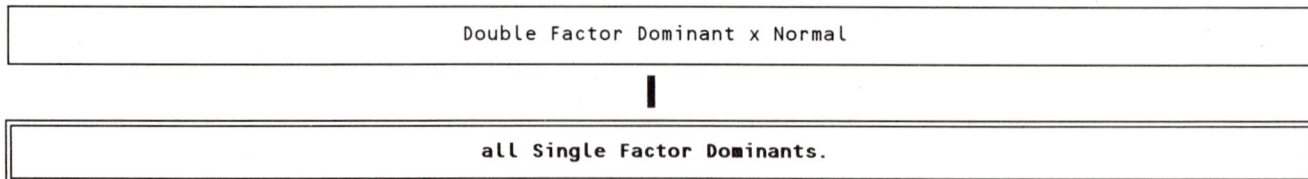

Second Season:

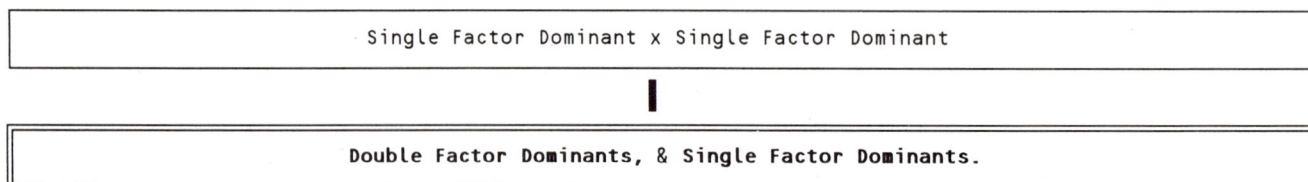

Single Factor Dominant x Single Factor Dominant

▌

Double Factor Dominants, & Single Factor Dominants.

Choosing Compatible Varieties

Some varieties combine to create further attractive colours, but it must be said that some combination or compound varieties turn out to be a waste of time and effort. A Pied variety combined with a ground colour modifier (Blue, Marine, White-faced, etc.) creates a range of subtle shades as well as bold patterns. Pied combined with the Dark Factor is striking; when the pattern of variegation is well balanced, strong contrasts are made with white, olive green, yellow and slate grey - depending on the species.

Pied combined with some Dilute varieties can lend a delicate subtlety of colour, or may create variation by laying down clear patches of ground colour surrounded by strong tints. Combining Cinnamon with the darker types of Dilute might be a worthwhile exercise with some species, as are the compound varieties which result from combinations with ground colour modifiers (Blue, Marine, etc.), with Cinnamon and Dilute.

Ground colour modifiers can also be combined with Ino to create Creamino, Ivorino and Albino. However, where two partial ground colour modifiers are concerned - such as Marine and Lavender - cross breeding seems a retrograde step and it is best to keep the two strictly apart; the two amalgamate and their individual nuances are lost.

Most varieties of the Cockatiel make good combinations; the melanin modifiers (Dilute, Cinnamon, Fallow and Ino), as well as Pied and Pearl all work together with a ground colour modifier to make a wide range of pleasing varieties.

Some years ago I spent much time and effort in combining the Dilute with the Dark Factor in the Peach-faced Lovebird, but was not pleased with the result - this was one of those occasion where my work was not rewarded. Each and every factor has its own use and will add a particular quality when combined with those varieties with which it is 'sympathetic', but it must be remembered that some combinations spoil rather than improve the overall appearance - and that others simply negate each others effect.

With the very basic and simple combinations there may be only one path to take, with intricate compound varieties there are often several possible avenues which lead to the same objective. Some may need to be long and meandering, but in others the breeder may discover ingenious short cuts by making full use of the patterns of inheritance as applied to the stock available for the project.

It must be asked what the purpose may be in making such time consuming efforts, where - in the common species and varieties - so many of these birds are now available. In answer: the novice breeder will gain satisfaction and knowledge by going through these various procedures, and be fully equipped to deal with other rarer varieties in the future. The advanced breeder may wish to instil special qualities found in individual specimens already to hand, which are not present in compound variety specimens freely available for purchase from other breeders; in order to achieve an envisaged ideal it may be necessary to start the chosen combination or compound variety from scratch. Improvements in size, type, stance, feather quality, length of crest, length of tail, brilliance of colour, hardiness and prolific nature - all or any may need to be introduced by selective breeding, and serious faults might need to be corrected (e.g. bald crowns in Cockatiels).

READER'S NOTES on SPECIES & VARIETIES KEPT

Species	Variety	Inheritance	Page No

5

KNOWN PRIMARY VARIETIES

THE PRIMARY MUTANTS listed here with a brief description of their effect on plumage and their recorded modes of inheritance, are either commonly bred, well established or in the initial stages of being established within aviculture − it is likely that more will occur in an increasing number of species with each year that passes.

LIST OF SPECIES (in alphabetical order)

Adelaide Rosella (Platycercus adelaidae)

Ino   *Inheritance: Autosomal Recessive*
Effect: Total lack of melanin gives yellow, cream and white plumage marked with orange and red; bill and feet, flesh coloured; eyes, red. (Lutino).

Cinnamon   *Inheritance: Sex−linked Recessive*
Effect: Change from melanin black to melanin brown, changes black areas (especially on mantle) to brown and fawn.

Alexandrine Parrakeet (Psittacula eupatria)

Ino   *Inheritance: Sex−linked Recessive*
Effect: Total lack of melanin changes green plumage to yellow; maroon shoulder patches made lighter red; pupil, red; bill, red with whitish tip; feet, flesh coloured. Cock's black neck ring changed to white but pink collar retained. (Lutino).

Blue   *Inheritance: Autosomal Recessive*
Effect: Total lack of psittacin changes green plumage to blue and ground colour to white; maroon shoulder patches changed to grey; red bill retained. Cock's black neck ring retained but pink collar changed to white.

Australian King Parrot (Alisterus scapularis)

Dilute   *Inheritance: Autosomal Recessive*
Effect: Almost complete lack of melanin changes green plumage to yellow with a lime tinge in some areas; red plumage retained and lightened.

Barnards Parrakeet (Barnardius barnardi)

Blue   *Inheritance: Autosomal Recessive*
Effect: Total lack of psittacin changes green plumage to various shades of blue and ground colour to white.

53

Black-cheeked Lovebird (Agapornis nigrigenis)

Dilute *Inheritance: Autosomal Recessive*
Effect: Partial loss of melanin changes green plumage to lime green, with black on face made brownish.

Blue *Inheritance: Autosomal Recessive*
Effect: Total lack of psittacin changes green plumage to blue and ground colour to white; red bill changed to pinkish.

Bourke's Grass Parrakeet (Neophema bourkii)

Dilute (Red-eyed) *Inheritance: Autosomal Recessive*
Effect: Almost complete reduction of melanin leaves plumage coloured in pale pinks, creams, white and fawn. Bill, pale brown; cere and feet, flesh coloured; eyes, red.

Cinnamon *Inheritance: Sex-linked Recessive*
Effect: Change from melanin black to melanin brown, changes black areas to brown and fawn. Slightly paler than Fallow, so that more pink ground colour shows through. Eyes, dark red.

Fallow *Inheritance: Autosomal Recessive*
Effect: Only slightly paler in colour than the wild type, but with plum red eyes.

Rosa *Inheritance: Sex-linked Recessive*
Effect: Apart from wings, almost complete lack of melanin in specific areas, coupled with greatly enhanced strawberry pink ground colour. Blue forehead band of cock reduced to scattered blue feathers.

Pied *Inheritance: Autosomal Dominant*
Effect: Patchy elimination of melanin, with variegated areas whitish.

Cockatiel (Nymphicus hollandicus)

Ino *Inheritance: Sex-linked Recessive*
Effect: Total lack of melanin changing grey plumage to yellow, cream and white; orange cheek patches retained; bill and feet, flesh coloured; eyes entirely red in immatures, red pupils and pale irides in adults. Yellow striations retained on hen's tail and flights. (Lutino).

Cinnamon *Inheritance: Sex-linked Recessive*
Effect: Change from melanin black to melanin brown, changes grey plumage to fawn-grey. Area of yellow on head and face greatly increased in hens.

Fallow *Inheritance: Autosomal Recessive*
Effect: Change from melanin black to melanin brown, with further reduction giving a buff or tan colour; eyes, red; bill and feet, pale. Hens have yellowish faces and cream-yellow plumage from breast to belly.

Dilute *Inheritance: Autosomal Incomplete Dominant*
Effect: Partial reduction of melanin in two shades. Single Factor less effective than Double Factor which makes plumage silvery grey. (English).

Dilute   *Inheritance: Autosomal Recessive*
Effect: Partial reduction of melanin which makes plumage silvery grey. The effect is variable and eyes may be pale to red.

Pied   *Inheritance: Autosomal Recessive*
Effect: Patchy elimination of melanin, making contrasting white patches on grey plumage and flesh coloured patches on bill and feet.

White-faced   *Inheritance: Autosomal Recessive*
Effect: Total lack of psittacin changes yellow and cream ground colour to white, and removes orange cheek patches completely.

Pale-faced   *Inheritance: Autosomal Recessive*
Effect: Partial lack of psittacin, changes yellow and cream ground colour to cream and white, and orange cheek patches to yellow-orange.

Pearl   *Inheritance: Sex-linked Recessive*
Effect: Melanin pigment removed from centres of feathers in specific areas of plumage, resulting in polka dot or laced effect. Hen: tail and crest, yellow feathers with dark quills. Cock: loses visual effect on maturity in most strains. Increased effect described as Laced.

Deep Yellow Suffusion   *Selective Breeding*
Effect: Enhancement of yellow and orange ground colour. Deepest yellow ground colour described as 'Buttercup', mid-range described as 'Primrose' - difficult to judge in reality.

Eastern Rosella (Platycercus eximius)

Ino   *Inheritance: Sex-linked Recessive*
                        and Autosomal Recessive forms
Effect: Total lack of melanin gives yellow, cream and white plumage; red made lighter; eyes, red; bill and feet, flesh coloured. (Lutino).

Cinnamon   *Inheritance: Sex-linked Recessive*
Effect: Change from melanin black to melanin brown, changes black areas (especially on mantle) to brown and fawn.

Dilute   *Inheritance: Autosomal Recessive*
Effect: Partial to almost complete lack of melanin changes green plumage to yellow with a lime tinge; black on mantle reduced to greygreen or pale green; red plumage retained and lightened. Effect variable with some birds almost totally lacking in melanin on back and wings - resulting in practically yellow backs.

Pied   *Inheritance: Autosomal Dominant*
Effect: Melanin lacking in patches, revealing yellow and white ground colour, but elimination of red in variegated areas is a detrimental trait.

Ruby   *Inheritance: Sex-linked Recessive*
Effect: Spread of red colour over all of underparts; red-pink tail with dark quill.

Melanistic   *Inheritance: Autosomal Recessive*
Effect: Spread of black or blackish plumage over most of bird; flecks of black in white cheek patches; some red on head and breast; hens blacker than cocks.

Elegant Grass Parakeet (Neophema elegans)

Ino
Inheritance: Autosomal Recessive

Effect: Yellow and white ground colour; doubt over variety, due to smutty wings/tails in some birds. Eyes, red; bill, feet - pinkish. (Lutino).

Cinnamon
Inheritance: Sex-linked Recessive

Effect: Melanin black changed to melanin brown, making plumage paler overall; flights brownish.

Pied
Inheritance: Autosomal Dominant

Effect: Patchy elimination of melanin which reveals yellow and white ground colour; paler bill and feet.

Fischer's Lovebird (Agapornis fischeri)

Ino
Inheritance: Autosomal Recessive

Effect: Total lack of melanin, changing green plumage to yellow; red-orange of head clarified and enhanced; red bill retained; eyes, red pupil and pink irides; feet, flesh coloured. (Lutino).

Dilute
Inheritance: Autosomal Recessive

Effect: Partial loss of melanin making green plumage lime green. Some European strains show almost total reduction of melanin, changing green to yellow. Almost certain to have been introduced via hybridization with Dilute Masked; evidence can be seen in transitional head colour of some specimens.

Blue
Inheritance: Autosomal Recessive

Effect: Total lack of psittacin, changing green plumage to blue; orange on head to white-grey; yellow ground colour to white. Bill, pale pink.

Indian Ringneck Parrakeet (Psittacula krameri manillensis)

Ino
Inheritance: Sex-linked Recessive

Effect: Total lack of melanin changes green plumage to yellow; pupil, red; bill, red with whitish tip; feet, flesh coloured. Cock's black neck ring changed to white but pink collar retained. (Lutino).

Cinnamon
Inheritance: Sex-linked Recessive

Effect: Melanin black changed to melanin brown, makes plumage slightly paler overall, but with little change to the cock's neck ring.

Clearhead
Inheritance: Autosomal Recessive

Effect: Melanin slightly reduced throughout makes plumage paler; adult cocks heads are yellowish due to almost total lack of melanin but pink and black collar retained; hens lack the clear head.

Dilute
Inheritance: Sex-linked Recessive

Effect: Almost complete reduction of melanin making green plumage yellow with lime tinge; head, yellow; cock's black neck ring changed to pale grey.

Pied
Inheritance: Autosomal Recessive

Effect: Patchy elimination of melanin reveals yellow ground colour; extensive spread over plumage; detrimental in causing break up or disappearance of cock's pink neck ring (as well as black).

Blue   *Inheritance: Autosomal Recessive*

Effect: Total lack of psittacin changes green plumage to blue and yellow ground colour to white; red bill retained. Cock's black neck ring retained but pink collar changed to white.

Marine   *Inheritance: Autosomal Recessive*

Effect: Partial lack of psittacin changes green plumage to green-blue and yellow ground colour to cream; red bill retained. Cock's black neck ring retained but pink collar made paler.

Grey   *Inheritance: Autosomal Complete Dominant*

Effect: Elimination of blue through negation of Tyndall effect changes green plumage to greygreen.

Lineolated Parrakeet (Bolborhynchus lineola)

Ino   *Inheritance: Sex-linked Recessive*

Effect: Total lack of melanin, changing green plumage to yellow; red bill retained; eyes, red; bill and feet, flesh coloured. (Lutino).

Marine   *Inheritance: Autosomal Recessive*

Effect: Almost complete lack of psittacin, changing green plumage to blue and yellow ground colour to cream.

Dark Factor   *Inheritance: Autosomal Incomplete Dominant*

Effect: Darkens plumage in two phases.

Masked Lovebird (Agapornis personata)

Ino   *Inheritance: Autosomal Recessive*

Effect: Total lack of melanin, changing green plumage to yellow; black of head changed to red-orange making the species practically indistinguishable from Lutino Fischer's; red bill retained; eyes, red pupil and pink irides; feet, flesh coloured; introduction of Ino via hybridization with Lutino Fischer's. (Lutino).

Dilute   *Inheritance: Autosomal Recessive*

Effect: Partial loss of melanin making green plumage lime green and black head brownish. Some European strains show almost total reduction of melanin, changing green to yellow. Hybridization with Dilute Fischer's has left specimens of intermediate colour; evidence can be seen in transitional head colour of some specimens.

Blue   *Inheritance: Autosomal Recessive*

Effect: Total lack of psittacin, changing green plumage to blue and yellow ground colour to white. Bill, pale pink.

Dark Factor   *Inheritance: Autosomal Incomplete Dominant*

Effect: Darkens plumage in two phases.

Nyasa Lovebird (Agapornis lilianae)

Ino   *Inheritance: Autosomal Recessive*

Effect: Total lack of melanin, changing green plumage to golden yellow; red-orange of head clarified and enhanced; pink and red bill retained; eyes, red pupil and pink irides; feet, flesh coloured. (Lutino).

Peach–faced Lovebird (Agapornis roseicollis)

Ino   *Inheritance: Sex–linked Recessive*
Effect: Total lack of melanin, changing green plumage to golden yellow; pink and red of head clarified and enhanced; bill, flesh coloured; eyes, red; feet, flesh coloured. (Lutino).

Dilute   *Inheritance: Autosomal Recessive*
Effect: Partial loss of melanin making green plumage lime yellow; grey lacing on wings; pink and red of head clarified and enhanced. Some forms or strains more yellow than others. (American).

Dilute   *Inheritance: Sex–linked Recessive*
Effect: Partial loss of melanin making green plumage lime yellow; flights light grey-fawn with no lacing; pink and red of head clarified and enhanced. (Australian).

Cinnamon   *Inheritance: Sex–linked Recessive*
Effect: Melanin black changed to melanin brown, making plumage paler overall; flights fawnish; pink and red of head clarified and enhanced; eyes, dark brown.

Fallow   *Inheritance: Autosomal Recessive*
Effect: Incomplete reduction of melanin, changing green plumage to lime; flights greyish fawn; pink and red of head clarified and enhanced; eyes, red.

Pied   *Inheritance: Autosomal Dominant*
Effect: Patchy elimination of melanin reveals ground colour; causes shrinkage of red and pink of head and throat; variable spread over plumage.

Pied   *Inheritance: Autosomal Recessive*
Effect: Patchy elimination of melanin reveals ground colour; causes shrinkage of red and pink of head and throat; variegation extends to most of plumage with a predominance of 'clear' birds; dark markings on some specimens is evidence of Pied trait. (Australia).

Marine   *Inheritance: Autosomal Recessive*
Effect: Partial lack of psittacin changes green to green-blue; red and pink areas changed to salmon pink and ivory.

Lavender   *Inheritance: Autosomal Recessive*
Effect: Almost complete lack of psittacin on underpart of abdomen changes green to blue; partial lack on upperparts changes green to green-blue; trace of pink remains on forehead.

Tangerine   *Inheritance: Autosomal Incomplete Dominant*
Effect: Change of red and pink on face to orange in Double Factor, Single Factor is mid-way.

Dark Factor   *Inheritance: Autosomal Incomplete Dominant*
Effect: Darkens plumage in two phases.

Violet   *Inheritance: Autosomal Complete Dominant*
Effect: Violet tint over plumage can be seen to greatest effect on rump area.

Red Suffusion   *Inheritance: Possibility unknown*
Effect: Change from yellow to red ground colour; variable in spread and increases with age.

58

Pennant's Rosella (Platycercus elegans)

Blue *Inheritance: Autosomal Recessive*
Effect: Total elimination of psittacin red; crimson areas changed to greyish white in some strains which possess less melanin, and grey in darker strains. Black areas retained and blue areas enhanced.

Princess of Wales Parrakeet (Polytelis alexandrae)

Ino *Inheritance: Autosomal Recessive*
Effect: Total lack of melanin reveals yellow and white ground colour; pink plumage enhanced; eyes, red; feet, flesh coloured; bill, pink. (Lutino).

Blue *Inheritance: Autosomal Recessive*
Effect: Total lack of psittacin, changing green plumage to blue; yellow and pink ground colour to white. Bill, pale pink.

Red Suffused *Selective Breeding*
Effect: Yellow ground colour changed to red, amount varies with the individual.

Port Lincoln Parrakeet (Barnardius zonarius zonarius)

Blue *Inheritance: Autosomal Recessive*
Effect: Total lack of psittacin, changing green plumage to blue and yellow ground colour to white.

Quaker Parrakeet (Myiopsitta monachus)

Blue *Inheritance: Autosomal Recessive*
Effect: Total lack of psittacin, changing green plumage to blue and yellow ground colour to white.

Dilute *Inheritance: Autosomal Recessive*
Effect: Almost complete loss of melanin making green plumage yellow; but retention of some pale grey on face and breast markings.

Red-fronted Kakariki (Cyanoramphus novaezelandiae)

Cinnamon *Inheritance: Sex-linked Recessive*
Effect: Melanin black changed to melanin brown, making plumage paler overall; flights grey-brown; red of head lighter; feet and cere paler; brown-black tip to bill.

Pied *Inheritance: Autosomal Dominant*
Effect: Patchy elimination of melanin reveals ground colour; causes shrinkage of red on head and throat; variable spread over plumage.

Red-rumped Parrakeet (Psephotus haematonotus)

Ino *Inheritance: Sex-linked Recessive*
Effect: Total lack of melanin reveals yellow and white ground colour; red rump clarified and enhanced; eyes, red; feet and bill flesh coloured. (Lutino).

Cinnamon   *Inheritance: Sex-linked Recessive*
Effect: Melanin black changed to melanin brown, makes plumage paler overall and flights grey-brown. (Australia).

Dilute   *Inheritance: Sex-linked Recessive*
Effect: Incomplete reduction of melanin changing hen's plumage to cream, and making dark green plumage lime green in cock; red of rump brightened.

Pied   *Inheritance: Autosomal Recessive*
Effect: Patchy elimination of melanin reveals yellow, cream and white ground colour; extensive spread over plumage; detrimental in causing difficulty in sexing, and red on cock's rump to change to yellow.

Blue   *Inheritance: Autosomal Recessive*
Effect: Total lack of psittacin changes green plumage to blue, and yellow ground colour to white; cock's red rump eliminated and changed to pure white in best specimens; hen's plumage changed to grey-fawn.

Marine   *Inheritance: Autosomal Recessive*
Effect: Partial lack of psittacin changes green to green-blue; changes yellow ground colour to cream; cock's red rump changed to pale orange; hen's olive plumage given greyish tone.

Roseate Cockatoo (Eolophus roseicapillus)

Ino   *Inheritance: Sex-linked Recessive*
Effect: Total lack of melanin changing grey plumage to white; rosy pink plumage brightened; bill and feet, flesh coloured; eyes, red, hen has pinkish iris. (Roseino).

Dilute   *Inheritance: Autosomal Recessive*
Effect: Partial reduction of melanin which makes grey plumage silvery grey.

White-faced   *Inheritance: Autosomal Recessive*
Effect: Total lack of psittacin changes pink ground colour to white.

Scaly-breasted Lorikeet (Trichoglossus chlorolepidotus)

Grey   *Inheritance: Autosomal Complete Dominant*
Effect: Elimination of blue through negation of Tyndall effect changes green plumage to greygreen.

Splendid Grass Parrakeet (Neophema splendida)

Cinnamon   *Inheritance: Sex-linked Recessive*
Effect: Melanin black changed to melanin brown, changes green plumage to lime green, blues made paler; flights to grey-brown; cock's breast to lighter scarlet; feet, bill and cere to flesh colour.

Dilute   *Inheritance: Sex-linked Recessive*
Effect: Slight loss of melanin making greens and blues slightly lighter; flights, dark grey; feet, bill and cere lighter than wild type.

Fallow   *Inheritance: Autosomal Recessive*
Effect: Slight reduction in melanin making blues and greens slightly paler; eyes, reddish.

Pied *Inheritance: Autosomal Dominant*
Effect: Patchy elimination of melanin reveals yellow and white ground colour; individuals vary in amount of variegation; retrograde side effect causes elimination of cock's scarlet breast where variegated.

Blue *Inheritance: Autosomal Recessive*
Effect: Total lack of psittacin changes green plumage to blue and yellow ground colour to white; scarlet chest area of cock changed to white.

Marine *Inheritance: Autosomal Recessive*
Effect: Partial lack of psittacin changes green plumage to green-blue and yellow ground colour to cream; scarlet breast of cock changed to salmon pink. Greener strain exists.

Red-bellied *Selective Breeding*
Effect: Yellow lower abdomen of cock and hen changed to red; natural trait which can be selectively bred.

Stanley Rosella (Platycercus icterotis)

Blue *Inheritance: Autosomal Recessive*
Effect: Total elimination of psittacin red and yellow changes scarlet areas to greyish white and green areas to blue. Black retained and blue areas enhanced.

Turquoisine Grass Parrakeet (Neophema pulchella)

Dilute *Inheritance: Autosomal Recessive*
Effect: Almost complete loss of melanin changing green to yellow with slight lime tinge on back and head; blues made pale; maroon wing bar changed to red; feet, bill and cere only slightly lighter than wild type.

Fallow *Inheritance: Autosomal Recessive*
Effect: Slight reduction in melanin making blues and greens slightly paler; eyes, red.

Pied *Inheritance: Autosomal Recessive*
Effect: Patchy elimination of melanin reveals yellow and white ground colour; individuals vary in amount of variegation; retrograde side effect causes elimination of cock's maroon wing bars where variegated.

Pearl *Inheritance: Sex-linked Recessive*
Effect: Melanin lacking from centres of individual feathers giving a pearl or laced effect; selective breeding increases amount of ground colour revealed on each feather. Hens are more yellow than cocks and have orange-red wing bars which causes uncertainty in sexing.

Marine *Inheritance: Autosomal Recessive*
Effect: Partial lack of psittacin changes green plumage to green-blue and yellow ground colour to cream; maroon wing bars duller.

Red-fronted *Selective Breeding*
Effect: Yellow areas of upper lower abdomen of cock and hen changed to orange-red.

Dark Factor *Inheritance: Autosomal Incomplete Dominant*
Effect: Darkens plumage in two phases.

Twenty-eight Parrakeet (Barnardius zonarius semitorquatus)

Blue   *Inheritance: Autosomal Recessive*

Effect: Total lack of psittacin, changing green plumage to blue and yellow ground colour to white.

Yellow Rosella (Platycercus flaveolus)

Dilute   *Inheritance: Autosomal Recessive*

Effect: Partial to almost complete lack of melanin makes yellow plumage more pure in colour. Black on mantle feathers reduced to pale grey-fawn; red frontal band retained. (Australia).

FOR FUTURE REVISIONS OF THIS MANUAL: the publishers will appreciate any news, photographs, slides, breeding results, descriptions and information relating to recently occurring primary colour varieties.

6

GLOSSARY of EQUIVALENT NAMES of VARIETIES

Australian King Parrot (Alisterus scapularis)

Dilute Normal = Yellow.

Black-cheeked Lovebird (Agapornis nigrigenis)

Dilute Green = Yellow.
Dilute Blue = White.

Bourke's Grass Parrakeet (Neophema bourkii)

Cinnamon = Isabel (Holland).
Dilute (Red-eyed) Brown = Yellow (Britain) or Cream (Australia).
Dilute Rosa Brown = Yellow Rosa (Britain) or Lacs (Holland).

Cockatiel (Nymphicus hollandicus)

Cinnamon Lutino = Cafe au lait or Lavender Wing (with controversy, Britain).
Dilute Normal = Silver.
Lutino = White or Albino.
Fallow Dilute = Platinum.
Pearl = Laced for exaggerated form.

Eastern Rosella (Platycercus eximius)

Cinnamon = Isabel.
Dilute Normal = Pastel or Yellow.
Melanistic = Black.
Pied = Silver-winged, and White-winged for heavily variegated form.
Ruby = Red or Opaline.

Fischer's Lovebird (Agapornis fischeri)

Dilute Green = Yellow.
Dilute Blue = White.

Lineolated Parrakeet (Bolborhynchus lineola)

Dark Marine = Cobalt.
Slate Marine = Mauve.

Masked Lovebird (Agapornis personata)

Dilute Green = Yellow.
Dilute Blue = White.
Dark Blue = Cobalt.
Slate Blue = Mauve.

Peach-faced Lovebird (Agapornis roseicollis)

Cinnamon = American Cinnamon.
Creamino = Albino (Holland and USA).
Dark Green = Jade or Medium Green (Holland, Australia and USA).
Dark Marine = Cobalt or Medium Dutch Blue (Holland and USA).
Dilute (Recessive) Green = Golden Cherry or American Yellow (Holland and USA).
Dilute (Recessive) Marine = Silver Cherry or American White (Holland and USA).
Dilute (Sex-linked) Green = Australian Cinnamon.
Dilute (Sex-linked) Marine = Ivory (Australia).
Dilute (Sex-linked) Olive Green = Mustard (Australia).
Lavender = White-faced Blue or White-masked.
Marine = Pastel Blue, Dutch Blue or Par-blue.
Marine-Lavender = White-faced Green (Britain) or Seagreen (Holland).
Olive Green = Dark Green (Holland and USA).
Pied (Recessive) Green = Australian Yellow or Yellow (Holland).
Red Suffusion = Red-pied, Red, or Red-spotted.
Slate Marine = Mauve or Dark Dutch Blue (Holland and USA).
Tangerine (Tang-) = Orange-faced.

Quaker Parrakeet (Myiopsitta monachus)

Dilute Green = Yellow.

Red-rumped Parrakeet (Psephotus haematonotus)

Dilute Green = Yellow.
Marine = Blue.

Indian Ringneck Parrakeet (Psittacula krameri manillensis)

Cinnamon = Isabel (Holland).
Cinnamon Blue = Airblue (Holland).
Cinnamon Greyblue = Silver (Holland).
Cinnamon Ino = Lacewing (Holland).
Cinnamon Olive = Golden Cherry (Holland).
Clearhead Green = Yellowhead.
Clearhead Blue = Whitehead.
Dilute Green = Buttercup (Belgium) or Yellowhead Cinnamon (Holland).
Greygreen = Olive.
Greyblue = Grey.
Greymarine = Pastelgrey (Holland).
Lutino = Yellow.
Marine = Turquoise, Green-blue or Pastel-blue (Holland).

64

Roseate Cockatoo (Eolophus roseicapillus)

Dilute Normal = Silver (Australia).
Roseino = Lutino (Australia).
White-faced = Grey and White.

Scaly-breasted Lorikeet (Trichoglossus chlorolepidotus)

Greygreen = Olive.

Splendid Grass Parrakeet (Neophema splendida)

Blue = White-breasted Blue.
Cinnamon Blue = Silver.
Cinnamon Dilute Blue = Ivory.
Cinnamon Dilute Green = Golden Yellow.
Dilute Green = Isabel (Holland).
Dilute Blue = Heaven Blue.
Marine = Blue (Britain); Pastelblue and Seagreen for a greener phase (Holland).

Turquoisine Grass Parrakeet (Neophema pulchella)

Dark Green = Jade.
Dilute Green = Yellow.
Marine = Blue or Pastel Blue.
Pearl = Pied.

Yellow Rosella (Platycercus flaveolus)

Dilute Normal = Yellow (Australia).

READER'S NOTES on NEW COLOUR VARIETIES

Species	Description of New Variety	Inheritance if Known
PLUM-HEADED PARRAKEET	LUTINO (INDIA)	AUTOSOMAL RECESSIVE
"	CINNAMON (INDIA)	SEX-LINKED RECESSIVE
CELESTIAL PARROTLET	BLUE (EUROPE)	AUTOSOMAL RECESSIVE
"	FALLOW (EUROPE)	AUTOSOMAL RECESSIVE

7

INHERITANCE of
KNOWN PRIMARY VARIETIES

PRELIMINARY NOTES

SEASONS

THROUGHOUT ALL the following pairings – and the Universal Breeding Programmes in section *8* – first, second and third seasons do *not* necessarily mean *consecutive* breeding seasons. They signify instead the next possible seasons the individual pair can be persuaded to breed. For instance, Lovebirds, Grass Parrakeets and Cockatiels could be expected to breed at one year old, so fresh young pairs could be set up each season – a *three* season breeding programme could be completed in *three* years. The larger species mentioned may take two, three, four years or more to reach maturity. Asiatic parrakeets taking *three* years to mature, would need a minimum of *nine* years to complete a three season breeding programme.

Provided that the breeder already holds the necessary birds, it may be possible to skip the first or even second breeding seasons and enter the suitable breeding programme at a more advanced position.

Percentages of Expected Young

Most writers on colour varieties refer in a precise way to the percentages of types of young which can be expected from given pairings – with great emphasis on the figures and theory. When these calculations are not borne out in practice, excuses have to be found for the failures of their predictions. I have always believed that the inclusion of exact percentages are a needless complication for breeders to take into account, especially for beginners who may be struggling with the basic rules of inheritance.

Unless obtained from pure theory, percentages are usually arrived at after breeding averages have been estimated. Averages are calculated from figures which must include maximums and minimums; so we return to the fact that maximums and minimums of numbers of varieties of nestlings are found in practical results!

The larger the number of visual varieties and splits that a breeding pair are able to produce, the less likely are actual percentages of expectations to be proven in practice. It is only possible to predict what is probable, not what is definitely going to be.

According to theory, it would be a very outside chance for a youngster exhibiting a certain hoped for set of factors to be produced from a breeding pair which (between the two partners) is split for several varieties. Even so, on a number of occasions, I have found that such long shots do occur, not only once but several times in the season – and off more than one pair. On the other hand, where – in theory – pairings should have produced substantial amounts of a particular single variety, none at all have been forthcoming over the entire season.

No percentages of expectations are quoted in the following pages, which also means that occasions where the Crossover Theory might apply need not be mentioned. It is impossible to predict percentages of Crossover young without knowing the Crossover Values and these can only be evaluated from extensive breeding results. At present, values have so far only been established for Budgerigars and there seems no reason to suppose these to be correct for other psittacines.

Pairing and Progeny Boxes

Throughout this section *(7)* and the following section *(8)*, on *Universal Breeding Programmes for Combination and Compound Varieties* – as with the previously 'boxed' examples of pairings and expectations in sections *3* and *4* – a single outline represents the breeding pair, a double outline represents the expected young, and the sought after young are printed in bold text, i.e.:

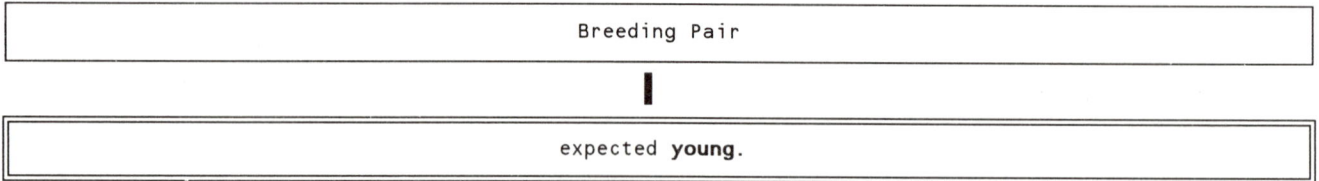

```
+--------------------------------------------------+
|                  Breeding Pair                   |
+--------------------------------------------------+
```

I

```
++------------------------------------------------++
||                expected young.                 ||
++------------------------------------------------++
```

Inheritance Codes

The inheritance of each variety is denoted by (AR) for Autosomal Recessive, (SLR) for Sex-linked Recessive, (AID) for Autosomal Incomplete Dominant, (ACD) for Autosomal Complete Dominant, and (S) for Selective Breeding. *See section 10 for ways in which these references can be used.*

THE STATE OF AVAILABILITY *of the following primary varieties and suggested combination and compound varieties – from the time of writing – may improve or even deteriorate as time passes. However, it is most likely that the coming years will see the list of species and varieties greatly increased.*

AUTOSOMAL RECESSIVE VARIETIES (AR)

Blue (AR)

The pure Blue (total elimination of psittacin) or its equivalent, is common in the Masked Lovebird, Indian Ringneck Parrakeet and Cockatiel **(White-faced)**; becoming more frequently available in Pennant's Rosella and Splendid Grass Parrakeet; scarce in the Quaker Parrakeet, Princess of Wales Parrakeet and Fischer's Lovebird; so far confined to Australia in the Red-rumped Parrakeet; rare or extremely rare in the Black-cheeked Lovebird, Alexandrine Parrakeet and Roseate Cockatoo. There have been other examples of Blue specimens, especially in South American species – macaws, amazons, parrakeets and parrotlets – but evidence as to their attempted establishment in aviculture is not forthcoming at present.

The ground colour of all *true* Blues is pure white. All Blues have so far proved to be Autosomal Recessive in their inheritance; the sex of individuals as related to Blue inheritance is immaterial, e.g.:

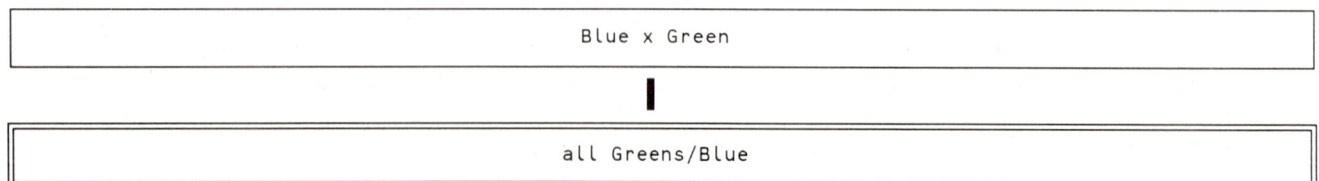

```
+--------------------------------------------------+
|                  Blue x Green                    |
+--------------------------------------------------+
```

I

```
++------------------------------------------------++
||                all Greens/Blue                 ||
++------------------------------------------------++
```

Green/Blue x Green/Blue

I

Greens, Greens/Blue, & Blues.

Green/Blue x Green

I

Greens/Blue, & Greens.

Blue x Green/Blue

I

Blues, & Greens/Blue.

Blue x Blue

I

all Blues.

For Cockatiels and Roseate Cockatoos: replace Blue with **White-faced**, and Green with **Normal.**

It is worthwhile including Blue in Combination or Compound varieties with the following existing factors:

Masked Lovebird: Ino (making Albino), Dilute and Dark Factor.
Fischer's Lovebird: Ino (making Albino) and Dilute.
Black-cheeked Lovebird: Dilute.
Indian Ringneck Parrakeet: Ino (making Albino), Cinnamon, Clearhead, Dilute, Pied and Grey.
Alexandrine Parrakeet: Ino (making Albino).
Splendid Grass Parrakeet: Cinnamon, Dilute and Pied.
Red-rumped Parrakeet: Ino (making Albino), Cinnamon, Dilute and Pied.
Princess of Wales Parrakeet: Ino (making Albino).
Cockatiel: Ino (making Albino), Cinnamon, Fallow, Dilute, Pied and Pearl.
Roseate Cockatoo: Ino (making Albino) and Dilute.
Quaker Parrakeet: Dilute.

Marine (AR)

The Marine (partial reduction in psittacin) or its equivalent, is common in the Peach-faced Lovebird and Splendid Grass Parrakeet (which exists in a Greener strain, probably an allele of Marine; i.e. lesser effect on psittacin); obscure or rare in the Indian Ringneck Parrakeet, Red-rumped Parrakeet, Turquoisine Grass Parrakeet (possibly introduced through hybridization with Marine Splendids), Cockatiel **(Pale-faced)** and Lineolated Parrakeet. There have been other rare examples of Marine specimens, including the Plum-headed Parrakeet, Alexandrine Parrakeet, and Port Lincoln Parrakeet.

The ground colour of Marine is cream. All Marines have so far proved to be Autosomal Recessive in their inheritance, so the sex of the above species as related to Marine inheritance is immaterial, e.g.:

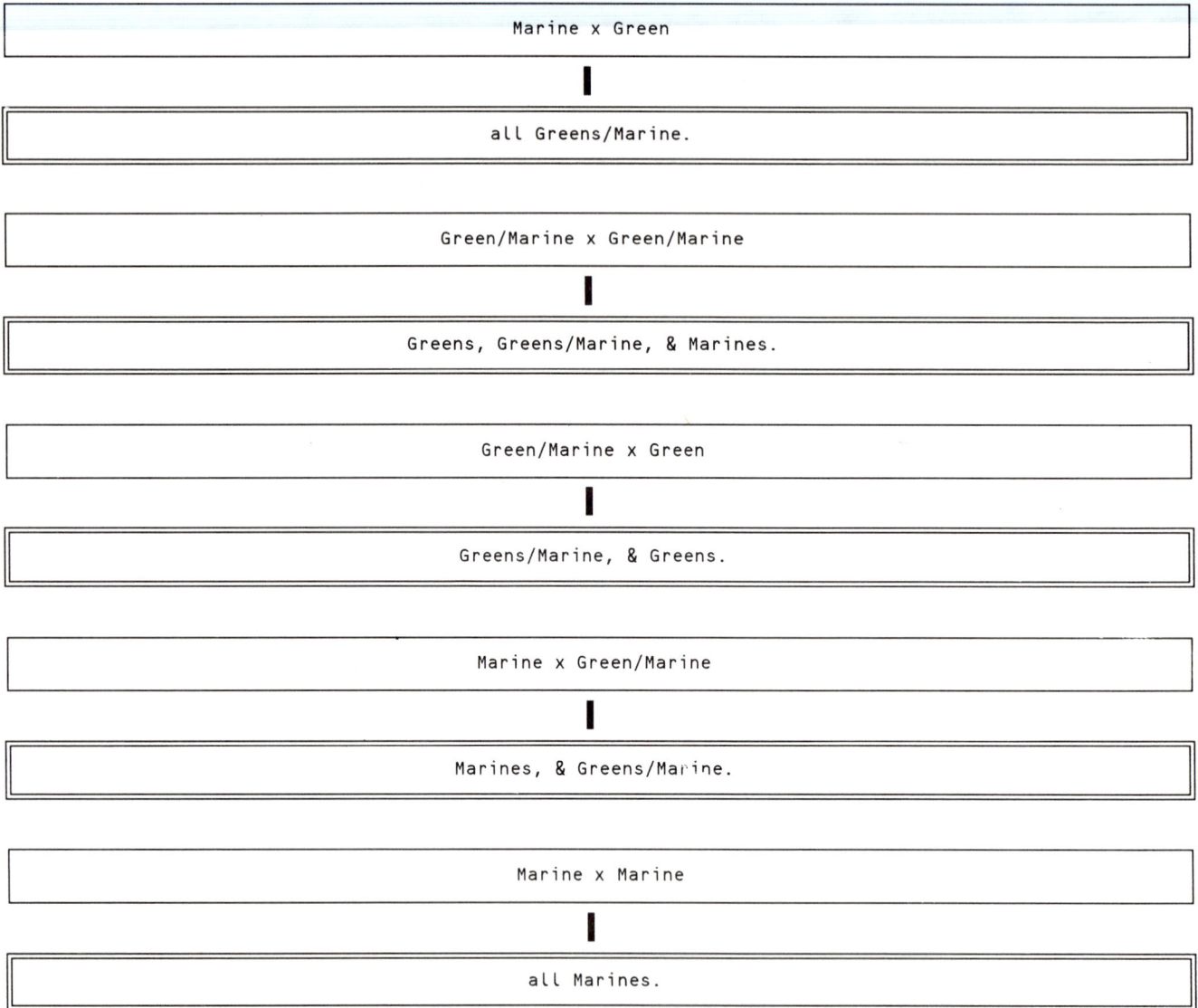

Marine x Green

↓

all Greens/Marine.

Green/Marine x Green/Marine

↓

Greens, Greens/Marine, & Marines.

Green/Marine x Green

↓

Greens/Marine, & Greens.

Marine x Green/Marine

↓

Marines, & Greens/Marine.

Marine x Marine

↓

all Marines.

The following pairings illustrate the relationship of *Marine* with *Blue*, Marine acts as the Dominant and Blue as the Recessive (see allelomorphs), e.g.:

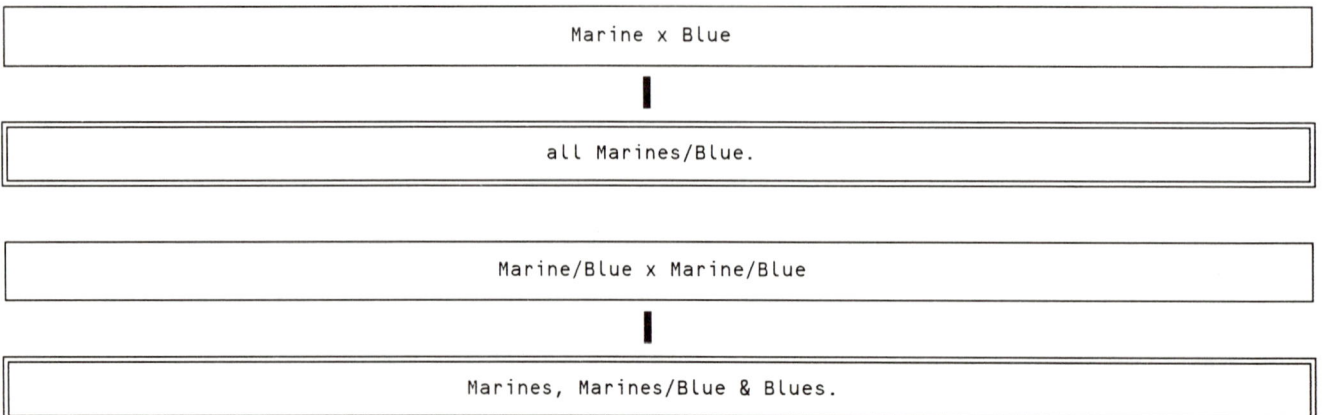

Marine x Blue

↓

all Marines/Blue.

Marine/Blue x Marine/Blue

↓

Marines, Marines/Blue & Blues.

```
┌──────────────────────────────────────────────────────────────────┐
│                      Marine/Blue x Marine                          │
└──────────────────────────────────────────────────────────────────┘
                                 █
┌──────────────────────────────────────────────────────────────────┐
│                    Marines/Blue, & Marines.                        │
└──────────────────────────────────────────────────────────────────┘

┌──────────────────────────────────────────────────────────────────┐
│                       Marine/Blue x Blue                           │
└──────────────────────────────────────────────────────────────────┘
                                 █
┌──────────────────────────────────────────────────────────────────┐
│                    Blues, & Marines/Blue.                          │
└──────────────────────────────────────────────────────────────────┘
```

For Cockatiels: replace Marine with **Pale-faced**, Blue with **White-faced**, and Green with **Normal** throughout the preceding pairings and expectations.

It is worthwhile including Marine in Combination or Compound varieties with the following existing factors:

Peach-faced Lovebird: Ino (making Creamino), Dilute, Cinnamon, Fallow, Pied, Tangerine, Dark Factor and Violet Factor. *(Note: crossing Marine with Lavender produces birds half way between the two in appearance - there is no point. See allelomorphs.)*

Indian Ringneck Parrakeet: Ino (making Creamino), Cinnamon, Clearhead, Dilute, Pied and Grey.

Splendid Grass Parrakeet: Cinnamon, Dilute, Pied and Red-bellied. *(Note: crossing Marine with the 'Greener' strain is said to produce examples of both types - there is no point. See allelomorphs.)*

Turquoisine Grass Parrakeet: Dilute, Fallow, Pied, Pearl, Dark Factor and Red-fronted.

Red-rumped Parrakeet: Ino (making Creamino), Dilute, Cinnamon and Pied.

Cockatiel: Ino (making Creamino), Cinnamon, Fallow, Dilute, Pied and Pearl.

Lineolated Parrakeet: Ino (making Creamino) and Dark Factor.

Lavender (AR)

The Lavender (more reduction of psittacin on face and belly than Marine, and less reduction of psittacin on back and wings) is found in the Peach-faced Lovebird and is scarce in its pure form, having been crossed frequently with Marine.

The ground colour of Lavender is ivory. Lavender has proved to be Autosomal Recessive in its inheritance, so the sex of the above species as related to Lavender inheritance is immaterial. To illustrate its relationship with Green, replace Marine with **Lavender** in the pairings and expectations given in the previous section on Marine.

It is worthwhile including Lavender in Combination or Compound varieties with the following existing factors:

Peach-faced Lovebird: Ino (making Ivorino), Dilute, Cinnamon, Fallow, Pied, Tangerine, Dark Factor and Violet Factor. *(Note: crossing Lavender with Marine produces birds half way between the two in appearance - there is no point. See allelomorphs.)*

Dilute (AR)

The Recessive Dilute (partial reduction of melanin) can take on any fixed phase of the various gradations between almost complete lack of melanin and only a slight

71

loss of melanin. The variety is common in the Peach-faced Lovebird, Fischer's Lovebird, Masked Lovebird and Turquoisine Grass Parrakeet; it is becoming more frequently available in the Bourke's Parrakeet (Red-eyed Dilute) and Eastern Rosella, it is scarce in the Cockatiel, and is a great rarity in the Australian King Parrot, Quaker Parrakeet, Black-cheeked Lovebird and Roseate Cockatoo.

The Dilute mutation is seen to be most effective at reducing melanin in the Bourke's Parrakeet, Turquoisine Grass Parrakeet, Australian King Parrot and Roseate Cockatoo; slightly less effective in the Peach-faced Lovebird and Quaker Parrakeet; even less so in the Masked and Fischer's Lovebirds (though there are paler strains), and variable to a great extent in the Eastern Rosella.

There are Dilute varieties which have different modes of inheritance, but those listed here are all Recessive to their appropriate wild type and so the sex of the above species as related to Dilute inheritance is immaterial, e.g.:

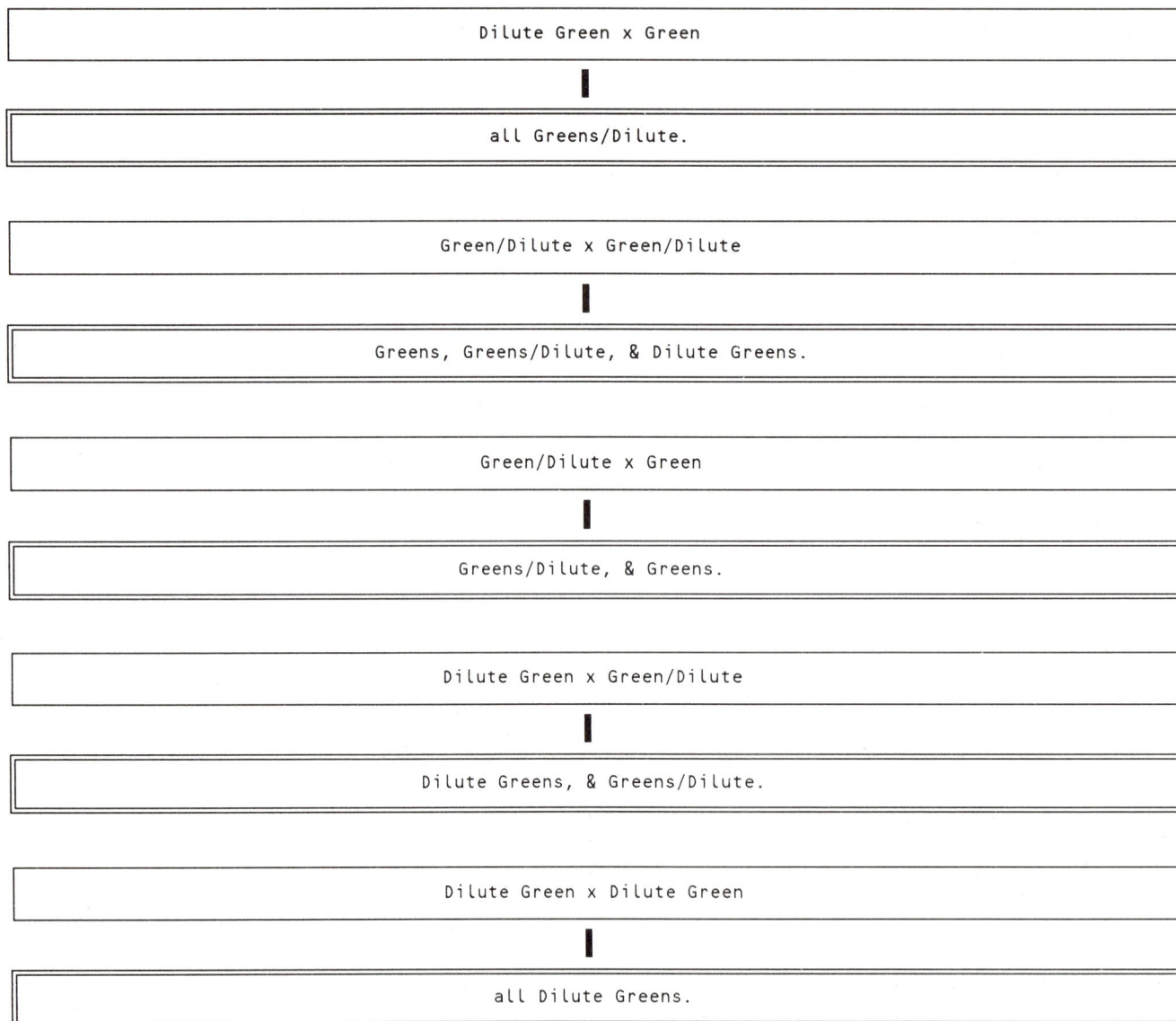

Dilute Green x Green

▮

all Greens/Dilute.

Green/Dilute x Green/Dilute

▮

Greens, Greens/Dilute, & Dilute Greens.

Green/Dilute x Green

▮

Greens/Dilute, & Greens.

Dilute Green x Green/Dilute

▮

Dilute Greens, & Greens/Dilute.

Dilute Green x Dilute Green

▮

all Dilute Greens.

For Eastern Rosella, Cockatiel and Roseate Cockatoo: replace Green with **Normal** throughout the preceding pairings and expectations.

For Bourke's Grass Parrakeet: replace Green with **Brown** throughout the preceding pairings and expectations. *(Note: apart from the Recessive Dilute Cockatiel which shows variable eye colour, the Red-eyed Dilute Bourke's is the odd one out in this section for obvious reasons. There may be a dark-eyed Dilute*

Bourke's in the future - but otherwise there seems little use in affording it an entire section on its own with no like kinds to keep it company).

It is worthwhile including Recessive Dilute in Combination or Compound varieties with the following existing factors:

Peach-faced Lovebird: Marine, Lavender, Cinnamon, Fallow, Pied, Tangerine, Dark Factor and Violet Factor.
Masked Lovebird: Blue and Dark Factor.
Fischer's Lovebird: Blue.
Black-cheeked Lovebird: Blue.
Bourke's Grass Parrakeet: Fallow, Cinnamon, Rosa and Pied.
Turquoisine Grass Parrakeet: Marine, Fallow, Pied, Pearl, Dark Factor and Red-fronted.
Eastern Rosella: Cinnamon and Ruby.
Australian King Parrot: as far as is known, none.
Cockatiel: White-faced, Pale-faced, Cinnamon, Fallow, Pied, Pearl and Deep Yellow Suffusion. Crossing with the Dominant Dilute will create confusion and is inadvisable.
Roseate Cockatoo: White-faced.
Quaker Parrakeet: Blue.

Clearhead (AR)

The Clearhead is a unique and rare variety of the Indian Ringneck Parrakeet (partial reduction of melanin, but with the cock's head practically reduced to ground colour).

Clearhead is Autosomal Recessive in its inheritance, so the sex of the birds as related to inheritance is immaterial. To illustrate its relationship with Green replace Dilute with **Clearhead** in the pairings and expectations given in the previous section on Dilute.

It is worthwhile including Clearhead in Combination or Compound varieties with the following existing factors:

Indian Ringneck Parrakeet: Blue, Marine and Grey.

Fallow (AR)

The Fallow (slight reduction of melanin in plumage, associated with red eyes) is obscure in the Bourke's Grass Parrakeet and Cockatiel; and rare and obscure in the Peach-faced Lovebird, Splendid and Turquoisine Grass Parrakeets. Its value as an addition to be incorporated in the framework of combination and compound varieties in the above species is not certain, but its pattern of matings and expectations with the wild type can be illustrated by replacing Dilute with **Fallow** in the pairings and expectations given in the previous section on Dilute.

For Cockatiels: replace Dilute with **Fallow** and Green with **Normal** throughout the preceding pairings and expectations in the section on Dilute.

For Bourke's Grass Parrakeet: replace Dilute with **Fallow** and Green with **Brown** throughout the preceding pairings and expectations in the section on Dilute.

It could be worthwhile including Fallow in Combination or Compound varieties with the following existing factors:

Peach-faced Lovebird: Marine, Lavender, Cinnamon, Dilute, Pied, Tangerine, Dark Factor and Violet Factor.
Bourke's Grass Parrakeet: Dilute, Cinnamon, Rosa and Pied.

Turquoisine Grass Parrakeet: Marine, Dilute, Pied, Pearl, Dark Factor and Red-fronted.

Splendid Grass Parrakeet: Blue, Marine, Cinnamon, Dilute, Pied and Red-bellied.

Cockatiel: White-faced, Pale-faced, Cinnamon, Dilute, Pied, Pearl and Deep Yellow Suffusion.

Ino (AR)

The Ino (total elimination of melanin) is generally thought of as a Sex-linked variety, in which genetic type it is easier to establish, but some notable Autosomal Recessive Lutinos exist. The Lutino Nyasa has existed for decades but is still an avicultural rarity; the variety is extremely rare in the Eastern and Adelaide Rosellas, scarce in the Princess of Wales Parrakeet but becoming more frequently available in the Elegant Grass Parrakeet. In these varieties its inheritance is as for the other Autosomal Recessives when interacting with Green, e.g.:

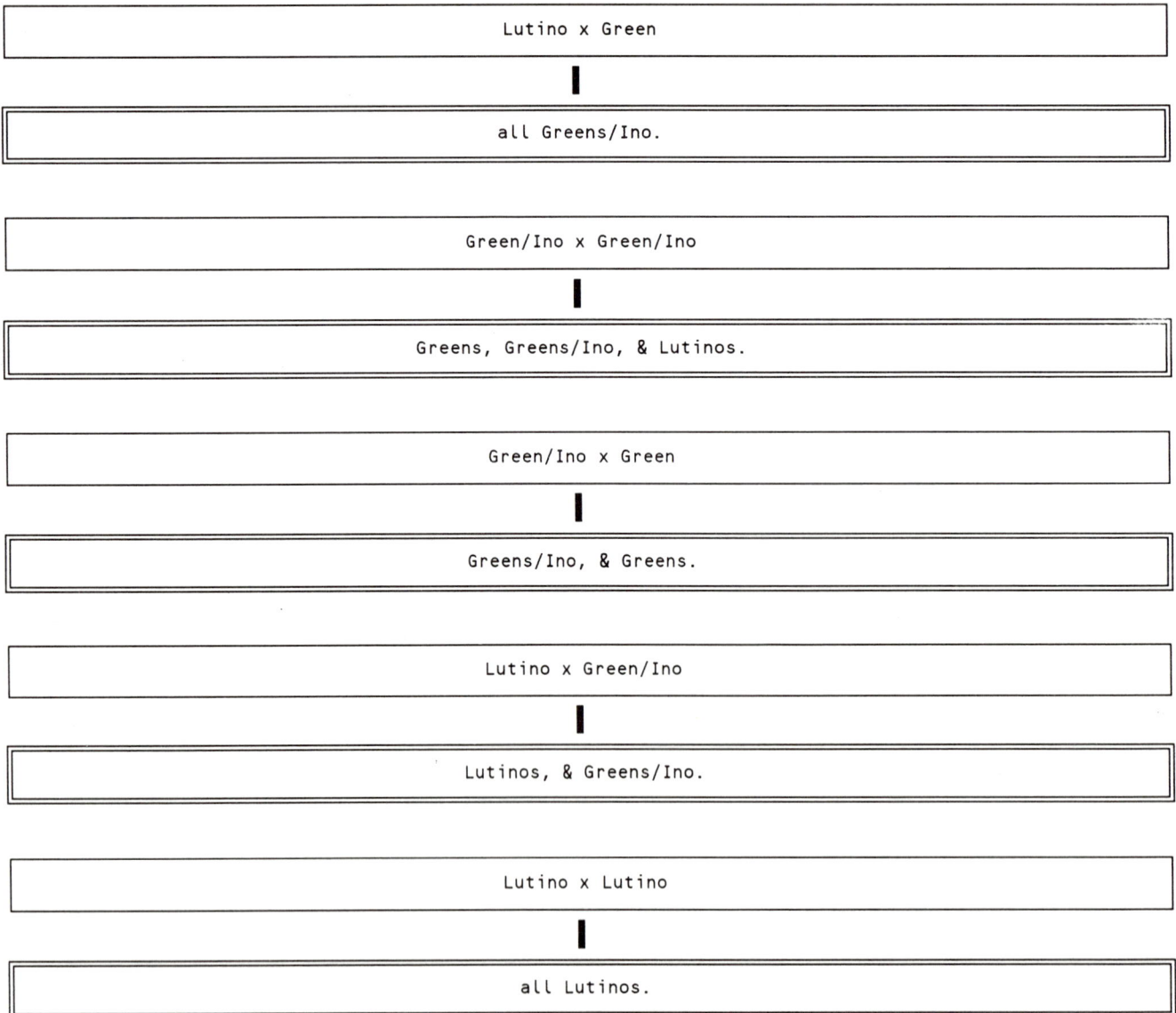

Lutino x Green

all Greens/Ino.

Green/Ino x Green/Ino

Greens, Greens/Ino, & Lutinos.

Green/Ino x Green

Greens/Ino, & Greens.

Lutino x Green/Ino

Lutinos, & Greens/Ino.

Lutino x Lutino

all Lutinos.

It is worthwhile including Recessive Ino in Combination varieties with the following existing factors:

Nyasa Lovebird: as far as is known, none.

Elegant Grass Parrakeet: Cinnamon (might have the same effect as Sex-linked Ino with Cinnamon).

Adelaide Rosella: Cinnamon (might have the same effect as Sex-linked Ino with Cinnamon).

Eastern Rosella: Ruby (making Rubino) and Cinnamon (might have the same effect as Sex-linked Ino with Cinnamon).

Princess of Wales Parrakeet: Blue (makes Albino).

Pied (AR)

The Recessive Pied (patchy elimination of melanin) is common in the Cockatiel (paradoxically, split Pied Cockatiels show a white patch on the back of the head, and this visual sign in other species is recognized as indication of a Dominant mutation); scarce in the Peach-faced, and obscure or rare in the Red-fronted Kakariki, Red-rumped Parrakeet (Europe), Indian Ringneck Parrakeet (USA) and Turquoisine Grass Parrakeet (Australia).

Question over the inheritance of Pied in the Red-fronted Kakariki exists; though listed as Autosomal Recessive, one specialist British breeder has noted: the very low incidence of Pied young from breeding pairs, eruption of pied markings on apparently normal birds at maturity, and lastly 'split' Pieds paired to known normal specimens producing Pied young – all indicative of an erratic nature which bears common ground with known Dominant Pied varieties.

The sex of the birds as related to inheritance of the variety in relation to Green is immaterial, e.g.:

Pied Green x Green

all Greens/Pied.

Green/Pied x Green/Pied

Greens, Greens/Pied, & Pied Greens.

Green/Pied x Green

Greens/Pied, & Greens.

Pied Green x Green/Pied

Pied Greens, & Greens/Pied.

Pied Green x Pied Green

↓

all Pied Greens.

For Cockatiels: replace Green with **Normal** throughout the preceding pairings and expectations.

It is worthwhile including Recessive Pied in Combination and Compound varieties with the following existing factors:

Peach-faced Lovebird: Marine, Lavender, Tangerine, Dark Factor and Violet Factor.
Red-fronted Kakariki: Cinnamon.
Indian Ringneck Parrakeet: Blue, Marine and Grey.
Red-rumped Parrakeet: Blue and Marine.
Cockatiel: White-faced, Pale-faced, Cinnamon, Dilute, Pearl and Deep Yellow Suffusion.

Melanistic (AR)

As far as is known, the rare Melanistic variety (increase of melanin pigment) exists only in the Eastern Rosella, though there have been reports of Black Splendid Grass Parrakeets in Europe. The sex of birds of this variety is immaterial as regards their inheritance, e.g.:

Melanistic x Normal

↓

all Normals/Melanistic.

Normal/Melanistic x Normal/Melanistic

↓

Normals, Normals/Melanistic, & Melanistics.

Normal/Melanistic x Normal

↓

Normals/Melanistic, & Normals.

Melanistic x Normal/Melanistic

↓

Melanistics, & Normals/Melanistic.

Melanistic x Melanistic

|
|---|

all Melanistics.

It would be worthwhile and interesting to attempt to include Melanistic in Combination and Compound varieties with the following existing factors:

Eastern Rosella: Cinnamon, Pied, Dilute and Ruby.

SEX–LINKED RECESSIVE VARIETIES (SLR)

It is important to remember that hens cannot be split for a Sex-linked Recessive variety.

Ino (SLR)

The Sex-linked Ino (Lutino) (total elimination of melanin pigment) is common in the Peach-faced Lovebird, Indian Ringneck Parrakeet and Cockatiel; well established in the Red-rumped Parrakeet (Australia only); extremely rare in the Alexandrine Parrakeet, Eastern Rosella (Europe), Roseate Cockatoo (**Roseino**) and Lineolated Parrakeet. Ino interacts with the wild type in the following way:

Lutino cock x Green hen

Lutino hens, & Green cocks/Ino.

Green cock/Ino x Green hen

Lutino hens, Green cocks & hens, & Green cocks/Ino.

Green cock/Ino x Lutino hen

Lutino cocks & hens, Green hens, & Greens cocks/Ino.

Green cock x Lutino hen

Green hens & Greens cocks/Ino.

```
┌─────────────────────────────────────────────────────────────┐
│                  Lutino cock x Lutino hen                     │
└─────────────────────────────────────────────────────────────┘
                               █
┌─────────────────────────────────────────────────────────────┐
│                        all Lutinos.                           │
└─────────────────────────────────────────────────────────────┘
```

For Cockatiel and Eastern Rosella: replace Green with **Normal**. For Roseate Cockatoo: replace Green with **Normal** and Lutino with **Roseino**.

It is worthwhile including Sex-linked Ino in Combination varieties with the following existing factors:

Peach-faced Lovebird: Marine (making Creamino), Lavender (making Ivorino) and Cinnamon.

Indian Ringneck Parrakeet: Blue (making Albino), Marine (making Creamino) and Cinnamon.

Alexandrine Parrakeet: Blue (making Albino).

Red-rumped Parrakeet: Blue (making Albino), Marine (making Creamino) and Cinnamon.

Eastern Rosella: Ruby (making Rubino) and Cinnamon.

Cockatiel: White-faced (making Albino), Pale-faced (making Creamino), Cinnamon and Pearl.

Roseate Cockatoo: White-faced (making Albino).

Lineolated Parrakeet: Marine (making Creamino).

Cinnamon (SLR)

The Cinnamon (changes melanin black to melanin brown) is common in the Peach-faced Lovebird, Cockatiel and Indian Ringneck Parrakeet; it is available in the Red-fronted Kakariki and Bourke's Grass Parrakeet; it is rare but likely to become available in the future in the Elegant and Splendid Grass Parrakeets, and just becoming established in the Red-rumped Parrakeet, Eastern and Adelaide Rosellas. The interaction of Cinnamon with the wild type is as follows:

```
┌─────────────────────────────────────────────────────────────┐
│             Cinnamon Green cock x Green hen                   │
└─────────────────────────────────────────────────────────────┘
                               █
┌─────────────────────────────────────────────────────────────┐
│      Cinnamon Green hens, & Green cocks/Cinnamon.             │
└─────────────────────────────────────────────────────────────┘


┌─────────────────────────────────────────────────────────────┐
│          Green cock/Cinnamon x Green hen                      │
└─────────────────────────────────────────────────────────────┘
                               █
┌─────────────────────────────────────────────────────────────┐
│  Cinnamon Green hens, Green cocks & hens, & Green cocks/Cinnamon. │
└─────────────────────────────────────────────────────────────┘


┌─────────────────────────────────────────────────────────────┐
│       Green cock/Cinnamon x Cinnamon Green hen                │
└─────────────────────────────────────────────────────────────┘
                               █
┌─────────────────────────────────────────────────────────────┐
│  Cinnamon Green cocks & hens, Green hens, & Green cocks/Cinnamon. │
└─────────────────────────────────────────────────────────────┘
```

78

Green cock x Cinnamon Green hen

I

Green hens & Green cocks/Cinnamon.

Cinnamon Green cock x Cinnamon Green hen

I

all Cinnamon Greens.

For the Cockatiel and Eastern Rosella: replace Green with **Normal** throughout the preceding pairings and expectations.

For Bourke's Grass Parrakeet: replace Green with **Brown** throughout the preceding pairings and expectations.

It is worthwhile including Cinnamon in Combination and Compound varieties with the following existing factors:

Peach-faced Lovebird: Marine, Lavender, Ino, Dilute, Tangerine, Dark Factor and Violet Factor.
Indian Ringneck Parrakeet: Blue, Marine, Ino, Dilute, Clearhead and Grey.
Red-fronted Kakariki: Pied.
Bourke's Grass Parrakeet: Dilute and Rosa.
Splendid Grass Parrakeet: Blue, Marine, Dilute and Red-bellied.
Elegant Grass Parrakeet: Ino (might have the same effect as Cinnamon with Sex-linked Ino).
Red-rumped Parrakeet: Blue, Marine, Ino and Dilute.
Eastern Rosella: Ino, Dilute, Ruby and Melanistic.
Cockatiel: White-faced, Pale-faced, Ino, Dilute, Pied, Pearl and Deep Yellow Suffusion.

Dilute (SLR)

The Dilute (partial reduction of melanin) is generally thought of as a Recessive variety, but Sex-linked Dilutes also exist in some species and these include the Peach-faced Lovebird and Red-rumped Parrakeet - both of which are reasonably freely available - and the Indian Ringneck Parrakeet and Splendid Grass Parrakeet, both of which are obscure at present.

To illustrate its relationship with Green, replace Cinnamon with **Dilute** in the pairings and expectations given in the previous section on Cinnamon.

It is worthwhile including Sex-linked Dilute in Combination and Compound varieties with the following existing factors:

Peach-faced Lovebird: Marine, Lavender, Cinnamon, Tangerine and Violet Factor.
Indian Ringneck Parrakeet: Blue, Marine, Cinnamon, Clearhead and Grey.
Splendid Grass Parrakeet: Blue, Marine, Cinnamon and Red-bellied.
Red-rumped Parrakeet: Blue, Marine and Cinnamon.

Peach-faced Lovebird and Indian Ringneck - special note: in these species, the Sex-linked Dilute has a particular relationship with Ino (the two are allelomorphic), Green cocks can be split for one variety or the other, but not

79

for both; as would be expected, hens cannot be split for either of these sex-linked varieties e.g.:

Dilute Green cock x Lutino hen

Dilute Green hens, & Dilute Green cocks/Ino.

Lutino cock x Dilute Green hen

Lutino hens, & Dilute Green cocks/Ino.

Green cock/Ino x Dilute Green hen

Lutino hens, Green hens, Dilute Green cocks/Ino, & Green cocks/Dilute.

Green cock/Dilute x Lutino hen

Dilute Green hens, Green hens, Dilute Green cocks/Ino, & Greens cocks/Ino.

Dilute Green cock/Ino x Lutino hen

Lutino cocks & hens, Dilute Green hens, & Dilute Green cocks/Ino.

Pearl (SLR)

The Pearl (partial elimination of melanin from the centres of individual feathers) is common in the Cockatiel, and scarce in the Turquoisine Grass Parrakeet. The effect can be improved by selective breeding, i.e. continually selecting the better marked birds for breeding results in an improvement with each generation. The variety interacts with the wild type in typical Sex-linked manner:

Pearl Normal cock x Normal hen

Pearl Normal hens, & Normal cocks/Pearl.

Normal cock/Pearl x Normal hen

▮

Pearl Normal hens, Normal cocks & hens, & Normal cocks/Pearl.

Normal cock/Pearl x Pearl Normal hen

▮

Pearl Normal cocks & hens, Normal hens, & Normal cocks/Pearl.

Normal cock x Pearl Normal hen

▮

Normal hens & Normal cocks/Pearl.

Pearl Normal cock x Pearl Normal hen

▮

all Pearl Normals.

For the Turquoisine Grass Parrakeet: replace Normal with **Green** throughout the preceding pairings and expectations.

It is worthwhile including Pearl in Combination and Compound varieties with the following existing factors:

Cockatiel: White-faced, Pale-faced, Ino, Dilute, Cinnamon, Pied and Deep Yellow Suffusion.

Turquoisine Grass Parrakeet: Marine, Pied, Red-fronted, Dark Factor and possibly Dilute.

Rosa and Ruby (SLR)

The extensive spread of original red or pink ground colour, to the detriment of yellow ground, is established - as far as is known - in a definite inheritable pattern in two psittacines. It is common in the Bourke's Grass Parrakeet (Rosa) and rare in the Eastern Rosella (Ruby). The Rosa Bourke interacts with the wild type as follows:

Rosa Brown cock x Brown hen

▮

Rosa Brown hens, & Brown cocks/Rosa.

81

Brown cock/Rosa x Brown hen

Rosa Brown hens, Brown cocks & hens, & Brown cocks/Rosa.

Brown cock/Rosa x Rosa Brown hen

Rosa Brown cocks & hens, Brown hens, & Brown cocks/Rosa.

Brown cock x Rosa Brown hen

Brown hens & Brown cocks/Rosa.

Rosa Brown cock x Rosa Brown hen

all Rosa Browns.

For the Eastern Rosella: replace Brown with **Normal** and Rosa with **Ruby** throughout the preceding pairings and expectations.

It is worthwhile including Rosa or Ruby in Combination and Compound varieties with the following existing factors:

Bourke's Grass Parrakeet: Dilute (Red-eyed), Cinnamon, Fallow and Pied.
Eastern Rosella: Dilute, Cinnamon and Melanistic.

AUTOSOMAL INCOMPLETE DOMINANT VARIETIES (AID)

Dark Factor (AID)

The Dark Factor (partial to complete negation of the Tyndall effect) is common in the Peach-faced Lovebird, becoming established in the Masked Lovebird, rare in the Turquoisine Grass Parrakeet and the Lineolated Parrakeet.

Its two phases - Dark Green and Olive Green - are also referred to as Single Dark Factor Green and Double Dark Factor Green. 'Dark' and 'Slate' are used in the Blue, Marine and Lavender series. The Dark Factor interacts with the wild type as follows:

Dark Green x Green

Continued on next page.

Dark Greens, & Greens.

Dark Green x Dark Green

Olive Greens, Dark Greens, & Greens.

Olive Green x Green

all Dark Greens.

Olive Green x Dark Green

Olive Greens, & Dark Greens.

Olive Green x Olive Green

all Olive Greens.

It is worthwhile including the Dark Factor in Combination or Compound varieties with the following existing factors:

Peach-faced Lovebird: Marine, Lavender, Cinnamon, Fallow, Pied, Tangerine and Violet Factor.
Masked Lovebird: Blue.
Turquoisine Grass Parrakeet: Marine, Fallow, Pied, Pearl and Red-fronted.
Lineolated Parrakeet: Marine.

Dilute (AID)

As far as is known the Dominant Dilute exists in only one species of psittacine, the Cockatiel, shows its presence in two depths - described as Single Factor and Double Factor - and reduces melanin. The reduction of this pigment is much greater in the Double Factor birds - shortened to (D)Dilute - so that they are markedly paler than the Single Factor birds - shortened to (S)Dilute. Interaction with Normals is as follows:

(S)Dilute Normal x Normal

Continued from previous page.

(S)Dilute Normals, & Normals.

(S)Dilute Normal x (S)Dilute Normal

(D)Dilute Normals, (S)Dilute Normals, & Normals.

(D)Dilute Normal x Normal

all (S)Dilute Normals.

(D)Dilute Normal x (S)Dilute Normal

(D)Dilute Normals, & (S)Dilute Normals.

(D)Dilute Normal x (D)Dilute Normal

all (D)Dilute Normals.

It is worthwhile including the Dominant Dilute in Combination or Compound varieties with the following existing factors:

Cockatiel: White-faced, Pale-faced, Cinnamon, Fallow, Pied, Pearl and Deep Yellow Suffusion.

Tangerine (AID)

The Tangerine (partial reversion of red ground colour to yellow ground colour) is only established in the Peach-faced Lovebird and is not freely available. While Single Factor birds show only a slight indication, Double Factor birds show the feature to its maximum extent. For ease of use in the pairings the names have been shortened to (S)Tang- and (D)Tang-, applied in the following way:

(S)Tang-Green x Green

(S)Tang-Greens, & Greens.

(S)Tang-Green x (S)Tang-Green

(D)Tang-Greens, (S)Tang-Greens, & Greens.

(D)Tang-Green x Green

all (S)Tang-Greens.

(D)Tang-Green x (S)Tang-Green

(D)Tang-Greens, & (S)Tang-Greens.

(D)Tang-Green x (D)Tang-Green

all (D)Tang-Greens.

It is worthwhile including Tangerine in Combination or Compound varieties with the following existing factors:

Peach-faced: Marine, Lavender, Ino, Dilute, Cinnamon, Dark Factor and Violet Factor.

AUTOSOMAL COMPLETE DOMINANT VARIETIES (ACD)

Pied (ACD)

The Dominant Pied (patchy elimination of melanin) is common in the Peach-faced Lovebird, established but obscure in the Eastern Rosella, Splendid, Elegant and Bourke's Grass Parrakeets. Though usually classed as Complete Dominant, the nature of this variety is highly unpredictable and has not been found to conform with usual Single-Double Factor theory. Neither does it adhere to the theory of Incomplete Dominance, in which there would be a predictable intermediate phase of effect. Future re-classification under a *new* category of **Autosomal Variable Dominant (AVD)** to give clearer indication of its different nature must be seriously considered.

Pied specimens which exhibit maximum variegation tend to produce a predominance of like young, but some of the progeny can be entirely normal. Even stranger; occasionally, normal looking young produced from Pied parents will moult out to acquire Pied markings at adulthood and be able to produce Pied youngsters; also, apparently normal looking birds bred off Pieds have been known

85

to produce Pieds when paired to other normal looking specimens. Of course, it may just be that the telltale mark of the Pied has been too small to be noticed, or could have been on a bill or a toe, which was disregarded. The tiniest visual evidence gives that bird the ability to pass on the variety in a more exaggerated form.

As a way of denoting the amount of Pied plumage displayed by individual birds, the usual descriptions to be used are: *Full Pied* or *Clear Pied* to describe those which lack melanin almost entirely; *Heavily Pied* to describe those which possess substantial variegation; and *Lightly Pied* for those of only slight variegation. An increase of variegation can be achieved over several generations by selective breeding.

Though Dominant Pied is now given an Inheritance Code of (ACD), for safety's sake, it is best to assume that this rather unstable factor is inherited in the following simple way:

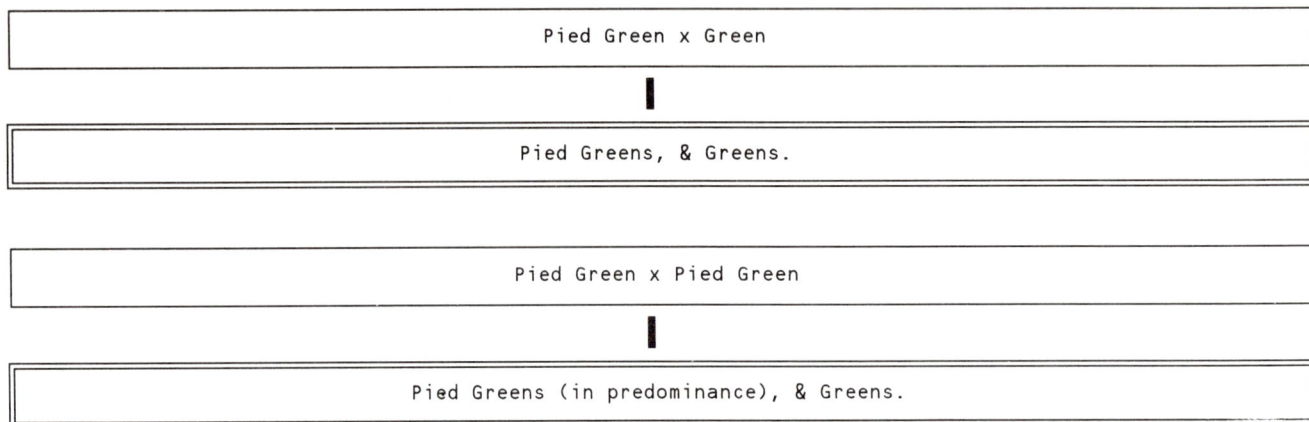

Pied Green x Green

|
|

Pied Greens, & Greens.

Pied Green x Pied Green

|
|

Pied Greens (in predominance), & Greens.

Traditional Dominant Pied theory – with Single and Double Factor being a measure of ability to pass on the variety, without any intention of reference to amount of variegation – proceeds as follows, with (S)Pied representing Single Factor and (D)Pied representing Double Factor:

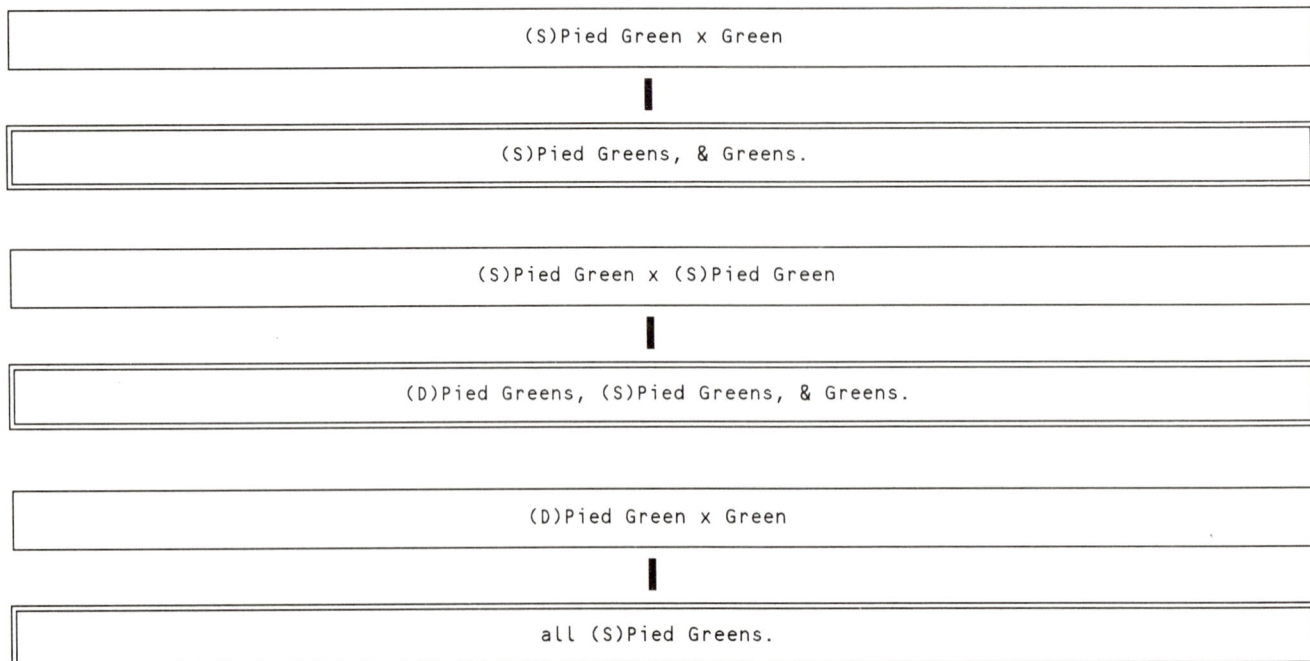

(S)Pied Green x Green

|
|

(S)Pied Greens, & Greens.

(S)Pied Green x (S)Pied Green

|
|

(D)Pied Greens, (S)Pied Greens, & Greens.

(D)Pied Green x Green

|
|

all (S)Pied Greens.

```
┌──────────────────────────────────────────────────────────┐
│            (D)Pied Green x (S)Pied Green                  │
└──────────────────────────────────────────────────────────┘
                            ▮
┌──────────────────────────────────────────────────────────┐
│          (D)Pied Greens, & (S)Pied Greens.               │
└──────────────────────────────────────────────────────────┘

┌──────────────────────────────────────────────────────────┐
│            (D)Pied Green x (D)Pied Green                  │
└──────────────────────────────────────────────────────────┘
                            ▮
┌──────────────────────────────────────────────────────────┐
│                  all (D)Pied Greens.                     │
└──────────────────────────────────────────────────────────┘
```

Of the five theoretical pairings above, three produce all Pied young, but in practice the writer has found that all breeding pairs of Dominant Pied Peach-faceds eventually produce at least some normal birds. This could also prove to be the case with the rarer Dominant Pied Parrakeets and, if so, re-classification as *Autosomal Variable Dominant* must be carried through.

For the Eastern Rosella: replace Green with **Normal** throughout the preceding pairings and expectations.

For Bourke's Grass Parrakeet: replace Green with **Brown** throughout the preceding pairings and expectations.

It is possibly worthwhile to include Dominant Pied in Combination or Compound varieties with the following existing factors:

Peach–faced: Marine, Lavender, Dilute, Dark Factor and Violet Factor.
Bourke's Grass Parrakeet: Dilute and Rosa.
Splendid Grass Parrakeet: Blue and Marine.
Elegant Grass Parrakeet: Cinnamon.
Eastern Rosella: Dilute, Ruby and Melanistic.

Grey (ACD)

Apart from the Budgerigar, the Grey (total negation of the Tyndall effect) has become widely available in the Indian Ringneck Parrakeet, is established in the Scaly-breasted Lorikeet (Australia only) – from which it has been introduced into other Lorikeets – and known to exist in the Plum-headed Parrakeet. For Grey colour to present itself, a Blue variety must exist, but none are so far established in the last two species. Single Factor – (S)Grey – and Double Factor – (D)Grey – are only measures of the individual's ability to pass on the variety to its progeny, and not gradations of affect. The Grey Factor interacts with Green as follows:

```
┌──────────────────────────────────────────────────────────┐
│              (S)Greygreen x Green                        │
└──────────────────────────────────────────────────────────┘
                            ▮
┌──────────────────────────────────────────────────────────┐
│            (S)Greygreens, & Greens.                      │
└──────────────────────────────────────────────────────────┘

┌──────────────────────────────────────────────────────────┐
│            (S)Greygreen x (S)Greygreen                   │
└──────────────────────────────────────────────────────────┘
                            ▮
┌──────────────────────────────────────────────────────────┐
│      (D)Greygreens, (S)Greygreens, & Greens.             │
└──────────────────────────────────────────────────────────┘
```

```
┌─────────────────────────────────────────────────────────────────┐
│                    (D)Greygreen x Green                           │
└─────────────────────────────────────────────────────────────────┘
                                │
┌─────────────────────────────────────────────────────────────────┐
│                    all (S)Greygreens.                             │
└─────────────────────────────────────────────────────────────────┘

┌─────────────────────────────────────────────────────────────────┐
│               (D)Greygreen x (S)Greygreen                         │
└─────────────────────────────────────────────────────────────────┘
                                │
┌─────────────────────────────────────────────────────────────────┐
│            (D)Greygreens, & (S)Greygreens.                        │
└─────────────────────────────────────────────────────────────────┘

┌─────────────────────────────────────────────────────────────────┐
│               (D)Greygreen x (D)Greygreen                         │
└─────────────────────────────────────────────────────────────────┘
                                │
┌─────────────────────────────────────────────────────────────────┐
│                    all (D)Greygreens.                             │
└─────────────────────────────────────────────────────────────────┘
```

It is worthwhile including Grey in Combination or Compound varieties with the following existing factors:

Indian Ringneck Parrakeet: Blue (making Greyblue), Marine (making Greymarine), Pied, Dilute, Cinnamon and Clearhead. If combined with Ino, the Grey Factor would cause a loss of iridescence and make the plumage matt - such birds are described as Ino masking Grey.

Violet Factor (ACD)

As far as can be discovered, the Violet Factor (thought to be due to structural difference in the barb and compacted melanin) is established in only one other species beside the Budgerigar - the Peach-faced Lovebird, in which it seems to be subject to the same theory of inheritance. Single Factor and Double Factor are represented by (S)Violet and (D)Violet:

```
┌─────────────────────────────────────────────────────────────────┐
│                 (S)Violet Green x Green                           │
└─────────────────────────────────────────────────────────────────┘
                                │
┌─────────────────────────────────────────────────────────────────┐
│              (S)Violet Greens, & Greens.                          │
└─────────────────────────────────────────────────────────────────┘

┌─────────────────────────────────────────────────────────────────┐
│            (S)Violet Green x (S)Violet Green                      │
└─────────────────────────────────────────────────────────────────┘
                                │
┌─────────────────────────────────────────────────────────────────┐
│        (D)Violet Greens, (S)Violet Greens, & Greens.              │
└─────────────────────────────────────────────────────────────────┘
```

(D)Violet Green x Green

|
|---|

all (S)Violet Greens.

(D)Violet Green x (S)Violet Green

|
|---|

(D)Violet Greens, & (S)Violet Greens.

(D)Violet Green x (D)Violet Green

|
|---|

all (D)Violet Greens.

According to theory, there is no visible difference between Single and Double Factor birds, however, Budgerigar breeders specializing in Violets have found that birds presumed to be Double Factor *do* have a more intense violet colour. At one time it was thought that Double Factor Violet constituted a lethal effect on embryos, but this possibility now seems to have been discounted.

The Budgerigar theory on Violet may or may not apply to the variety as it exists in the Peach-faced Lovebird, but their original breeder believed that Violet was cumulative - like the Dark Factor - and that Single and Double Factor birds could be distinguished by their greater or lesser intensity.

In Budgerigars the true Violet colour can only be exhibited to the full in birds which also possess the Blue Factor and a single Dark Factor, so this was taken as the goal. The Violet was combined with the nearest varieties to Blue in the Peach-faced - the Marine and the Lavender.

From breeding results achieved, it was thought that combination of Violet and the Dark Factor was not a complete success; (D)Violet Dark Green seemed to be of equal appearance to (D)Violet Green, (D)Violet Dark Marine looked the same as (D)Violet Marine, Violet Olive Greens were of the same appearance as Olive Greens, and Violet Slate Marines were the same as Slate Marines. This information lead to the conclusion that the combination of Violet with the Dark Factor had been proved fruitless; however this is not so with the combination of Violet and Marine, or Violet and Lavender.

It is worthwhile including Violet in Combination or Compound varieties with the following existing factors:

Peach-faced Lovebird: Marine, Lavender, Pied, Dilute, Cinnamon, Tangerine, and the Dark Factor if enhancement is possible.

SELECTIVE BREEDING (S)

Red and Deep Yellow Suffusion (S)

Red Suffusion in Peach-faced Lovebirds is common but an inheritable trait for the effect has not so far been proved to exist. Deep Yellow Suffusion in Cockatiels,

Red Suffusion in Turquoisine Grass Parrakeets (Red-fronted) and Splendid Grass Parrakeets (Red-bellied) is well established in these species, but extremely rare in Princess of Wales Parrakeets. The effect can be reproduced and increased by Selective Breeding, e.g.:

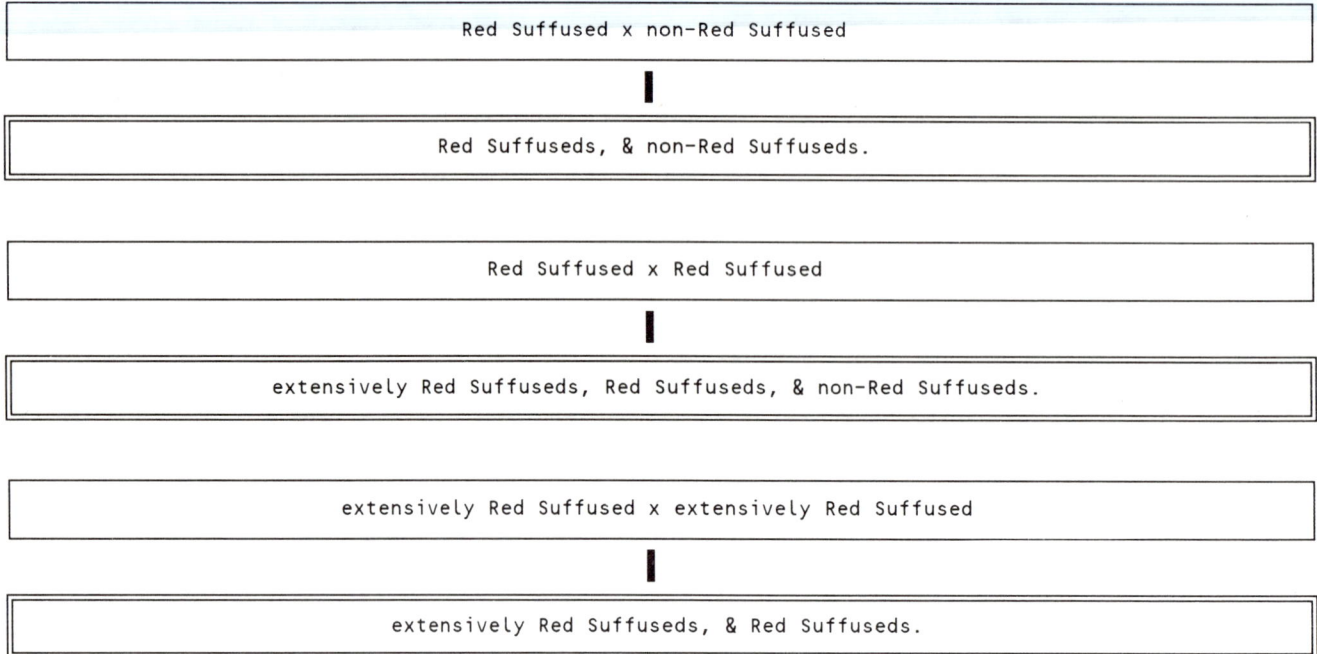

Red Suffused x non-Red Suffused

Red Suffuseds, & non-Red Suffuseds.

Red Suffused x Red Suffused

extensively Red Suffuseds, Red Suffuseds, & non-Red Suffuseds.

extensively Red Suffused x extensively Red Suffused

extensively Red Suffuseds, & Red Suffuseds.

For further information on Red and Deep Yellow Suffusion and worthwhile existing factors to be used in Combination and Compound varieties, see *section 8, Universal Breeding Programmes for Combination and Compound Varieties, Red and Deep Yellow Suffusion in Combination & Compound Varieties.* For Cockatiels: replace Red Suffused with **Deep Yellow Suffused.**

8

UNIVERSAL BREEDING PROGRAMMES
for COMBINATION & COMPOUND VARIETIES

INHERITANCE CODES

*THE INHERITANCE of each variety (factor) is denoted by (AR) for Autosomal Recessive, (SLR) for Sex-linked Recessive, (AID) for Autosomal Incomplete Dominant, (ACD) for Autosomal Complete Dominant, and (S) for Selective Breeding. The type of inheritance of each factor which goes to make up a combination or compound variety follows the name of that variety; for example, **(SLR+AR)** is the Inheritance Code for Albino (Sex-linked), **(SLR+ACD+AR)** is the Inheritance Code for Cinnamon Greyblue, etc., etc.. See section 10 for use of Inheritance Codes.*

ALBINO, CREAMINO, IVORINO & RUBINO

Albino (Sex-linked) (SLR+AR)

Species: *Indian Ringneck Parrakeet, Alexandrine Parrakeet, Red-rumped Parrakeet (Australian Sex-linked Ino), Cockatiel and Roseate Cockatoo. For the Cockatiel replace Green with **Normal** and Blue with **White-faced** throughout the following. For the Roseate Cockatoo replace Green with **Normal**, Lutino with **Roseino** and Blue with **White-faced** throughout the following.*

Firstly, cocks which are split for both Ino and Blue (or White-faced in Cockatiels and Roseate Cockatoos) are needed. These can be provided in several ways but it will be obvious that pairing (a) is preferable because the split cocks can be identified from the Lutino hens by eye colour as soon as they are hatched – which is of great benefit.

First Season:
(a)

Lutino cock x Blue hen

▌

Lutino hens/Blue, & **Green cocks/Ino+Blue.**

(b)

Blue cock x Lutino hen

▌

Green hens/Blue, & **Green cocks/Ino+Blue.**

(c)

Green cock/Ino x Blue hen

Green hens/Blue, Lutino hens/Blue, **Green cocks/Ino+Blue**, & Green cocks/Blue.

Second Season; the split cocks can be paired to Blue hens or Lutino hens/Blue:

(a)

Green cock/Ino+Blue x Blue hen

cocks & hens: Blues, & Greens/Blue.   hens: **Albinos**, & Lutinos/Blue.   cocks: Blues/Ino, & Greens/Ino+Blue.

(b)

Green cock/Ino+Blue x Lutino hen/Blue

cocks & hens: **Albinos**, Lutinos/Blue, & Lutinos.   hens: Blues, Greens/Blue, & Greens.   cocks: Blues/Ino, Greens/Ino+Blue, & Greens/Ino.

By now a wide selection of stock should be available for breeding in the third season, and a predominance of Albinos can be achieved by the following pairings – other than Albino x Albino.

Third Season; a selection of pairings:
(a)

Albino cock x Lutino hen/Blue

cocks & hens: **Albinos**, & Lutinos/Blue.

(b)

Lutino cock/Blue x Albino hen

cocks & hens: **Albinos,** & Lutinos/Blue.

(c)

Lutino cock/Blue x Lutino hen/Blue

cocks & hens: **Albinos**, Lutinos/Blue, & Lutinos.

(d)

Blue cock/Ino x Albino hen

I

Albino cocks & hens, Blue hens, & Blue cocks/Ino.

(e)

Lutino cock/Blue x Blue hen

I

Albino hens, Lutino hens/Blue, Blue cocks/Ino, & Green cocks/Ino+Blue.

Creamino (Sex–linked) (SLR+AR)

Species: *Indian Ringneck Parrakeet, Red–rumped Parrakeet, Cockatiel, Lineolated Parrakeet and Peach–faced Lovebird.*

To illustrate the matings and expectations which show the production of this combination variety, replace Blue with **Marine**, and Albino with **Creamino** in the entire preceding section on **Albino (Sex–linked)**. For Cockatiels, replace Green with **Normal**, Blue with **Pale–faced**, and Albino with **Creamino.**

Ivorino (Sex–linked) (SLR+AR)

Species: *Peach–faced Lovebird.*

To illustrate the matings and expectations which show the production of this combination variety, replace Blue with **Lavender**, and Albino with **Ivorino** in the entire preceding section on **Albino (Sex–linked)**.

Rubino (Sex–linked) (SLR+SLR)

Species: *Eastern Rosella Parrakeet (European Sex–linked Ino).*

First Season; cocks split for Ino and Ruby are needed, and these can be provided in two ways:

(a)

Lutino cock x Ruby Normal hen

I

Lutino hens, & **Normal cocks/Ino+Ruby.**

(b)

Ruby Normal cock x Lutino hen

I

Ruby Normal hens, & **Normal cocks/Ino+Ruby.**

Second Season; the split cocks can be paired to Lutino hens or Ruby Normal hens:

(a)

Normal cock/Ino+Ruby x Lutino hen

↓

hens: **Rubinos,** Lutinos, Ruby Normals, & Normals. cocks: Lutinos/Ruby, Lutinos, Normals/Ino+Ruby, & Normals/Ino.

(b)

Normal cock/Ino+Ruby x Ruby Normal hen

↓

hens: **Rubinos,** Lutinos, Ruby Normals, & Normals. cocks: Ruby Normals/Ino, Ruby Normals, Normals/Ino+Ruby, & Normals/Ruby.

The following cocks can be selected from the two previous pairings for use with the young Rubino hens in the third season: **Lutinos** (hoping those chosen are split Ruby) and **Ruby Normals** (hoping those chosen are split Ino). Should this be the case a greater amount of Rubinos (cocks and hens) is likely to be produced.

Third Season; two suggested pairings:

(a)

Lutino cock/Ruby x Rubino hen

↓

Rubino cocks & hens, Lutino hens, & Lutino cocks/Ruby.

(b)

Ruby Normal cock/Ino x Rubino hen

↓

Rubino cocks & hens, Ruby Normal hens, & Ruby Normal cocks/Ino.

Albino (Recessive) (AR+AR)

Species: *Masked Lovebird, Fischer's Lovebird, Red-rumped Parrakeet (European Recessive Ino) and Princess of Wales Parrakeet.*

First Season:

Lutino x Blue

↓

all **Greens/Ino+Blue**

Second Season:

Green/Ino+Blue x Green/Ino+Blue

▮

Albinos, Lutinos/Blue, Lutinos, Blues/Ino, Greens/Ino+Blue, Greens/Ino, Blues, Greens/Blue, & Greens.

Third Season onwards; the following examples of useful pairings can be made from the young provided in the second season;

(a)

Albino x Lutino

▮

all Lutinos/Blue

(b)

Albino x Lutino/Blue

▮

Albinos, & Lutinos/Blue.

(c)

Albino x Blue/Ino

▮

Albinos, & Blues/Ino.

(d)

Albino x Albino

▮

all **Albinos**.

Creamino (Recessive) (AR+AR)

Species: *Red-rumped Parrakeet (European Recessive Ino).*
    To illustrate the matings and expectations which show the production of this combination variety, replace Blue with **Marine**, and Albino with **Creamino** in the entire preceding section on **Albino (Recessive)**.

Rubino (Recessive) (SLR+AR)

Species: *Eastern Rosella (Australian Ino).*

Firstly, Normal cocks split Ino and Ruby, and Ruby Normal hens split Ino are needed. These can be provided in several ways but it will be obvious that pairing (a) is preferable because *both* required types are provided and they can be sexed while in nest feather.

First Season:

(a)

Ruby Normal cock x Lutino hen

I

Ruby Normal hens/Ino, & Normal cocks/Ruby+Ino.

(b)

Lutino cock x Ruby Normal hen

I

Normal hens/Ino, & **Normal cocks/Ruby+Ino.**

(c)

Normal cock/Ruby x Lutino hen

I

Normal hens/Ino, **Ruby Normal hens/Ino, Normal cocks/Ruby+Ino,** & Normal cocks/Ino.

Second Season; the split cocks can be paired to Lutino hens or Ruby Normal hens/Ino:

(a)

Normal cock/Ruby+Ino x Lutino hen

I

cocks & hens: Lutinos, & Normals/Ino. hens: **Rubinos,** & Ruby Normals/Ino. cocks: Lutinos/Ruby, & Normals/Ruby+Ino.

(b)

Normal cock/Ruby+Ino x Ruby Normal hen/Ino

I

cocks & hens: **Rubinos,** Ruby Normals/Ino, & Ruby Normals. hens: Lutinos, Normals/Ino, & Normals. cocks: Lutinos/Ruby, Normals/Ruby+Ino, & Normals/Ruby.

By now a wide selection of stock should be available for breeding in the third season, and a predominance of Rubinos can be achieved by the following pairings – other than Rubino x Rubino.

Third Season; a selection of pairings:

(a)

Rubino cock x Ruby Normal hen/Ino

▮

cocks & hens: **Rubinos,** & Ruby Normals/Ino.

(b)

Ruby Normal cock/Ino x Rubino hen

▮

cocks & hens: **Rubinos,** & Ruby Normals/Ino.

(c)

Ruby Normal cock/Ino x Ruby Normal hen/Ino

▮

cocks & hens: **Rubinos,** Ruby Normals/Ino, & Ruby Normals.

(d)

Lutino cock/Ruby x Rubino hen

▮

Rubino cocks & hens, Lutino hens, & Lutino cocks/Ruby.

(e)

Ruby Normal cock/Ino x Lutino hen

▮

Rubino hens, Ruby Normal hens/Ino, Lutino cocks/Ruby, & Normal cocks/Ruby+Ino.

CINNAMON BLUE (& CINNAMON WHITE–FACED)

Cinnamon Blue (SLR+AR)

Species: *Indian Ringneck Parrakeet, Red–rumped Parrakeet, Splendid Grass Parrakeet and Cockatiel. For Cockatiels (***Cinnamon White–faced***) replace Green with* **Normal** *and Blue with* **White–faced** *throughout the following.*

Firstly, cocks which are split for both Cinnamon and Blue (or White-faced in Cockatiels) are needed. These can be provided in several ways but it will be obvious that pairing (a) is preferable because the split cocks can be identified by eye colour as soon as they are hatched - which is of great benefit.

First Season:

(a)

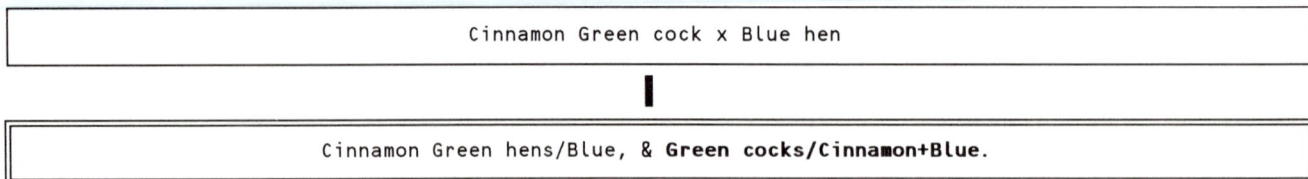

(b)

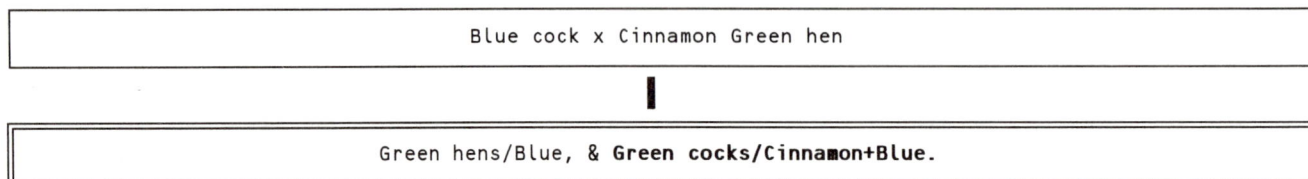

(c)

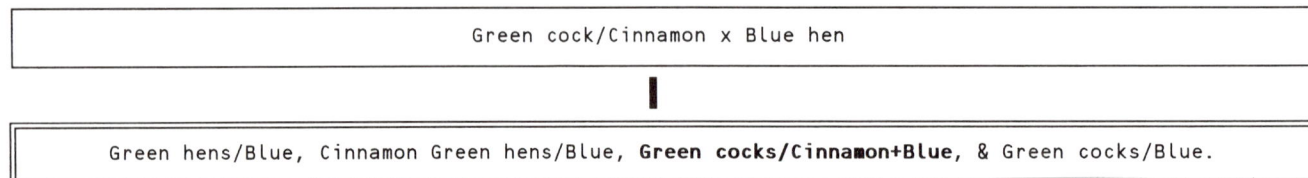

Second Season: two possible pairings. The split cocks can be paired to Blue hens or Cinnamon Green hens/Blue:

(a)

(b)

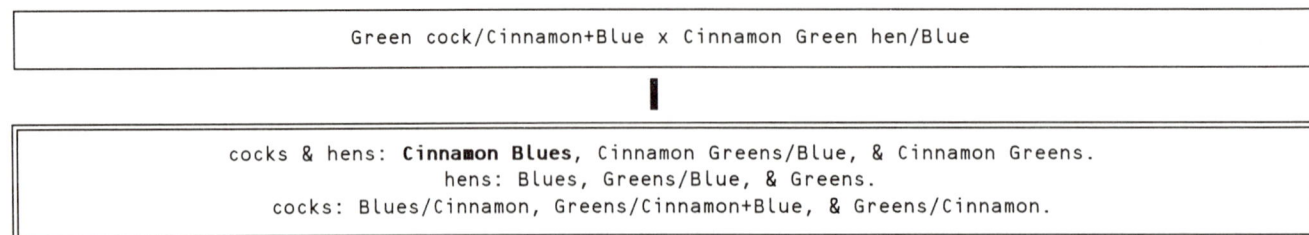

By now a wide selection of stock should be available for breeding in the third season, and a predominance of Cinnamon Blues can be achieved by the following pairings - other than Cinnamon Blue x Cinnamon Blue. It should be noted that although no Cinnamon Blue cocks are bred from pairing (a) there is likely to be a larger predominance of Blue birds than would be produced from pairing (b).

Third Season; a selection of pairings:

(a)

Cinnamon Blue cock x Cinnamon Green hen/Blue

|

cocks & hens: **Cinnamon Blues**, & Cinnamon Greens/Blue.

(b)

Cinnamon Green cock/Blue x Cinnamon Blue hen

|

cocks and hens: **Cinnamon Blues**, & Cinnamon Greens/Blue.

(c)

Cinnamon Green cock/Blue x Cinnamon Green hen/Blue

|

cocks & hens: **Cinnamon Blues**, Cinnamon Greens/Blue, & Cinnamon Greens.

(d)

Blue cock/Cinnamon x Cinnamon Blue hen

|

Cinnamon Blue cocks & hens, Blue hens, & Blue cocks/Cinnamon.

(e)

Cinnamon Green cock/Blue x Blue hen

|

Cinnamon Blue hens, Cinnamon Green hens/Blue, Blue cocks/Cinnamon, & Green cocks/Cinnamon+Blue.

Cinnamon Marine (SLR+AR)

Species: *Indian Ringneck Parrakeet, Red-rumped Parrakeet, Splendid Grass Parrakeet, Peach-faced Lovebird and Cockatiel **(Cinnamon Pale-faced).***

To illustrate the matings and expectations which show the production of this combination variety, replace Blue with **Marine** in the entire preceding section on **Cinnamon Blue.** For Cockatiels, replace Green with **Normal** and Blue with **Pale-faced.**

Cinnamon Lavender (SLR+AR)

Species: *Peach-faced Lovebird.*
To illustrate the matings and expectations which show the production of this combination variety, replace Blue with **Lavender** in the entire preceding section on **Cinnamon Blue.**

CINNAMON DILUTE

Cinnamon Dilute (Sex-linked) Blue (SLR+SLR+AR) (& Green) (SLR+SLR)

Species: *Indian Ringneck Parrakeet, Red-rumped Parrakeet and Splendid Grass Parrakeet.*

First Season; four suggested pairings. Cocks which are split for Dilute, Cinnamon and Blue are needed, and these can be produced in several ways:

(a)

Dilute Green cock x Cinnamon Blue hen

▌

Dilute Green hens/Blue & **Green cocks/Dilute+Cinnamon+Blue.**

(b)

Cinnamon Blue cock x Dilute Green hen

▌

Cinnamon Green hens/Blue, & **Green cocks/Dilute+Cinnamon+Blue.**

(c)

Dilute Blue cock x Cinnamon Green hen

▌

Dilute Green hens/Blue, & **Green cocks/Dilute+Cinnamon+Blue.**

(d)

Cinnamon Green cock x Dilute Blue hen

▌

Cinnamon Green hens/Blue, & **Green cocks/Dilute+Cinnamon+Blue.**

Second Season; the split cocks can be paired to either Dilute Blue hens or Cinnamon Blue hens:

Green cock/Dilute+Cinnamon+Blue x Dilute Blue hen

▌

100

Continued from previous page.

> **hens:**
> **Cinnamon Dilute Blues, Cinnamon Dilute Greens/Blue,** Dilute Blues, Dilute Greens/Blue,
> Cinnamon Blues, Cinnamon Greens/Blue, Blues, & Greens/Blue.
> **cocks:**
> *Dilute Blues/Cinnamon, *Dilute Greens/Cinnamon+Blue, *Dilute Blues, *Dilute Greens/Blue,
> Blues/Dilute+Cinnamon, Greens/Dilute+Cinnamon+Blue, *Blues/Dilute, & *Greens/Dilute+Blue.

By using a **Cinnamon Blue hen** in the above pairing instead of a **Dilute Blue hen**, those cock birds marked with an asterisk (*) will be omitted from the expectations and replaced by the following:

> Cinnamon Blues/Dilute, Cinnamon Greens/Dilute+Blue,
> Cinnamon Blues, Cinnamon Greens/Blue, Blues/Cinnamon, & Greens/Cinnamon+Blue.

The following cocks can be selected from both types of pairings for use with the young Cinnamon Dilute hens in the third season: **Dilute Blues** (hoping those chosen are split Cinnamon), **Dilute Greens** (hoping those chosen are split Cinnamon and Blue), **Cinnamon Blues** (hoping those chosen are split Dilute), and **Cinnamon Greens** (hoping those chosen are split Dilute and Blue). Should this be the case a greater amount of Cinnamon Dilutes (cocks and hens) is likely to be produced.

Third Season; four examples:

(a)

> Dilute Blue cock/Cinnamon x Cinnamon Dilute Blue hen

> **Cinnamon Dilute Blue cocks & hens,** Dilute Blue hens, & Dilute Blue cocks/Cinnamon.

(b)

> Dilute Green cock/Cinnamon+Blue x Cinnamon Dilute Blue hen

> cocks & hens: **Cinnamon Dilute Blues, & Cinnamon Dilute Greens/Blue.**
> hens: Dilute Blues, & Dilute Greens/Blue.
> cocks: Dilute Blues/Cinnamon, & Dilute Greens/Cinnamon+Blue.

(c)

> Cinnamon Blue cock/Dilute x Cinnamon Dilute Green hen/Blue

> cocks & hens: **Cinnamon Dilute Blues, & Cinnamon Dilute Greens/Blue.**
> hens: Cinnamon Blues, & Cinnamon Greens/Blue.
> cocks: Cinnamon Blues/Dilute, & Cinnamon Greens/Dilute+Blue.

(d)

> Cinnamon Green cock/Dilute+Blue x Cinnamon Dilute Blue hen

Continued on next page.

▐

```
cocks & hens: Cinnamon Dilute Blues, & Cinnamon Dilute Greens/Blue.
        hens: Cinnamon Blues, & Cinnamon Greens/Blue.
       cocks: Cinnamon Blues/Dilute, & Cinnamon Greens/Dilute+Blue.
```

Cinnamon Dilute (Sex–linked) Marine (SLR+SLR+AR) (& Green) (SLR+SLR)

Species: *Indian Ringneck Parrakeet, Red–rumped Parrakeet, Splendid Grass Parrakeet and Peach–faced Lovebird.*
To illustrate the matings and expectations which show the production of this compound variety, replace Blue with **Marine** in the entire preceding section on **Cinnamon Dilute (Sex–linked) Blue (& Green)**.

Cinnamon Dilute (Sex–linked) Lavender (SLR+SLR+AR) (& Green) (SLR+SLR)

Species: *Peach–faced Lovebird.*
To illustrate the matings and expectations which show the production of this compound variety, replace Blue with **Lavender** in the entire preceding section on **Cinnamon Dilute (Sex–linked) Blue (& Green)**.

Cinnamon Dilute (Recessive) Normal (SLR+AR)

Species: *Eastern Rosella and Bourke's Grass Parrakeet. For Bourke's: replace Normal, as used for Eastern Rosellas, with* **Brown.**

First Season; cocks split for Cinnamon and Dilute are needed:

```
Cinnamon Normal cock x Dilute Normal hen
```

▐

```
Cinnamon Normal hens/Dilute, & Normal cocks/Cinnamon+Dilute.
```

Second Season; both cocks and hens bred from the type of pairing used in the first season can be used, as well as Dilute Normal hens; two suggested pairings:

(a)

```
Normal cock/Cinnamon+Dilute x Cinnamon Normal hen/Dilute
```

▐

```
cocks & hens: Cinnamon Dilute Normals, Cinnamon Normals/Dilute, & Cinnamon Normals.
        hens: Dilute Normals, Normals/Dilute, & Normals.
       cocks: Dilute Normals/Cinnamon, Normals/Cinnamon+Dilute, & Normals/Cinnamon.
```

(b)

```
Normal cock/Cinnamon+Dilute x Dilute Normal hen
```

▐

Continued from previous page.

```
        cocks & hens: Dilute Normals, & Normals/Dilute.
      hens: Cinnamon Dilute Normals, & Cinnamon Normals/Dilute.
      cocks: Dilute Normals/Cinnamon, & Normals/Cinnamon+Dilute.
```

The first pairing (a) offers the possibility of providing Cinnamon Dilute Normal **cocks and hens**, while pairing (b) can provide only **hens** of the required combination.

Third Season; to consolidate the stock:

```
        Cinnamon Dilute Normal cock x Cinnamon Dilute Normal hen
```

```
                    all Cinnamon Dilute Normals.
```

All Dilute Normal cocks produced from pairing (a) in the second season must be split Cinnamon, so these are also useful:

```
        Dilute Normal cock/Cinnamon x Cinnamon Dilute Normal hen
```

```
  Cinnamon Dilute Normal cocks & hens, Dilute Normal hens, & Dilute Normal cocks/Cinnamon.
```

Cinnamon Dilute (Recessive) Marine (SLR+AR+AR) (& Green) (SLR+AR)

Species: *Peach-faced Lovebird.*

*First Season: if the pairing **Cinnamon Marine cock x Dilute Green hen** were used, the results would be the same as those below. Cocks split for Cinnamon, Dilute and Marine are needed:*

```
                Cinnamon Green cock x Dilute Marine hen
```

```
   Green cocks/Cinnamon+Dilute+Marine, & Cinnamon Green hens/Dilute+Marine.
```

*Second Season; the split cocks could be paired to Dilute hens, but would have no chance of producing Cinnamon Dilute cocks – only **hens**, i.e.:*

```
        Green cock/Cinnamon+Dilute+Marine x Dilute Marine hen
```

Continued from previous page.

```
cocks & hens:
Dilute Marines, Dilute Greens/Marine, Marines/Dilute, & Greens/Dilute+Marine.
                            hens:
     Cinnamon Dilute Marines, Cinnamon Dilute Greens/Marine,
    Cinnamon Marines/Dilute, & Cinnamon Greens/Dilute+Marine.
                            cocks:
     Dilute Marines/Cinnamon, Dilute Greens/Cinnamon+Marine,
    Marines/Cinnamon+Dilute, & Greens/Cinnamon+Dilute+Marine.
```

To provide a chance of breeding both **cock and hen** Cinnamon Dilutes, the following pairing can be made by using the birds produced in the first season:

```
Green cock/Cinnamon+Dilute+Marine x Cinnamon Green hen/Dilute+Marine
```

```
cocks & hens:
Cinnamon Dilute Marines, Cinnamon Dilute Greens/Marine, Cinnamon Dilute Greens,
 Cinnamon Marines/Dilute, Cinnamon Greens/Dilute+Marine, Cinnamon Greens/Dilute,
      Cinnamon Marines, Cinnamon Greens/Marine, & Cinnamon Greens.
                            hens:
      Dilute Marines, Dilute Greens/Marine, Dilute Greens,
      Marines/Dilute, Greens/Dilute+Marine, Greens/Dilute,
               Marines, Greens/Marine, & Greens.
                            cocks:
Dilute Marines/Cinnamon, Dilute Greens/Cinnamon+Marine, Dilute Greens/Cinnamon,
Marines/Cinnamon+Dilute, Greens/Cinnamon+Dilute+Marine, Greens/Cinnamon+Dilute,
      Marines/Cinnamon, Greens/Cinnamon+Marine, & Greens/Cinnamon.
```

As can be seen from the large scope of types which can be bred, this pairing is an outside chance – but the sought after compound varieties can arise. In the third season, any **Dilute Marine cocks/Cinnamon** from the above pairing would be a useful choice to pair to the **Cinnamon Green hens/Dilute & Marine** produced in the first season if Cinnamon Dilute Marines were not available – e.g. pairing (a) third season.

Alternatively, the **Dilute cocks** (which must all be split Cinnamon, and, if Green, may be split Marine) can be paired to any **Cinnamon Dilute hens** (which if Green may be split Marine), or the **Cinnamon Marine hens/Dilute** and **Cinnamon Green hens/Dilute and Marine** from the first pairing of the second season; e.g. pairings (b) and (c).

Third Season; three examples:
(a)

```
Dilute Marine cock/Cinnamon x Cinnamon Green hen/Dilute+Marine
```

```
cocks & hens:
    Cinnamon Dilute Marines, Cinnamon Dilute Greens/Marine,
    Cinnamon Marines/Dilute, & Cinnamon Greens/Dilute+Marine.
                        hens:
Dilute Marines, Dilute Greens/Marine, Marines/Dilute, & Greens/Dilute+Marine.
                        cocks:
     Dilute Marines/Cinnamon, Dilute Greens/Cinnamon+Marine,
    Marines/Cinnamon+Dilute, & Greens/Cinnamon+Dilute+Marine.
```

(b)

Dilute Marine cock/Cinnamon x Cinnamon Dilute Green hen/Marine

I

cocks & hens: **Cinnamon Dilute Marines, & Cinnamon Dilute Greens/Marine.** hens: Dilute Marines, & Dilute Greens/Marine. cocks: Dilute Marines/Cinnamon, & Dilute Greens/Cinnamon+Marine.

(c)

Dilute Green cock/Cinnamon+Marine x Cinnamon Marine hen/Dilute

I

cocks & hens: **Cinnamon Dilute Marines, Cinnamon Dilute Greens/Marine,** Cinnamon Marines/Dilute, & Cinnamon Greens/Dilute+Marine. hens: Dilute Marines, Dilute Greens/Marine, Marines/Dilute, & Greens/Dilute+Marine. cocks: Dilute Marines/Cinnamon, Dilute Greens/Cinnamon+Marine, Marines/Cinnamon+Dilute, & Greens/Cinnamon+Dilute+Marine.

Cinnamon Dilute (Recessive) Lavender (SLR+AR+AR) (& Green) (SLR+AR)

Species: Peach-faced Lovebird.
To illustrate the matings and expectations which show the production of this compound variety, replace Marine with **Lavender** in the entire preceding section on **Cinnamon Dilute (Recessive) Marine (& Green)**.

Cinnamon Clearhead Blue (SLR+AR+AR) (& Green) (SLR+AR)

Species: Indian Ringneck Parrakeet.
To illustrate the matings and expectations which show the production of this compound variety, replace Marine with **Blue** and Dilute with **Clearhead** in the entire preceding section on **Cinnamon Dilute (Recessive) Marine (& Green)**.

Cinnamon Clearhead Marine (SLR+AR+AR) (& Green) (SLR+AR)

Species: Indian Ringneck Parrakeet.
To illustrate the matings and expectations which show the production of this compound variety, replace Dilute with **Clearhead** in the entire preceding section on **Cinnamon Dilute (Recessive) Marine (& Green)**.

Cinnamon Dilute (Sex-linked) Greyblue (SLR+SLR+ACD+AR)

Grey: (S)= Single Factor   (D)= Double Factor

Species: Indian Ringneck Parrakeet.
In order to obtain an end result of Cinnamon Dilutes in both Greyblue *and* Greygreen, the first season pairings (below) would both need to include one partner which was of the Green series, so that the young would be *all* of the

105

Green series split Blue. If this were to be the case the expectations of the first season would be multiplied by two because for every type in the Blue series there would be an equivalent type in the Green split Blue series. In the second season – by using parents which were both of the Green split Blue series – the expectations would be multiplied by three because there would be equivalent types in the Blue, the Green split Blue *and* the Green series. The production of the variety in the Blue series is illustrated below.

First Season; two suggested pairings:

(a)

Dilute Blue cock x Cinnamon (D)Greyblue hen

Dilute (S)Greyblue hens, & (S)Greyblue cocks/Dilute+Cinnamon.

(b)

Cinnamon Blue cock x Dilute (D)Greyblue hen

Cinnamon (S)Greyblue hens, & (S)Greyblue cocks/Dilute+Cinnamon.

Second Season:

(S)Greyblue cock/Dilute+Cinnamon x Dilute (S)Greyblue hen

hens:
Cinnamon Dilute (D)Greyblues, Cinnamon Dilute (S)Greyblues, Cinnamon Dilute Blues, Dilute (D)Greyblues, Dilute (S)Greyblues, Dilute Blues, Cinnamon (D)Greyblues, Cinnamon (S)Greyblues, Cinnamon Blues, (D)Greyblues, (S)Greyblues, & Blues.
cocks:
*Dilute (D)Greyblues/Cinnamon, *Dilute (S)Greyblues/Cinnamon, *Dilute Blues/Cinnamon, *Dilute (D)Greyblues, *Dilute (S)Greyblues, *Dilute Blues, (D)Greyblues/Cinnamon+Dilute, (S)Greyblues/Cinnamon+Dilute, Blues/Cinnamon+Dilute, *(D)Greyblues/Dilute, *(S)Greyblues/Dilute, & *Blues/Dilute.

By using a **Cinnamon (S)Greyblue hen** instead of a Dilute (S)Greyblue hen in the above pairing, those cocks marked with an asterisk (*) will be omitted and replaced with the following:

Cinnamon (D)Greyblues/Dilute, Cinnamon (S)Greyblues/Dilute, Cinnamon Blues/Dilute, Cinnamon (D)Greyblues, Cinnamon (S)Greyblues, Cinnamon Blues, (D)Greyblues/Cinnamon, (S)Greyblues/Cinnamon, & Blues/Cinnamon.

The following cocks can be selected from the two types of pairings to be mated with any young Cinnamon Dilute Greyblue hens in the third season:– **Dilute Greyblues** (in the hope that those chosen are Double Factor Grey and split

Cinnamon), and **Cinnamon Greyblues** (in the hope that those chosen are Double Factor Grey and split Dilute). Should this be so, the following results could be obtained:

Third Season:

(a)

Dilute (D)Greyblue cock/Cinnamon x Cinnamon Dilute (D)Greyblue hen

I

Cinnamon Dilute (D)Greyblue cocks & hens, Dilute (D)Greyblue hens, & Dilute (D)Greyblue cocks/Cinnamon.

(b)

Cinnamon (D)Greyblue cock/Dilute x Cinnamon Dilute (D)Greyblue hen

I

Cinnamon Dilute (D)Greyblue cocks & hens, Cinnamon (D)Greyblue hens, & Cinnamon (D)Greyblue cocks/Dilute.

Cinnamon Dilute (Sex-linked) Greymarine (SLR+SLR+ACD+AR)

Species: Indian Ringneck Parrakeet.

To illustrate the matings and expectations which show the production of this compound variety, replace Blue with **Marine** and Greyblue with **Greymarine** in the entire preceding section on **Cinnamon Dilute (Sex-linked) Greyblue.**

Cinnamon Dilute (Sex-linked) Greygreen (SLR+SLR+ACD)

Species: Indian Ringneck Parrakeet.

To illustrate the production of *only* Cinnamon Dilute Greygreens, replace Blue with **Green** and Greyblue with **Greygreen** in the preceding section on **Cinnamon Dilute (Sex-linked) Greyblue.**

Cinnamon Dilute (Dominant) White-faced (SLR+AID+AR) (& Normal) (SLR+AID)

Species: Cockatiel.

Dilute: (S): Single Factor   (D): Double Factor

First Season:

Cinnamon White-faced cock x (D)Dilute Normal hen

I

Cinnamon (S)Dilute Normal hens/White-faced, & (S)Dilute Normal cocks/Cinnamon+White-faced.

Second Season; three suggested pairings:

(a)

(S)Dilute Normal cock/Cinnamon+White-faced x Cinnamon (S)Dilute Normal hen/White-faced

▮

cocks & hens: Cinnamon (D)Dilute White-faceds, Cinnamon (S)Dilute White-faceds, Cinnamon White-faceds, Cinnamon (D)Dilute Normals/White-faced, Cinnamon (S)Dilute Normals/White-faced, Cinnamon Normals/White-faced, Cinnamon (D)Dilute Normals, Cinnamon (S)Dilute Normals, & Cinnamon Normals. hens: (D)Dilute White-faceds, (S)Dilute White-faceds, White-faceds, (D)Dilute Normals/White-faced, (S)Dilute Normals/White-faced, Normals/White-faced, (D)Dilute Normals, (S)Dilute Normals, & Normals. cocks: (D)Dilute White-faceds/Cinnamon, (S)Dilute White-faceds/Cinnamon, White-faceds/Cinnamon, (D)Dilute Normals/Cinnamon+White-faced, (S)Dilute Normals/Cinnamon+White-faced, Dilute Normals/Cinnamon+White-faced, (D)Dilute Normals/Cinnamon, (S)Dilute Normals/Cinnamon, & Normals/Cinnamon.

(b)

(S)Dilute Normal cock/Cinnamon+White-faced x (D)Dilute White-faced hen

▮

cocks & hens: (D)Dilute White-faceds, (S)Dilute White-faceds, (D)Dilute Normals/White-faced, & (S)Dilute Normals/White-faced. hens: Cinnamon (D)Dilute White-faceds, Cinnamon (S)Dilute White-faceds, Cinnamon (D)Dilute Normals/White-faced, Cinnamon (S)Dilute Normals/White-faced, cocks: (D)Dilute White-faceds/Cinnamon, (S)Dilute White-faceds/Cinnamon (D)Dilute Normals/Cinnamon+White-faced, (S)Dilute Normals/Cinnamon+White-faced,

(c)

(S)Dilute Normal cock/Cinnamon+White-faced x Cinnamon White-faced hen

▮

cocks & hens: Cinnamon (S)Dilute White-faceds, Cinnamon White-faceds, Cinnamon (S)Dilute Normals/White-faced, & Cinnamon Normals/White-faced. hens: (S)Dilute White-faceds, White-faceds, (S)Dilute Normals/White-faceds, & Normals/White-faced. cocks: (S)Dilute White-faceds/Cinnamon, White-faceds/Cinnamon, (S)Dilute Normals/Cinnamon+White-faced, & Normals/Cinnamon+White-faced.

Consolidation and increase in production of Cinnamon Dilutes can take place in the third season by using by-products of the second season's breeding, as well as the Cinnamon Dilutes. The most useful cocks would be the following: from pairing (a), **(D)Dilute White-faced split Cinnamon**, and **(D)Dilute Normals split Cinnamon and White-faced**; from pairing (c), **(S)Dilute White-faceds split Cinnamon** and **(S)Dilute Normal split Cinnamon and White-faced**.

Third Season; best example:

> (D)Dilute White-faced cock/Cinnamon x Cinnamon (D)Dilute Normal hen/White-faced

I

> cocks & hens: **Cinnamon (D)Dilute White-faceds, & Cinnamon (D)Dilute Normals/White-faced.**
> hens: (D)Dilute White-faceds, & (D)Dilute Normals/White-faced.
> cocks: (D)Dilute White-faceds/Cinnamon, & (D)Dilute Normals/Cinnamon+White-faced.

Cinnamon Dilute (Dominant) Pale-faced (SLR+AID+AR) (& Normal) (SLR+AID)

Species: *Cockatiel.*

To illustrate the matings and expectations which show the production of this compound variety, replace White-faced with **Pale-faced** throughout the entire preceding section on **Cinnamon Dilute (Dominant) White-faced (& Normal).**

CINNAMON GREY

Cinnamon Greyblue (SLR+ACD+AR) (& Greygreen) (SLR+ACD)

Species: *Indian Ringneck Parrakeet.*

Grey: (S)= Single Factor Grey   (D)= Double Factor Grey

First Season; two suggested pairings:

(a)
Note: **Cinnamon Green cock x (D)Greyblue hen** *gives the same results as the pairing below.*

> Cinnamon Blue cock x (D)Greygreen hen

I

> **Cinnamon (S)Greygreen hens/Blue, & (S)Greygreen cocks/Cinnamon+Blue.**

(b)
Note: **(D)Greyblue cock x Cinnamon Green hen** *gives the same results as the pairing below.*

> (D)Greygreen cock x Cinnamon Blue hen

I

> (S)Greygreen hens/Blue, & **(S)Greygreen cocks/Cinnamon+Blue.**

Second Season; two suggested pairings:
(a)

> (S)Greygreen cock/Cinnamon+Blue x Cinnamon (S)Greygreen hen/Blue

I

109

Continued from previous page.

```
                              cocks & hens:
         Cinnamon (D)Greyblues, Cinnamon (S)Greyblues, Cinnamon Blues,
  Cinnamon (D)Greygreens/Blue, Cinnamon (S)Greygreens/Blue, Cinnamon Greens/Blue,
      Cinnamon (D)Greygreens, Cinnamon (S)Greygreens, & Cinnamon Greens.
                                  hens:
                    (D)Greyblues, (S)Greyblues, Blues,
             (D)Greygreens/Blue, (S)Greygreens/Blue, Greens/Blue,
                  (D)Greygreens, (S)Greygreens, & Greens.
                                  cocks:
           (D)Greyblues/Cinnamon, (S)Greyblues/Cinnamon, Blues/Cinnamon,
   (D)Greygreens/Cinnamon+Blue, (S)Greygreens/Cinnamon+Blue, Greens/Cinnamon+Blue,
        (D)Greygreens/Cinnamon, (S)Greygreens/Cinnamon, & Greens/Cinnamon.
```

(b)

```
            (S)Greygreen cock/Cinnamon+Blue x (D)Greyblue hen
```

```
                              cocks & hens:
      (D)Greyblues, (D)Greygreens/Blue, (S)Greyblues, & (S)Greygreens/Blue.
                                  hens:
           Cinnamon (D)Greyblues, Cinnamon (D)Greygreens/Blue,
         Cinnamon (S)Greyblues, & Cinnamon (S)Greygreens/Blue.
                                  cocks:
            (D)Greyblues/Cinnamon, (D)Greygreens/Cinnamon+Blue,
          (S)Greyblues/Cinnamon, & (S)Greygreens/Cinnamon+Blue.
```

It should be noted that although no Cinnamon Greyblue *cocks* are likely to be bred from pairing (b), there should be a larger number of Greyblue birds than would be bred off pairing (a). From these pairings enough Cinnamon Greyblues as would enable stock to be consolidated during subsequent seasons should be produced.

Cinnamon Greymarine (SLR+ACD+AR) (& Greygreen) (SLR+ACD)

Species: Indian Ringneck Parrakeet.
To illustrate the matings and expectations which show the production of this compound variety, replace Blue with **Marine** throughout the entire preceding section on **Cinnamon Greyblue (& Greygreen)**.

DILUTE GREY

Dilute (Sex-linked) Greyblue (SLR+ACD+AR) (& Greygreen) (SLR+ACD)

Species: Indian Ringneck Parrakeet
To illustrate the matings and expectations which show the production of this compound variety, replace Cinnamon with **Dilute** throughout the entire preceding section on **Cinnamon Greyblue (& Greygreen)**.

Dilute (Sex-linked) Greymarine (SLR+ACD+AR) (& Greygreen) (SLR+ACD)

Species: *Indian Ringneck Parrakeet.*

To illustrate the matings and expectations which show the production of this compound variety, replace Blue with **Marine**, and Cinnamon with **Dilute** throughout the entire preceding section on **Cinnamon Greyblue (& Greygreen).**

CLEARHEAD GREY

Clearhead Greyblue (AR+ACD+AR) (& Greygreen) (AR+ACD)

Species: *Indian Ringneck Parrakeet.*

Grey: (S)= Single Factor Grey   (D)= Double Factor Grey

First Season:

```
Clearhead Green x (D)Greyblue
```

▮

```
all (S)Greygreens/Clearhead+Blue.
```

Second Season:

(a)

```
(S)Greygreen/Clearhead+Blue x (S)Greygreen/Clearhead+Blue
```

▮

```
Clearhead (D)Greyblues, Clearhead (D)Greygreens/Blue, Clearhead (D)Greygreens,
Clearhead (S)Greyblues, Clearhead (S)Greygreens/Blue, Clearhead (S)Greygreens,
Clearhead Blues, Clearhead Greens/Blue, Clearhead Greens,
(D)Greyblues/Clearhead, (D)Greygreens/Clearhead+Blue, (D)Greygreens/Clearhead,
(S)Greyblues/Clearhead, (S)Greygreens/Clearhead+Blue, (S)Greygreens/Clearhead,
Blues/Clearhead, Greens/Clearhead+Blue, Greens/Clearhead,
(D)Greyblues, (D)Greygreens/Blue, (D)Greygreens,
(S)Greyblues, (S)Greygreens/Blue, (S)Greygreens,
Blues, Greens/Blue, & Greens.
```

To increase the incidence of this compound variety, the following 'by-product' types which could be paired to any young Clearhead Greyblues include the **Clearhead Greygreens** (in the hope that they are Double Factor Grey and split Blue), and the **Greyblues** (in the hope that they are Double Factor Grey and split Clearhead). The splits from the first season continue to be useful and, failing all else, any **Clearhead Greygreens** (in the hope that they are split Blue) could be paired to Clearhead Blues.

Third Season; four suggested pairings:

(a)

```
Clearhead (D)Greygreen/Blue x Clearhead (D)Greyblue
```

▮

Continued from previous page.

Clearhead (D)Greyblues, & Clearhead (D)Greygreens/Blue.

(b)

(D)Greyblue/Clearhead x Clearhead (D)Greyblue

Clearhead (D)Greyblues, & (D)Greyblues/Clearhead.

(c)

Clearhead (D)Greygreen/Blue x Clearhead Blue

Clearhead (S)Greyblues, & Clearhead (S)Greygreens/Blue.

(d)

Clearhead (D)Greyblue x Clearhead (D)Greyblue

all **Clearhead (D)Greyblues**.

Clearhead Greymarine (AR+ACD+AR) (& Greygreen) (AR+ACD)

Species: *Indian Ringneck Parrakeet.*

To illustrate the matings and expectations which show the production of this compound variety, replace Blue with **Marine** in the preceding section on **Clearhead Greyblue (& Greygreen).**

CINNAMON INO

Cinnamon Albino (Sex-linked) (SLR+SLR+AR) (& Lutino) (SLR+SLR)

Species: *Indian Ringneck Parrakeet, Red-rumped Parrakeet and Cockatiel; for Cockatiels replace Green with* **Normal,** *and Blue with* **White-faced.**

At first evaluation, there would seem to be little point in combining Cinnamon and Ino, as logic would suppose that Ino would simply negate the action of Cinnamon. However, in practice the Cinnamon factor has a partially inhibiting effect on Ino; remnants of melanin brown leave ghost traces against markings or areas which contain most melanin in the wild type, while darkest blue areas still show slight indication of their colour or are tinted with grey.

First Season; four suggested pairings; cocks which are split for Ino, Cinnamon and Blue are needed, and these can be produced in several ways:
(a)

Lutino cock x Cinnamon Blue hen

112

Continued from previous page.

```
Lutino hens/Blue, & Green cocks/Ino+Cinnamon+Blue.
```

(b)

```
Cinnamon Blue cock x Lutino hen
```

```
Cinnamon Green hens/Blue, & Green cocks/Ino+Cinnamon+Blue.
```

(c)

```
Albino cock x Cinnamon Green hen
```

```
Lutino hens/Blue, & Green cocks/Ino+Cinnamon+Blue.
```

(d)

```
Cinnamon Green cock x Albino hen
```

```
Cinnamon Green hens/Blue, & Green cocks/Ino+Cinnamon+Blue.
```

Second Season; the split cocks can be paired to either Albino hens or Cinnamon Blue hens:

```
Green cock/Ino+Cinnamon+Blue x Albino hen
```

```
hens:
Cinnamon Albinos, Cinnamon Lutinos/Blue, Albinos, Lutinos/Blue,
Cinnamon Blues, Cinnamon Greens/Blue, Blues, & Greens/Blue.
cocks:
*Albinos/Cinnamon, *Lutinos/Cinnamon+Blue, *Albinos, *Lutinos/Blue,
Blues/Ino+Cinnamon, Greens/Ino+Cinnamon+Blue, *Blues/Ino, & *Greens/Ino+Blue.
```

By using a **Cinnamon Blue hen** in the above pairing instead of an **Albino hen**, those cock birds marked with an asterisk (*) will be omitted from the expectations and replaced by the following:

```
Cinnamon Blues/Ino, Cinnamon Greens/Ino+Blue, Cinnamon Blues, Cinnamon Greens/Blue,
Blues/Cinnamon, & Greens/Cinnamon+Blue.
```

The following cocks can be selected from both types of pairings for use with the young Cinnamon Ino hens in the third season: **Albinos** (hoping those chosen are split Cinnamon), **Lutinos** (hoping those chosen are split Cinnamon and Blue), **Cinnamon Blues** (hoping those chosen are split Ino), and **Cinnamon Greens** (hoping

113

those chosen are split Ino and Blue). Should this be the case a greater amount of Cinnamon Inos (cocks and hens) is likely to be produced.

Third Season; four examples:
(a)

Albino cock/Cinnamon x Cinnamon Albino hen

▮

Cinnamon Albino cocks & hens, Albino hens, and Albino cocks/Cinnamon.

(b)

Lutino cock/Cinnamon+Blue x Cinnamon Albino hen

▮

cocks & hens: **Cinnamon Albinos, & Cinnamon Lutinos/Blue.** hens: Albinos, & Lutinos/Blue. cocks: Albinos/Cinnamon, & Lutinos/Cinnamon+Blue.

(c)

Cinnamon Blue cock/Ino x Cinnamon Lutino hen/Blue

▮

cocks & hens: **Cinnamon Albinos, & Cinnamon Lutinos/Blue.** hens: Cinnamon Blues, & Cinnamon Greens/Blue. cocks: Cinnamon Blues/Ino, & Cinnamon Greens/Ino+Blue.

(d)

Cinnamon Green cock/Ino+Blue x Cinnamon Albino hen

▮

cocks & hens: **Cinnamon Albinos, & Cinnamon Lutinos/Blue.** hens: Cinnamon Blues, & Cinnamon Greens/Blue. cocks: Cinnamon Blues/Ino, & Cinnamon Greens/Ino+Blue.

Cinnamon Creamino (Sex–linked) (SLR+SLR+AR)

Species: Indian Ringneck Parrakeet, Red-rumped Parrakeet, Peach-faced Lovebird and Cockatiel.

To illustrate the matings and expectations which show the production of this combination variety, replace Blue with **Marine** and Albino with **Creamino** in the entire preceding section on **Cinnamon Albino and Lutino (Sex-linked).** For Cockatiels replace Green with **Normal,** Blue with **Pale–faced** and Albino with **Creamino.**

Cinnamon Ivorino (Sex–linked) (SLR+SLR+AR)

Species: Peach–faced Lovebird.

To illustrate the matings and expectations which show the production of this combination variety, replace Blue with **Lavender** and Albino with **Ivorino** in the entire preceding section on **Cinnamon Albino & Lutino (Sex–linked).**

Cinnamon Lutino (Sex–linked) (SLR+SLR)

Species: *Eastern Rosella (European Ino).*

First Season; cocks split for Ino and Cinnamon are needed, and these can be provided in two ways:

(a)

Lutino cock x Cinnamon Normal hen

▐

Lutino hens, & **Normal cocks/Ino+Cinnamon**.

(b)

Cinnamon Normal cock x Lutino hen

▐

Cinnamon Normal hens, & **Normal cocks/Ino+Cinnamon**.

Second Season; the split cocks can be paired to either Lutino hens or Cinnamon Normal hens:

Normal cock/Ino+Cinnamon x Lutino hen

▐

hens: **Cinnamon Lutinos,** Lutinos, Cinnamon Normals, & Normals. cocks: Lutinos/Cinnamon, Lutinos, Normals/Ino+Cinnamon, & Normals/Ino.

By replacing the parent Lutino hen with a **Cinnamon Normal hen** in the above pairing, the young Lutino cocks/Cinnamon will be replaced by **Cinnamon Normal cocks/Ino**, and the young Lutino cocks by **Cinnamon Normal cocks**.

The following cocks can be selected from these two pairings for use with the young Cinnamon Lutino hens in the third season: **Lutinos** (hoping those chosen are split Cinnamon) and **Cinnamon Normals** (hoping those chosen are split Ino). Should this be the case a greater amount of Cinnamon Lutinos (cocks and hens) is likely to be produced.

Third Season; two suggested pairings:

(a)

Lutino cock/Cinnamon x Cinnamon Lutino hen

▐

Cinnamon Lutino cocks & hens, Lutino hens, & Lutino cocks/Cinnamon.

(b)

Cinnamon Normal cock/Ino x Cinnamon Lutino hen

▐

115

Continued from previous page.

Cinnamon Lutino cocks & hens, Cinnamon Normal hens, & Cinnamon Normal cocks/Ino.

Fourth Season; Cinnamon Lutinos can be paired together and will breed true.

Cinnamon Lutino (Recessive) (SLR+AR)

Species: *Elegant Grass Parrakeet, Adelaide Rosella and Eastern Rosella (Australian Ino). For the Eastern Rosella and Adelaide Rosella, replace Green with* **Normal** *throughout this entire section.*

Firstly, Green cocks split Ino and Cinnamon, and Cinnamon Green hens split Ino are needed. These can be provided in several ways but it will be obvious that pairing (a) is preferable because both required types are provided and they can be sexed from eye colour on hatching – which is of great benefit.

First Season:

(a)

Cinnamon Green cock x Lutino hen

Cinnamon Green hens/Ino, & Green cocks/Cinnamon+Ino.

(b)

Lutino cock x Cinnamon Green hen

Green hens/Ino, **& Green cocks/Cinnamon+Ino.**

(c)

Green cock/Cinnamon x Lutino hen

Green hens/Ino, **Cinnamon Green hens/Ino,** Green cocks/Cinnamon+Ino, & Green cocks/Ino.

Second Season; the split cocks can be paired to Lutino hens or Cinnamon Green hens/Ino:

(a)

Green cock/Cinnamon+Ino x Lutino hen

cocks & hens: Lutinos, & Greens/Ino. hens: **Cinnamon Lutinos,** & Cinnamon Greens/Ino. cocks: Lutinos/Cinnamon, & Greens/Cinnamon+Ino.

(b)

> Green cock/Cinnamon+Ino x Cinnamon Green hen/Ino

▮

> cocks & hens: **Cinnamon Lutinos,** Cinnamon Greens/Ino, & Cinnamon Greens.
> hens: Lutinos, Greens/Ino, & Greens.
> cocks: Lutinos/Cinnamon, Greens/Cinnamon+Ino, & Greens/Cinnamon.

By now a wide selection of stock should be available for breeding in the third season, and a predominance of Cinnamon Lutinos can be achieved by the following pairings – other than Cinnamon Lutino x Cinnamon Lutino.

Third Season; a selection of pairings:
(a)

> Cinnamon Lutino cock x Cinnamon Green hen/Ino

▮

> cocks & hens: **Cinnamon Lutinos,** & Cinnamon Greens/Ino.

(b)

> Cinnamon Green cock/Ino x Cinnamon Lutino hen

▮

> cocks & hens: **Cinnamon Lutinos,** & Cinnamon Greens/Ino.

(c)

> Cinnamon Green cock/Ino x Cinnamon Green hen/Ino

▮

> cocks & hens: **Cinnamon Lutinos,** Cinnamon Greens/Ino, & Cinnamon Greens.

(d)

> Lutino cock/Cinnamon x Cinnamon Lutino hen

▮

> **Cinnamon Lutino cocks & hens,** Lutino hens, & Lutino cocks/Cinnamon.

(e)

> Cinnamon Green cock/Ino x Lutino hen

▮

> **Cinnamon Lutino hens,** Cinnamon Green hens/Ino, Lutino cocks/Cinnamon, & Green cocks/Cinnamon+Ino.

CINNAMON MELANISTIC (SLR+AR)

Species: *Eastern Rosella.*

Firstly, Normal cocks split Cinnamon and Melanistic, and Cinnamon Normal hens split Melanistic are needed. These can be provided in several ways but it will be obvious that pairing (a) is preferable because both required types are produced and they can be sexed from eye colour on hatching - which is of great benefit.

First Season:

(a)

Cinnamon Normal cock x Melanistic hen

Cinnamon Normal hens/Melanistic, & Normal cocks/Cinnamon+Melanistic.

(b)

Melanistic cock x Cinnamon Normal hen

Normal hens/Melanistic, & **Normal cocks/Cinnamon+Melanistic.**

(c)

Normal cock/Cinnamon x Melanistic hen

Normal hens/Melanistic, **Cinnamon Normal hens/Melanistic,** **Normal cocks/Cinnamon+Melanistic,** & Normal cocks/Melanistic.

Second Season; the split cocks can be paired to Melanistic hens or Cinnamon Normal hens/Melanistic:

(a)

Normal cock/Cinnamon+Melanistic x Melanistic hen

cocks & hens: Melanistics, & Normals/Melanistic. hens: **Cinnamon Melanistics,** & Cinnamon Normals/Melanistic. cocks: Melanistics/Cinnamon, & Normals/Cinnamon+Melanistic.

(b)

Normal cock/Cinnamon+Melanistic x Cinnamon Normal hen/Melanistic

cocks & hens: **Cinnamon Melanistics,** Cinnamon Normals/Melanistic, & Cinnamon Normals. hens: Melanistics, Normals/Melanistic, & Normals. cocks: Melanistics/Cinnamon, Normals/Cinnamon+Melanistic, & Normals/Cinnamon.

By now a wide selection of stock should be available for breeding in the third season, and a predominance of Cinnamon Melanistics can be achieved by the following pairings – other than Cinnamon Melanistic x Cinnamon Melanistic.

Third Season; a selection of pairings:
(a)

Cinnamon Melanistic cock x Cinnamon Normal hen/Melanistic

cocks & hens: **Cinnamon Melanistics**, & Cinnamon Normals/Melanistic.

(b)

Cinnamon Normal cock/Melanistic x Cinnamon Melanistic hen

cocks & hens: **Cinnamon Melanistics**, & Cinnamon Normals/Melanistic.

(c)

Cinnamon Normal cock/Melanistic x Cinnamon Normal hen/Melanistic

cocks & hens: **Cinnamon Melanistics**, Cinnamon Normals/Melanistic, & Cinnamon Normals.

(d)

Melanistic cock/Cinnamon x Cinnamon Melanistic hen

Cinnamon Melanistic cocks & hens, Melanistic hens, & Melanistic cocks/Cinnamon.

(e)

Cinnamon Normal cock/Melanistic x Melanistic hen

Cinnamon Melanistic hens, Cinnamon Normal hens/Melanistic, Melanistic cocks/Cinnamon, & Normal cocks/Cinnamon+Melanistic.

CINNAMON ROSA & CINNAMON RUBY

Cinnamon Rosa (SLR+SLR)

Species: *Bourke's Grass Parrakeet (**Brown** = Normal).*

First Season; cocks split for Rosa and Cinnamon can be provided in two ways:
(a)

Rosa Brown cock x Cinnamon Brown hen

Continued from previous page.

Rosa Brown hens, & **Brown cocks/Rosa+Cinnamon.**

(b)

Cinnamon Brown cock x Rosa Brown hen

Cinnamon Brown hens, & **Brown cocks/Rosa+Cinnamon.**

Second Season; the split cocks can be paired to either Rosa Brown hens or Cinnamon Brown hens:

(a)

Brown cock/Rosa+Cinnamon x Rosa Brown hen

hens: **Cinnamon Rosa Browns,** Rosa Browns, Cinnamon Browns, & Browns. cocks: Rosa Browns/Cinnamon, Rosa Browns, Browns/Rosa+Cinnamon, & Browns/Rosa.

(b)

Brown cock/Rosa+Cinnamon x Cinnamon Brown hen

hens: **Cinnamon Rosa Browns,** Rosa Browns, Cinnamon Browns, & Browns. cocks: Cinnamon Browns/Rosa, Cinnamon Browns, Browns/Rosa+Cinnamon, & Browns/Cinnamon.

The following cocks can be selected from the two previous pairings for use with the young Cinnamon Rosa Brown hens in the third season: **Rosa Browns** (hoping those chosen are split Cinnamon) and **Cinnamon Browns** (hoping those chosen are split Rosa). Should this be the case a greater amount of Cinnamon Rosa Browns (cocks and hens) is likely to be produced.

Third Season; two suggested pairings:
(a)

Rosa Brown cock/Cinnamon x Cinnamon Rosa Brown hen

Cinnamon Rosa Brown cocks & hens, Rosa Brown hens, & Rosa Brown cocks/Cinnamon.

(b)

Cinnamon Brown cock/Rosa x Cinnamon Rosa Brown hen

Cinnamon Rosa Brown cocks & hens, Cinnamon Brown hens, & Cinnamon Brown cocks/Rosa.

Fourth Season; Cinnamon Rosa Browns can be paired together and will breed true.

Cinnamon Ruby (SLR+SLR)

Species: *Eastern Rosella*

To illustrate the matings and expectations which show the production of this combination variety, replace Brown with **Normal** and Rosa with **Ruby** in the entire preceding section on **Cinnamon Rosa.**

DILUTE BLUE (& DILUTE WHITE-FACED)

Dilute (Sex-linked) Blue (SLR+AR)

Species: *Indian Ringneck Parrakeet, Red-rumped Parrakeet and Splendid Grass Parrakeet.*

Firstly, cocks which are split for both Dilute and Blue are needed. These can be provided in several ways but it will be obvious that pairing (a) is preferable because the split cocks can be identified by eye colour as soon as they are hatched - which is of great benefit.

First Season:

(a)

Dilute Green cock x Blue hen

▌

Dilute Green hens/Blue, & **Green cocks/Dilute+Blue**.

(b)

Blue cock x Dilute Green hen

▌

Green hens/Blue, & **Green cocks/Dilute+Blue**.

(c)

Green cock/Dilute x Blue hen

▌

Green hens/Blue, Dilute Green hens/Blue, **Green cocks/Dilute+Blue**, & Green cocks/Blue.

Second Season; the split cocks can be paired to Blue hens or Dilute Green hens/Blue; two possible pairings:

(a)

Green cock/Dilute+Blue x Blue hen

▌

121

Continued from previous page.

> cocks & hens: Blues, & Greens/Blue.
> hens: **Dilute Blues,** & Dilute Greens/Blue.
> cocks: Blues/Dilute, & Greens/Dilute+Blue.

(b)

> Green cock/Dilute+Blue x Dilute Green hen/Blue

> cocks & hens: **Dilute Blues,** Dilute Greens/Blue, & Dilute Greens.
> hens: Blues, Greens/Blue, & Greens.
> cocks: Blues/Dilute, Greens/Dilute+Blue, & Greens/Dilute.

By now a wide selection of stock should be available for breeding in the third season, and a predominance of Dilute Blues can be achieved by the following pairings - other than Dilute Blue x Dilute Blue. It should be noted that although no Dilute Blue cocks are bred from pairing (a) there is likely to be a larger predominance of Blue birds than would be produced from pairing (b).

Third Season; a selection of pairings:
(a)

> Dilute Blue cock x Dilute Green hen/Blue

> cocks & hens: **Dilute Blues,** & Dilute Greens/Blue.

(b)

> Dilute Green cock/Blue x Dilute Blue hen

> cocks and hens: **Dilute Blues,** & Dilute Greens/Blue.

(c)

> Dilute Green cock/Blue x Dilute Green hen/Blue

> cocks & hens: **Dilute Blues,** Dilute Greens/Blue, & Dilute Greens.

(d)

> Blue cock/Dilute x Dilute Blue hen

> **Dilute Blue cocks & hens,** Blue hens, & Blue cocks/Dilute.

(e)

> Dilute Green cock/Blue x Blue hen

Continued from previous page.

▌

> **Dilute Blue hens**, Dilute Green hens/Blue, Blue cocks/Dilute, & Green cocks/Dilute+Blue.

Dilute (Sex–linked) Marine (SLR+AR)

Species: *Indian Ringneck Parrakeet, Red-rumped Parrakeet, Splendid Grass Parrakeet and Peach-faced Lovebird.*

To illustrate the matings and expectations which show the production of this combination variety, replace Blue with **Marine** in the entire preceding section on **Dilute (Sex–linked) Blue.**

Dilute (Sex–linked) Lavender (SLR+AR)

Species: *Peach-faced Lovebird.*

To illustrate the matings and expectations which show the production of this combination variety, replace Blue with **Lavender** in the entire preceding section on **Dilute (Sex–linked) Blue.**

Dilute (Dominant) White–faced (AID+AR)

Species: *Cockatiel.*

Dilute: (S)= Single Factor   (D)= Double Factor

First Season:

> (D)Dilute Normal x White-faced

▌

> all **(S)Dilute Normals/White-faced**.

Second Season:

> (S)Dilute Normal/White-faced x (S)Dilute Normal/White-faced

▌

> **(D)Dilute White-faceds, (S)Dilute White-faceds**, White-faceds,
> (D)Dilute Normals/White-faced, (S)Dilute Normals/White-faced, Normals/White-faced,
> (D)Dilute Normals, (S)Dilute Normals, & Normals.

In subsequent breeding seasons, Dilute White–faceds can be paired together to increase the stock, or paired to those splits produced in the first season, e.g.:

> (D)Dilute White-faced x (S)Dilute Normal/White-faced

▌

> **(D)Dilute White-faceds, (S)Dilute White-faceds,**
> (D)Dilute Normals/White-faced, & (S)Dilute Normals/White-faced.

Dilute (Dominant) Pale-faced (AID+AR)

Species: *Cockatiel.*

To illustrate the matings and expectations which show the production of this combination, replace White-faced with **Pale-faced** throughout the entire preceding section on **Dilute (Dominant) White-faced.**

Dilute (Recessive) Blue (AR+AR)

Species: *Quaker Parrakeet, Masked Lovebird, Fischer's Lovebird, Black-cheeked Lovebird and Roseate Cockatoo. For Roseate Cockatoos, replace Green with **Normal**, and Blue with **White-faced** throughout the following.*

First Season:

Dilute Green x Blue

|

all **Greens/Dilute+Blue**.

Second Season:

Green/Dilute+Blue x Green/Dilute+Blue

|

Dilute Blues, Dilute Greens/Blue, Dilute Greens, Blues/Dilute, Greens/Dilute+Blue, Greens/Dilute, Blues, Greens/Blue, & Greens.

Third Season; the following examples of useful pairings can be made from the young provided in the second season:

(a)

Dilute Blue x Dilute Green

|

all Dilute Greens/Blue.

(b)

Dilute Blue x Dilute Green/Blue

|

Dilute Blues, & Dilute Greens/Blue.

(c)

Dilute Blue x Blue/Dilute

|

Continued from previous page.

Dilute Blues, & Blues/Dilute.

(d)

Dilute Blue x Dilute Blue

all Dilute Blues.

Dilute (Recessive) Marine (AR+AR)

Species: *Turquoisine Grass Parrakeet and Peach-faced Lovebird.*
To illustrate the matings and expectations which show the production of this combination, replace Blue with **Marine** in the entire preceding section on **Dilute (Recessive) Blue.**

Dilute (Recessive) Lavender (AR+AR)

Species: *Peach-faced Lovebird.*
To illustrate the matings and expectations which show the production of this combination, replace Blue with **Lavender** in the entire preceding section on **Dilute (Recessive) Blue.**

DILUTE DARK FACTOR

Dilute (Recessive) Dark Factor Blue (AR+AID+AR) (& Green) (AR+AID)

Species: *Masked Lovebird.*

First Season:
Apart from the unconfirmed theoretical possibility of percentages of expectations being affected by crossover, if the pairing **Dilute Green x Slate Blue** were used instead, their progeny would be identical in appearance to those in the pairing below, and the results obtained from *their* progeny in following seasons would be identical to those which follow:

Dilute Blue x Olive Green

all Dark Greens/Dilute+Blue.

Second Season:

Dark Green/Dilute+Blue x Dark Green/Dilute+Blue

Continued on next page.

|
| :--- |
| **Dilute Slate Blues**, **Dilute Dark Blues**, Dilute Blues, |
| **Dilute Olive Greens/Blue**, **Dilute Dark Greens/Blue**, Dilute Greens/Blue, |
| **Dilute Olive Greens**, **Dilute Dark Greens**, Dilute Greens, |
| Slate Blues/Dilute, Dark Blues/Dilute, Blues/Dilute, |
| Olive Greens/Dilute+Blue, Dark Greens/Dilute+Blue, Greens/Dilute+Blue, |
| Olive Greens/Dilute, Dark Greens/Dilute, Greens/Dilute, |
| Slate Blues, Dark Blues, Blues, |
| Olive Greens/Blue, Dark Greens/Blue, Greens/Blue, |
| Olive Greens, Dark Greens, & Greens. |

From the above expectations, it will be seen that the likelihood of producing Dilute Dark Factor *Blues* is very small, but other 'by-product' varieties can be used in future pairings to heighten the probability of their production; i.e. any **Dilute Olive Greens** or **Dilute Dark Greens** (in the hope that they are split Blue), and any **Slate Blues** or **Dark Greens** (in the hope that they are split Dilute).

Third Season; two examples:

(a)

Dilute Olive Green/Blue x Dilute Dark Blue

|
| :--- |
| **Dilute Slate Blues**, **Dilute Dark Blues**, Dilute Olive Greens/Blue, & Dilute Dark Greens/Blue. |

(b)

Slate Blue/Dilute x Dark Blue/Dilute

|
| :--- |
| **Dilute Slate Blues**, **Dilute Dark Blues**, |
| Slate Blues/Dilute, Dark Blues/Dilute, Slate Blues, & Dark Blues. |

Dilute (Recessive) Dark Factor Marine (AR+AID+AR) (& Green) (AR+AID)

Species: *Turquoisine Grass Parrakeet and Peach-faced Lovebird.*
To illustrate the matings and expectations which show the production of this combination, replace Blue with **Marine** in the entire preceding section on **Dilute (Recessive) Dark Factor Blue.**

Dilute (Recessive) Dark Factor Lavender (AR+AID+AR) (& Green) (AR+AID)

Species: *Peach-faced Lovebird.*
To illustrate the matings and expectations which show the production of this combination, replace Blue with **Lavender** in the entire preceding section on **Dilute (Recessive) Dark Factor Blue.**

126

DILUTE ROSA & DILUTE RUBY

Dilute Rosa (AR+SLR)

Species: Bourke's Grass Parrakeet.

Firstly, cocks which are split for both Rosa and Dilute are needed. These can be provided in several ways but it will be obvious that pairing (a) is preferable because the split cocks can be identified in nest feather – which is of great benefit.

First Season:

(a)

```
Rosa Brown cock x Dilute Brown hen
```
▮
```
Rosa Brown hens/Dilute, & Brown cocks/Rosa+Dilute.
```

(b)

```
Dilute Brown cock x Rosa Brown hen
```
▮
```
Brown hens/Dilute, & Brown cocks/Rosa+Dilute.
```

(c)

```
Brown cock/Rosa x Dilute Brown hen
```
▮
```
Brown hens/Dilute, Rosa Brown hens/Dilute, Brown cocks/Rosa+Dilute, & Brown cocks/Dilute.
```

Second Season; the split cocks can be paired to Dilute Brown hens or Rosa Brown hens/Dilute:

(a)

```
Brown cock/Rosa+Dilute x Dilute Brown hen
```
▮
```
cocks & hens: Dilute Browns, & Browns/Dilute.
hens: Dilute Rosa Browns, & Rosa Browns/Dilute.
cocks: Dilute Browns/Rosa, & Browns/Rosa+Dilute.
```

(b)

```
Brown cock/Rosa+Dilute x Rosa Brown hen/Dilute
```
▮

Continued on next page.

127

|
```
cocks & hens: Dilute Rosa Browns, Rosa Browns/Dilute, & Rosa Browns.
         hens: Dilute Browns, Browns/Dilute, & Browns.
        cocks: Dilute Browns/Rosa, Browns/Rosa+Dilute, & Browns/Rosa.
```

By now a wide selection of stock should be available for breeding in the third season, and a predominance of Dilute Rosa Browns can be achieved by the following pairings – other than Dilute Rosa Brown x Dilute Rosa Brown.

Third Season; a selection of pairings:

(a)
```
Dilute Rosa Brown cock x Rosa Brown hen/Dilute
```
|
```
cocks & hens: Dilute Rosa Browns, & Rosa Browns/Dilute.
```

(b)
```
Rosa Brown cock/Dilute x Dilute Rosa Brown hen
```
|
```
cocks & hens: Dilute Rosa Browns, & Rosa Browns/Dilute.
```

(c)
```
Rosa Brown cock/Dilute x Rosa Brown hen/Dilute
```
|
```
cocks & hens: Dilute Rosa Browns, Rosa Browns/Dilute, & Rosa Browns.
```

(d)
```
Dilute Brown cock/Rosa x Dilute Rosa Brown hen
```
|
```
Dilute Rosa Brown cocks & hens, Dilute Brown hens, & Dilute Brown cocks/Rosa.
```

(e)
```
Rosa Brown cock/Dilute x Dilute Brown hen
```
|
```
Dilute Rosa Brown hens, Rosa Brown hens/Dilute, Dilute Brown cocks/Rosa, & Brown cocks/Rosa+Dilute.
```

Dilute Ruby (AR+SLR)

Species: Eastern Rosella

To illustrate the matings and expectations which show the production of this combination, replace Rosa with **Ruby** throughout the entire preceding section on **Dilute Rosa.**

FALLOW BLUE (& FALLOW WHITE-FACED)

Fallow Blue (AR+AR)

Species: Splendid Grass Parrakeet.

First Season:

```
Fallow Green x Blue
```

|

```
all Greens/Fallow+Blue
```

Second Season:

```
Green/Fallow+Blue x Green/Fallow+Blue
```

|

```
Fallow Blues, Fallow Greens/Blue, Fallow Greens,
Blues/Fallow, Greens/Fallow+Blue, Greens/Fallow,
Blues, Greens/Blue, & Greens.
```

Third Season; the following examples of useful pairings can be made from the young provided in the second season:

(a)

```
Fallow Blue x Fallow Green
```

|

```
all Fallow Greens/Blue.
```

(b)

```
Fallow Blue x Fallow Green/Blue
```

|

```
Fallow Blues, & Fallow Greens/Blue.
```

(c)

```
Fallow Blue x Blue/Fallow
```

|

```
Fallow Blues, & Blues/Fallow.
```

(d)

Fallow Blue x Fallow Blue

I

all **Fallow Blues**.

Fallow Marine (AR+AR)

Species: Splendid Grass Parrakeet, Turquoisine Grass Parrakeet and Peach-faced Lovebird.

To illustrate the matings and expectations which show the production of this combination, replace Blue with **Marine** throughout the entire preceding section on **Fallow Blue**.

Fallow Lavender (AR+AR)

Species: Peach-faced Lovebird.

To illustrate the matings and expectations which show the production of this combination, replace Blue with **Lavender** throughout the entire preceding section on **Fallow Blue**.

Fallow White-faced (AR+AR)

Species: Cockatiel.

To illustrate the matings and expectations which show the production of this combination, replace Blue with **White-faced** and Green with **Normal** throughout the entire preceding section on **Fallow Blue**.

Fallow Pale-faced (AR+AR)

Species: Cockatiel.

To illustrate the matings and expectations which show the production of this combination, replace Blue with **Pale-faced** and Green with **Normal** throughout the entire preceding section on **Fallow Blue**.

CLEARHEAD BLUE

Clearhead Blue (AR+AR)

Species: Indian Ringneck Parrakeet

First Season:

Clearhead Green x Blue

I

all **Greens/Clearhead+Blue**.

Second Season:

```
Green/Clearhead+Blue x Green/Clearhead+Blue
```

I

```
Clearhead Blues, Clearhead Greens/Blue, Clearhead Greens,
Blues/Clearhead, Greens/Clearhead+Blue, Greens/Clearhead,
Blues, Greens/Blue, & Greens.
```

From the third season onwards, the following examples of useful pairings can be made from the young provided in the second season. Any Clearhead Blues produced could be paired to: **Clearhead Greens** (in hope that those chosen are split Blue), **Blues** (in hope that those chosen are split Clearhead), and **Greens** (in hope that those chosen are split Clearhead and Blue).

Third Season:

(a)

```
Clearhead Blue x Clearhead Green
```

I

```
all Clearhead Greens/Blue.
```

(b)

```
Clearhead Blue x Clearhead Green/Blue
```

I

```
Clearhead Blues, & Clearhead Greens/Blue.
```

(c)

```
Clearhead Blue x Blue/Clearhead
```

I

```
Clearhead Blues, & Blues/Clearhead.
```

(d)

```
Clearhead Blue x Clearhead Blue
```

I

```
all Clearhead Blues.
```

Clearhead Marine (AR+AR)

Species: *Indian Ringneck.*

To illustrate the matings and expectations which show the production of this combination, replace Blue with **Marine** throughout the entire preceding section on **Clearhead Blue.**

FALLOW DILUTE

Fallow Dilute (Dominant) White-faced (AR+AID+AR) (& Normal) (AR+AID)

Species: Cockatiel.

Dilute: (S)= Single Factor   (D)= Double Factor

First Season:

Fallow White-faced x (D)Dilute Normal

|

all **(S)Dilute Normals/Fallow+White-faced.**

If the pairing **Fallow Normal x (D)Dilute White-faced** were used, the result would be identical to the one above.

Second Season:

(S)Dilute Normal/Fallow+White-faced x (S)Dilute Normal/Fallow+White-faced

|

Fallow (D)Dilute White-faceds, Fallow (S)Dilute White-faceds, Fallow White-faceds, **Fallow (D)Dilute Normals/White-faced, Fallow (S)Dilute Normals/White-faced,** Fallow Normals/White-faced, **Fallow (D)Dilute Normals, Fallow (S)Dilute Normals,** Fallow Normals, (D)Dilute White-faceds/Fallow, (S)Dilute White-faceds/Fallow, White-faceds/Fallow, (D)Dilute Normals/Fallow+White-faced, (S)Dilute Normals/Fallow+White-faced, Normals/Fallow+White-faced, (D)Dilute Normals/Fallow, (S)Dilute Normals/Fallow, Normals/Fallow, (D)Dilute White-faceds, (S)Dilute White-faceds, White-faceds, (D)Dilute Normals/White-faced, (S)Dilute Normals/White-faced, Normals/White-faced, (D)Dilute Normals, (S)Dilute Normals, & Normals.

To increase the incidence of Fallow Dilutes, any that are bred should be paired together during the third season, or paired to the **(S)Dilute Normals split Fallow (and White-faced)** which were bred in the first season.

Third Season;
best example:

Fallow (D)Dilute White-faced x (S)Dilute Normal/Fallow+White-faced

|

Fallow (D)Dilute White-faceds, Fallow (S)Dilute White-faceds, Fallow (D)Dilute Normals/White-faced, Fallow (S)Dilute Normals/White-faced, (D)Dilute White-faceds/Fallow, (S)Dilute White-faceds/Fallow, (D)Dilute Normals/Fallow+White-faced, & (S)Dilute Normals/Fallow+White-faced.

Fallow Dilute (Dominant) Pale–faced (AR+AID+AR) (& Normal) (AR+AID)

Species: *Cockatiel*

To illustrate the matings and expectations which show the production of this compound variety, replace White-faced with **Pale–faced** in the entire preceding section on **Fallow Dilute (Dominant) White–faced (& Normal).**

TANGERINE COMBINATION & COMPOUND VARIETIES

*IN ORDER to simplify and shorten the following pairings and expectations, Tangerine has been shortened to **Tang–;** Tangerine could be used to create other compound varieties beside those shown below; these would include Cinnamon Tang-Lutino, Cinnamon Dilute Tang-Green and Pied (Dominant) Tang-Olive Green.*

Tang–Lutino (AID+SLR)

Species: *Peach-faced Lovebird.*

Tang: (S)= Single Factor (D)= Double Factor

First Season:

Lutino cock x (D)Tang-Green

I

(S)Tang–Lutino hens, & (S)Tang–Green cocks/Ino.

Second Season; two suggested pairings:

(a)

(S)Tang-Green cock/Ino x (D)Tang-Green hen

I

cocks & hens: (D)Tang-Greens, & (S)Tang-Greens. hens: **(D)Tang-Lutinos**, & (S)Tang-Lutinos. cocks: (D)Tang-Greens/Ino, & (S)Tang-Greens/Ino.

(b)

(S)Tang-Green/Ino x (S)Tang-Lutino hen

I

cocks & hens: **(D)Tang-Lutinos**, (S)Tang-Lutinos, & Lutinos. hens: (D)Tang-Greens, (S)Tang-Greens, & Greens. cocks: (D)Tang-Greens/Ino, (S)Tang-Greens/Ino, & Greens/Ino.

Tang—Creamino (AID+SLR)

Species: *Peach-faced Lovebird*

Tang: (S)= Single Factor   (D)= Double Factor

This compound variety could be produced by first crossing **(D)Tang—Lutino with Creamino** (in which case the sex of the colour varieties would be irrelevant), or making a first cross of **Creamino cock with (D)Tang—Green hen.**

First Method:
First Season:

```
                    (D)Tang-Lutino x Creamino
```

```
                    all (S)Tang-Lutinos/Marine.
```

Second Season:

```
          (S)Tang-Lutino/Marine x (S)Tang-Lutino/Marine
```

```
            (D)Tang-Creaminos, (S)Tang-Creaminos, Creaminos,
        (D)Tang-Lutinos/Marine, (S)Tang-Lutinos/Marine, Lutinos/Marine,
              (D)Tang-Lutinos, (S)Tang-Lutinos, & Lutinos.
```

Second Method:
First Season:

```
              Creamino cock x (D)Tang-Green hen
```

```
    (S)Tang-Lutino hens/Marine, & (S)Tang-Green cocks/Ino+Marine.
```

Second Season:

```
      (S)Tang-Green cock/Ino+Marine x (S)Tang-Lutino hen/Marine
```

```
                          cocks & hens:
              (D)Tang-Creaminos, (S)Tang-Creaminos, Creaminos,
          (D)Tang-Lutinos/Marine, (S)Tang-Lutinos/Marine, Lutinos/Marine,
                (D)Tang-Lutinos, (S)Tang-Lutinos, & Lutinos.
                              hens:
                (D)Tang-Marines, (S)Tang-Marines, Marines,
          (D)Tang-Greens/Marine, (S)Tang-Greens/Marine, Greens/Marine,
                (D)Tang-Greens, (S)Tang-Greens, & Greens.
                              cocks:
            (D)Tang-Marines/Ino, (S)Tang-Marines/Ino, Marines/Ino,
      (D)Tang-Greens/Ino+Marine, (S)Tang-Greens/Ino+Marine, Greens/Ino+Marine,
            (D)Tang-Greens/Ino, (S)Tang-Greens/Ino, & Greens/Ino.
```

Tang–Ivorino (AID+SLR)

Species: Peach-faced Lovebird

To illustrate the matings and expectations which show the production of this compound variety, replace Marine with **Lavender** in the entire preceding section on **Tang–Creamino.**

Dilute (Recessive) Tang–Marine (AR+AID+AR) (& Green) (AR+AID)

Species: Peach-faced Lovebird.

Tang: (S)= Single Factor   (D)= Double Factor

First Season:

```
                    Dilute Marine x (D)Tang-Green
```

```
              all (S)Tang-Greens/Dilute+Marine.
```

If the pairing **Dilute Green x (D)Tang–Marine** were used, the result would be identical to the one above.

Second Season:

```
        (S)Tang-Green/Dilute+Marine x (S)Tang-Green/Dilute+Marine
```

```
        Dilute (D)Tang-Marines, Dilute (S)Tang-Marines, Dilute Marines,
   Dilute (D)Tang-Greens/Marine, Dilute (S)Tang-Greens/Marine, Dilute Greens/Marine,
        Dilute (D)Tang-Greens, Dilute (S)Tang-Greens, Dilute Greens,
        (D)Tang-Marines/Dilute, (S)Tang-Marines/Dilute, Marines/Dilute,
   (D)Tang-Greens/Dilute+Marine, (S)Tang-Greens/Dilute+Marine, Greens/Dilute+Marine,
        (D)Tang-Greens/Dilute, (S)Tang-Greens/Dilute, Greens/Dilute,
              (D)Tang-Marines, (S)Tang-Marines, Marines,
        (D)Tang-Greens/Marine, (S)Tang-Greens/Marine, Greens/Marine,
              (D)Tang-Greens, (S)Tang-Greens, & Greens.
```

To increase the incidence of Dilute (D)Tangerines, any that are bred should be paired together during the third season, or paired to the **(S)Tang–Greens split Dilute (and Marine)** which were bred in the first season.

Third Season; best example:

```
        Dilute (D)Tang-Marine x (S)Tang-Green/Dilute+Marine
```

```
        Dilute (D)Tang-Marines, Dilute (S)Tang-Marines,
     Dilute (D)Tang-Greens/Marine, Dilute (S)Tang-Greens/Marine,
        (D)Tang-Marines/Dilute, (S)Tang-Marines/Dilute,
     (D)Tang-Greens/Dilute+Marine, & (S)Tang-Greens/Dilute+Marine.
```

135

Dilute (Recessive) Tang–Lavender (AR+AID+AR) (& Green) (AR+AID)

Species: *Peach-faced Lovebird*
 To illustrate the matings and expectations which show the production of this compound variety, replace Marine with **Lavender** in the entire preceding section on **Dilute (Recessive) Tang–Marine (& Green).**

Fallow Tang–Marine (AR+AID+AR) (& Green) (AR+AID)

Species: *Peach-faced Lovebird*
 To illustrate the matings and expectations which show the production of this compound variety, replace Dilute with **Fallow** in the entire preceding section on **Dilute (Recessive) Tang–Marine (& Green).**

Fallow Tang–Lavender (AR+AID+AR) (& Green) (AR+AID)

Species: *Peach-faced Lovebird*
 To illustrate the matings and expectations which show the production of this compound variety, replace Dilute with **Fallow** and Marine with **Lavender** in the entire preceding section on **Dilute (Recessive) Tang–Marine (& Green).**

Pied (Recessive) Tang–Marine (AR+AID+AR) (& Green) (AR+AID)

Species: *Peach-faced Lovebird*
 To illustrate the matings and expectations which show the production of this compound variety, replace Dilute with **Pied** in the entire preceding section on **Dilute (Recessive) Tang–Marine (& Green).**

Pied (Recessive) Tang–Lavender (AR+AID+AR) (& Green) (AR+AID)

Species: *Peach-faced Lovebird.*
 To illustrate the matings and expectations which show the production of this compound variety, replace Dilute with **Pied** and Marine with **Lavender** in the entire preceding section on **Dilute (Recessive) Tang–Marine (& Green).**

Cinnamon Tang–Marine (SLR+AID+AR) (& Green) (SLR+AID)

Species: *Peach-faced Lovebird.*

Tang: (S)= Single Factor   (D)= Double Factor

Though this compound variety could be produced by first breeding Cinnamon (D)Tang-Greens and then crossing these with Cinnamon Marines (in which case the sex of the individuals would be irrelevant), the variety could also be produced by making a first cross of **Cinnamon Marine cock with (D)Tang-Green hen.**

First Method:
First Season:

Cinnamon (D)Tang-Green x Cinnamon Marine

Continued from previous page.

▐

all **Cinnamon (S)Tang-Green/Marines.**

Second Season:

Cinnamon (S)Tang-Green/Marine x Cinnamon (S)Tang-Green/Marine

▐

Cinnamon (D)Tang-Marines, Cinnamon (S)Tang-Marines, Cinnamon Marines,
Cinnamon (D)Tang-Greens/Marine, Cinnamon (S)Tang-Greens/Marine, Cinnamon Greens/Marine,
Cinnamon (D)Tang-Greens, Cinnamon (S)Tang-Greens, & Cinnamon Greens.

Second Method:
First Season:

Cinnamon Marine cock x (D)Tang-Green hen

▐

Cinnamon (S)Tang-Green hens/Marine, & **(S)Tang-Green cocks/Cinnamon+Marine.**

Second Season; two suggested pairings:
(a)

(S)Tang-Green cock/Cinnamon+Marine x Cinnamon (S)Tang-Green hen/Marine

▐

cocks & hens:
Cinnamon (D)Tang-Marines, Cinnamon (S)Tang-Marines, Cinnamon Marines,
Cinnamon (D)Tang-Greens/Marine, Cinnamon (S)Tang-Greens/Marine, Cinnamon Greens/Marine,
Cinnamon (D)Tang-Greens, Cinnamon (S)Tang-Greens, & Cinnamon Greens.
hens:
(D)Tang-Marines, (S)Tang-Marines, Marines,
(D)Tang-Greens/Marine, (S)Tang-Greens/Marine, Greens/Marine,
(D)Tang-Greens, (S)Tang-Greens, & Greens.
cocks:
(D)Tang-Marines/Cinnamon, (S)Tang-Marines/Cinnamon, Marines/Cinnamon,
(D)Tang-Greens/Cinnamon+Marine, (S)Tang-Greens/Cinnamon+Marine, Greens/Cinnamon+Marine,
(D)Tang-Greens/Cinnamon, (S)Tang-Greens/Cinnamon, & Greens/Cinnamon.

(b)

(S)Tang-Green cock/Cinnamon+Marine x (D)Tang-Marine hen

▐

hens:
Cinnamon (D)Tang-Marines, Cinnamon (S)Tang-Marines,
Cinnamon (D)Tang-Greens/Marine, Cinnamon (S)Tang-Greens/Marine,
(D)Tang-Marines, (S)Tang-Marines,
(D)Tang-Greens/Marine, & (S)Tang-Greens/Marine.
cocks:
(D)Tang-Marines/Cinnamon, (S)Tang-Marines/Cinnamon
(D)Tang-Greens/Cinnamon+Marine, (S)Tang-Greens/Cinnamon+Marine,
(D)Tang-Marines, (S)Tang-Marines,
(D)Tang-Greens/Marine, & (S)Tang-Greens/Marine.

Consolidation and increase in production of Cinnamon (D)Tangerines can take place in the third season by using by-products of the second season's breeding – as well as the Cinnamon (D)Tangerines. The most useful cocks would be from pairing (a):- **(D)Tang-Marines split Cinnamon**, and **(D)Tang-Greens split Cinnamon and Marine.**

Third Season; best example:

(D)Tang-Marine cock/Cinnamon x Cinnamon (D)Tang-Green hen/Marine

|

cocks & hens: **Cinnamon (D)Tang-Marines, & Cinnamon (D)Tang-Greens/Marine.**   hens: (D)Tang-Marines, & (D)Tang-Greens/Marine.   cocks: (D)Tang-Marines/Cinnamon, & (D)Tang-Greens/Cinnamon+Marine.

Cinnamon Tang-Lavender (SLR+AID+AR) (& Green) (SLR+AID)

Species: Peach-faced Lovebird.
   To illustrate the matings and expectations which show the production of this compound variety, replace Marine with **Lavender** throughout the entire preceding section on **Cinnamon Tang-Marine (& Green).**

Dilute (Sex-linked) Tang-Marine (SLR+AID+AR) (& Green) (SLR+AID)

Species: Peach-faced Lovebird.
   To illustrate the matings and expectations which show the production of this compound variety, replace Cinnamon with **Dilute** throughout the entire preceding section on **Cinnamon Tang-Marine (& Green).**

Dilute (Sex-linked) Tang-Lavender (SLR+AID+AR) (& Green) (SLR+AID)

Species: Peach-faced Lovebird.
   To illustrate the matings and expectations which show the production of this compound variety, replace Cinnamon with **Dilute** and Marine with **Lavender** throughout the entire preceding section on **Cinnamon Tang-Marine (& Green).**

Pied (Dominant) Tang-Marine (ACD+AID+AR) (& Green) (ACD+AID)

Species: Peach-faced Lovebird.

Tang: (S)= Single Factor   (D)= Double Factor

First Season:

Pied Marine x (D)Tang-Green

|

Pied (S)Tang-Greens/Marine, & (S)Tang-Greens/Marine.

138

Second Season:

```
Pied (S)Tang-Green/Marine x Pied (S)Tang-Green/Marine
```

▮

```
Pied (D)Tang-Marines, Pied (S)Tang-Marines, Pied Marines,
Pied (D)Tang-Greens/Marine, Pied (S)Tang-Greens/Marine, Pied Greens/Marine,
Pied (D)Tang-Greens, Pied (S)Tang-Greens, Pied Greens,
(D)Tang-Marines, (S)Tang-Marines, Marines,
(D)Tang-Greens/Marine, (S)Tang-Greens/Marine, Greens/Marine,
(D)Tang-Greens, (S)Tang-Greens, & Greens.
```

Pied (Dominant) Tang–Lavender (ACD+AID+AR) (& Green) (ACD+AID)

Species: *Peach-faced Lovebird.*

To illustrate the matings and expectations which show the production of this compound variety, replace Marine with **Lavender** throughout the entire preceding section on **Pied (Dominant) Tang–Marine (& Green).**

Tang–Marine (AID+AR)

Species: *Peach-faced Lovebird.*

Tang: (S)= Single Factor   (D)= Double Factor

First Season:

```
(D)Tang-Green x Marine
```

▮

```
all (S)Tang-Greens/Marine.
```

Second Season:

```
(S)Tang-Green/Marine x (S)Tang-Green/Marine
```

▮

```
(D)Tang-Marines, (S)Tang-Marines, Marines,
(D)Tang-Greens/Marine, (S)Tang-Greens/Marine, Greens/Marine,
(D)Tang-Greens, (S)Tang-Greens, & Greens.
```

In subsequent breeding seasons, the Tang–Marines can be paired together to increase the stock, or paired to those splits produced in the first season, e.g.:

```
(D)Tang-Marine x (S)Tang-Green/Marine
```

▮

```
(D)Tang-Marines, (S)Tang-Marines,
(D)Tang-Greens/Marine, (S)Tang-Greens/Marine,
(D)Tang-Greens, & (S)Tang-Greens.
```

Tang–Lavender (AID+AR)

Species: *Peach–faced Lovebird.*

To illustrate the matings and expectations which show the production of this compound variety, replace Marine with **Lavender** throughout the entire preceding section on **Tang–Marine.**

Dark Factor Tang–Marine (AID+AID+AR) (& Green) (AID+AID)

Species: *Peach–faced Lovebird.*

Tang: (S)= Single Factor   (D)= Double Factor

First Season:

```
                    Slate Marine x (D)Tang-Green
```

```
                    all Dark (S)Tang-Greens/Marine.
```

Second Season:

```
        Dark (S)Tang-Green/Marine x Dark (S)Tang-Green/Marine
```

```
            Slate (D)Tang-Marines, Slate (S)Tang-Marines, Slate Marines,
         Dark (D)Tang-Marines, Dark (S)Tang-Marines, Dark Marines,
                (D)Tang-Marines, (S)Tang-Marines, Marines,
    Olive (D)Tang-Greens/Marine, Olive (S)Tang-Greens/Marine, Olive Greens/Marine,
     Dark (D)Tang-Greens/Marine, Dark (S)Tang-Greens/Marine, Dark Greens/Marine,
          (D)Tang-Greens/Marine, (S)Tang-Greens/Marine, Greens/Marine,
            Olive (D)Tang-Greens, Olive (S)Tang-Greens, Olive Greens,
          Dark (D)Tang-Greens, Dark (S)Tang-Greens, Dark Greens,
              (D)Tang-Greens, (S)Tang-Greens, & Greens.
```

Third Season; the Dark Factor and Tangerine can be concentrated by pairing together only birds showing both varieties to some degree. One example:

```
            Dark (S)Tang-Marine x Olive (D)Tang-Green/Marine
```

```
            Slate (D)Tang-Marines, Slate (S)Tang-Marines,
            Dark (D)Tang-Marines, Dark (S)Tang-Marines,
        Olive (D)Tang-Greens/Marine, Olive (S)Tang-Greens/Marine,
        Dark (D)Tang-Greens/Marine, & Dark (S)Tang-Greens/Marine.
```

Dark Factor Tang–Lavender (AID+AID+AR) (& Green) (AID+AID)

Species: *Peach–faced Lovebird.*

To illustrate the matings and expectations which show the production of this compound variety, replace Marine with **Lavender** throughout the entire preceding section on **Dark Factor Tang–Marine (& Green).**

VIOLET FACTOR COMBINATION & COMPOUND VARIETIES

Violet Factor Marine (ACD+AR)

Species: Peach-faced Lovebird.

Violet: (S)= Single Factor (D)= Double Factor

First Season:

```
(D)Violet Green x Marine
```

```
all (S)Violet Greens/Marine.
```

Second Season; two suggested pairings:
(a)

```
(S)Violet Green/Marine x (S)Violet Green/Marine
```

```
(D)Violet Marines, (S)Violet Marines, Marines,
(D)Violet Greens/Marine, (S)Violet Greens/Marine, Greens/Marine,
(D)Violet Greens, (S)Violet Greens, & Greens.
```

(b)

```
(S)Violet Green/Marine x Marine
```

```
(S)Violet Marines, Marines, (S)Violet Greens/Marine, & Greens/Marine.
```

In subsequent breeding seasons, the Violet Marines can be paired together to increase the stock, or may be paired to the **(S)Violet Greens split Marine** produced in the first season.

Third Season:
(a)

```
(D)Violet Marine x (D)Violet Marine
```

```
all (D)Violet Marines.
```

(b)

```
(D)Violet Marine x (S)Violet Marine
```

```
(D)Violet Marines, & (S)Violet Marines.
```

141

(c)

(S)Violet Marine x (S)Violet Marine

|
|

(D)Violet Marines, (S)Violet Marines, & Marines.

(d)

(D)Violet Marine x (S)Violet Green/Marine

|
|

(D)Violet Marines, (S)Violet Marines, (D)Violet Greens/Marine, & (S)Violet Greens/Marine.

Violet Factor Lavender (ACD+AR)

Species: *Peach-faced Lovebird.*

To illustrate the matings and expectations which show the production of this compound variety, replace Marine with **Lavender** throughout the entire preceding section on **Violet Factor Marine.**

Violet Dark Factor Marine (ACD+AID+AR)

Species: *Peach-faced Lovebird.*

Violet: (S)= Single Factor   (D)= Double Factor

Elsewhere, it has been warned that some breeders have found the combination of Violet Marine with the Dark Factor to be of no consequence where the Peach-faced is concerned, others say that it brings about the desired effect – so if the breeder wishes to attempt to prove its usefulness the following programme can be applied.

*It is worth remembering that, in Budgerigar culture, the Violet Factor in combination with the Blue Factor and (S)Dark Factor creates the **true** violet coloured bird; though Violet (D)Dark Blues (known by Budgerigar breeders as Violet Mauves) are valuable as breeding stock, they do not show the Violet Factor at its visual best.*

First Season:

(D)Violet Marine x Slate Marine

|
|

all **(S)Violet Dark Marines.**

Second Season; three suggested pairings:
(a)

(S)Violet Dark Marine x (S)Violet Dark Marine

|
|

Continued from previous page.

(D)Violet Slate Marines, (S)Violet Slate Marines, Slate Marines,
(D)Violet Dark Marines, **(S)Violet Dark Marines,** Dark Marines,
(D)Violet Marines, (S)Violet Marines, & Marines.

(b)

(S)Violet Dark Marine x Slate Marine

(S)Violet Slate Marines, Slate Marines, **(S)Violet Dark Marines,** & Dark Marines.

(c)

(S)Violet Dark Marine x (D)Violet Marine

(D)Violet Dark Marines, (S)Violet Dark Marines, (D)Violet Marines, & **(S)Violet Marines.**

Violet Dark Factor Lavender (ACD+AID+AR)

Species: *Peach-faced Lovebird.*

To illustrate the matings and expectations which show the production of this compound variety, replace Marine with **Lavender** throughout the entire preceding section on **Violet Dark Factor Marine.**

Cinnamon Violet Factor Marine (SLR+ACD+AR) (& Green) (SLR+ACD)

Species: *Peach-faced Lovebird.*

Violet: (S)= Single Factor   (D)= Double Factor

First Season; **Cinnamon Green cock x (D)Violet Marine hen** *gives the same results as the pairing below; two suggested pairings:*

(a)

Cinnamon Marine cock x (D)Violet Green hen

Cinnamon (S)Violet Green hens/Marine, & (S)Violet Green cocks/Cinnamon+Marine.

(b)
Note: **(D)Violet Marine cock x Cinnamon Green hen** *gives the same results as the pairing below:*

(D)Violet Green cock x Cinnamon Marine hen

(S)Violet Green hens/Marine, & **(S)Violet Green cocks/Cinnamon+Marine.**

143

Second Season; two suggested pairings:

(a)

(S)Violet Green cock/Cinnamon+Marine x Cinnamon (S)Violet Green hen/Marine

———————I———————

cocks & hens:
Cinnamon (D)Violet Marines, Cinnamon (S)Violet Marines, Cinnamon Marines,
Cinnamon (D)Violet Greens/Marine, Cinnamon (S)Violet Greens/Marine, Cinnamon Greens/Marine,
Cinnamon (D)Violet Greens, Cinnamon (S)Violet Greens, & Cinnamon Greens.
hens:
(D)Violet Marines, (S)Violet Marines, Marines,
(D)Violet Greens/Marine, (S)Violet Greens/Marine, Greens/Marine,
(D)Violet Greens, (S)Violet Greens, & Greens.
cocks:
(D)Violet Marines/Cinnamon, (S)Violet Marines/Cinnamon, Marines/Cinnamon,
(D)Violet Greens/Cinnamon+Marine, (S)Violet Greens/Cinnamon+Marine, Greens/Cinnamon+Marine,
(D)Violet Greens/Cinnamon, (S)Violet Greens/Cinnamon, & Greens/Cinnamon.

(b)

(S)Violet Green cock/Cinnamon+Marine x (D)Violet Marine hen

———————I———————

cocks & hens:
(D)Violet Marines, (D)Violet Greens/Marine,
(S)Violet Marines, & (S)Violet Greens/Marine.
hens:
Cinnamon (D)Violet Marines, Cinnamon (D)Violet Greens/Marine,
Cinnamon (S)Violet Marines, & **Cinnamon (S)Violet Greens/Marine.**
cocks:
(D)Violet Marines/Cinnamon, (D)Violet Greens/Cinnamon+Marine,
(S)Violet Marines/Cinnamon, & (S)Violet Greens/Cinnamon+Marine.

It should be noted that although no Cinnamon Violet Marine *cocks* are likely to be bred from pairing (b), there should be a larger number of Violet Marine birds than would be bred off pairing (a). From these pairings enough Cinnamon Violet Marines as would enable stock to be consolidated during subsequent seasons should be produced.

Cinnamon Violet Factor Lavender (SLR+ACD+AR) (& Green) (SLR+ACD)

Species: *Peach-faced Lovebird.*
To illustrate the matings and expectations which show the production of this compound variety, replace Marine with **Lavender** throughout the entire preceding section on **Cinnamon Violet Factor Marine (& Green)**.

Dilute (Sex-linked) Violet Factor Marine (SLR+ACD+AR) (& Green) (SLR+ACD)

Species: *Peach-faced Lovebird.*
To illustrate the matings and expectations which show the production of this compound variety, replace Cinnamon with **Dilute** throughout the entire preceding section on **Cinnamon Violet Factor Marine (& Green)**.

Dilute (Sex–linked) Violet Factor Lavender (SLR+ACD+AR) (& Green) (SLR+ACD)

Species: *Peach–faced Lovebird.*

To illustrate the matings and expectations which show the production of this compound variety, replace Cinnamon with **Dilute** and Marine with **Lavender** throughout the entire preceding section on **Cinnamon Violet Factor Marine (& Green).**

Dilute (Recessive) Violet Factor Marine (AR+ACD+AR) (& Green) (AR+ACD)

Species: *Peach–faced Lovebird.*

Violet: (S)= Single Factor   (D)= Double Factor

First Season; if the pairing **Dilute Marine x (D)Violet Green** *were used, the results would be the same as those below:*

```
                  Dilute Green x (D)Violet Marine
```

```
              all (S)Violet Greens/Dilute+Marine.
```

Second Season:

```
   (S)Violet Green/Dilute+Marine x (S)Violet Green/Dilute+Marine
```

```
    Dilute (D)Violet Marines, Dilute (D)Violet Greens/Marine, Dilute (D)Violet Greens,
    Dilute (S)Violet Marines, Dilute (S)Violet Greens/Marine, Dilute (S)Violet Greens,
              Dilute Marines, Dilute Greens/Marine, Dilute Greens,
    (D)Violet Marines/Dilute, (D)Violet Greens/Dilute+Marine, (D)Violet Greens/Dilute,
    (S)Violet Marines/Dilute, (S)Violet Greens/Dilute+Marine, (S)Violet Greens/Dilute,
              Marines/Dilute, Greens/Dilute+Marine, Greens/Dilute,
          (D)Violet Marines, (D)Violet Greens/Marine, (D)Violet Greens,
          (S)Violet Marines, (S)Violet Greens/Marine, (S)Violet Greens,
                   Marines, Greens/Marine, & Greens.
```

To increase the incidence of this compound variety, the following 'by-product' types which could be paired to any young Dilute Violet Marines include the **Dilute Violet Greens** (in the hope that they are Double Factor Violet and split Marine), and the **Violet Marines** (in the hope that they are Double Factor Violet and split Dilute). The splits from the first season continue to be useful and, failing all else, any **Dilute Violet Greens** (in the hope that they are split Marine) could be paired to **Dilute Marines.**

Third Season; four suggested pairings:

(a)

```
       Dilute (D)Violet Green/Marine x Dilute (D)Violet Marine
```

```
       Dilute (D)Violet Marines, & Dilute (D)Violet Greens/Marine.
```

(b)

| (D)Violet Marine/Dilute x Dilute (D)Violet Marine |

▮

| **Dilute (D)Violet Marines, & (D)Violet Marines/Dilute.** |

(c)

| Dilute (D)Violet Green/Marine x Dilute Marine |

▮

| **Dilute (S)Violet Marines, & Dilute (S)Violet Greens/Marine.** |

(d)

| Dilute (D)Violet Marine x Dilute (D)Violet Marine |

▮

| all **Dilute (D)Violet Marines.** |

Dilute (Recessive) Violet Factor Lavender (AR+ACD+AR) (& Green) (AR+ACD)

Species: Peach-faced Lovebird.
   To illustrate the matings and expectations which show the production of this compound variety, replace Marine with **Lavender** throughout the entire preceding section on **Dilute (Recessive) Violet Factor Marine (& Green).**

Fallow Violet Factor Marine (AR+ACD+AR) (& Green) (AR+ACD)

Species: Peach-faced Lovebird.
   To illustrate the matings and expectations which show the production of this compound variety, replace Dilute with **Fallow** throughout the entire preceding section on **Dilute (Recessive) Violet Factor Marine (& Green).**

Fallow Violet Factor Lavender (AR+ACD+AR) (& Green) (AR+ACD)

Species: Peach-faced Lovebird.
   To illustrate the matings and expectations which show the production of this compound variety, replace Dilute with **Fallow** and Marine with **Lavender** throughout the entire preceding section on **Dilute (Recessive) Violet Factor Marine (& Green).**

Pied (Recessive) Violet Factor Marine (AR+ACD+AR) (& Green) (AR+ACD)

Species: Peach-faced Lovebird.
   To illustrate the matings and expectations which show the production of this compound variety, replace Dilute with **Pied** throughout the entire preceding section on **Dilute (Recessive) Violet Factor Marine (& Green).**

Pied (Recessive) Violet Factor Lavender (AR+ACD+AR) (& Green) (AR+ACD)

Species: Peach-faced Lovebird.

To illustrate the matings and expectations which show the production of this compound variety, replace Dilute with **Pied** and Marine with **Lavender** throughout the entire preceding section on **Dilute (Recessive) Violet Factor Marine (& Green)**.

Pied (Dominant) Violet Factor Marine (ACD+ACD+AR) (& Green) (ACD+ACD)

Species: Peach-faced Lovebird.

Violet: (S)= Single Factor   (D)= Double Factor

First Season; if the pairing **Pied Marine x (D)Violet Green** *were used, the results would be the same as those below:*

```
                      Pied Green x (D)Violet Marine
```

▮

```
         Pied (S)Violet Greens/Marine, & (S)Violet Greens/Marine.
```

Second Season:

```
      Pied (S)Violet Green/Marine x Pied (S)Violet Green/Marine
```

▮

```
    Pied (D)Violet Marines, Pied (D)Violet Greens/Marine, Pied (D)Violet Greens,
    Pied (S)Violet Marines, Pied (S)Violet Greens/Marine, Pied (S)Violet Greens,
            Pied Marines, Pied Greens/Marine, Pied Greens,
         (D)Violet Marines, (D)Violet Greens/Marine, (D)Violet Greens,
         (S)Violet Marines, (S)Violet Greens/Marine, (S)Violet Greens,
               Marines, Greens/Marine, & Greens.
```

Pied (Dominant) Violet Factor Lavender (ACD+ACD+AR) (& Green) (ACD+ACD)

Species: Peach-faced Lovebird.

To illustrate the matings and expectations which show the production of this compound variety, replace Marine with **Lavender** throughout the entire preceding section on **Pied (Dominant) Violet Factor Marine (& Green)**.

Violet Factor Tang-Marine (ACD+AID+AR)

Species: Peach-faced Lovebird.

Violet: (S)= Single Factor   (D)= Double Factor

Tang: (S)= Single Factor   (D)= Double Factor

First Season:

```
                  (D)Violet Marine x (D)Tang-Marine
```

▮

Continued from previous page.

```
┌─────────────────────────────────────────────────────────────┐
│                all (S)Violet (S)Tang-Marines.                │
└─────────────────────────────────────────────────────────────┘
```

Second Season; three suggested pairings:

(a)

```
┌─────────────────────────────────────────────────────────────┐
│      (S)Violet (S)Tang-Marine x (S)Violet (S)Tang-Marine     │
└─────────────────────────────────────────────────────────────┘
```

```
┌─────────────────────────────────────────────────────────────┐
│  (D)Violet (D)Tang-Marines, (S)Violet (D)Tang-Marines, (D)Tang-Marines,  │
│  (D)Violet (S)Tang-Marines,  (S)Violet (S)Tang-Marines, (S)Tang-Marines, │
│          (D)Violet Marines, (S)Violet Marines, & Marines.    │
└─────────────────────────────────────────────────────────────┘
```

(b)

```
┌─────────────────────────────────────────────────────────────┐
│       (S)Violet (S)Tang-Marine x (D)Tang-Marine              │
└─────────────────────────────────────────────────────────────┘
```

```
┌─────────────────────────────────────────────────────────────┐
│  (S)Violet (D)Tang-Marines, (D)Tang-Marines, (S)Violet (S)Tang-Marines, & (S)Tang-Marines. │
└─────────────────────────────────────────────────────────────┘
```

(c)

```
┌─────────────────────────────────────────────────────────────┐
│       (S)Violet (S)Tang-Marine x (D)Violet Marine            │
└─────────────────────────────────────────────────────────────┘
```

```
┌─────────────────────────────────────────────────────────────┐
│  (D)Violet (S)Tang-Marines, (S)Violet (S)Tang-Marines, (D)Violet Marines, & (S)Violet Marines. │
└─────────────────────────────────────────────────────────────┘
```

Third Season:

```
┌─────────────────────────────────────────────────────────────┐
│     (D)Violet (S)Tang-Marine x (S)Violet (D)Tang-Marine      │
└─────────────────────────────────────────────────────────────┘
```

```
┌─────────────────────────────────────────────────────────────┐
│   (D)Violet (D)Tang-Marines, (D)Violet (S)Tang-Marines,      │
│   (S)Violet (D)Tang-Marines, & (S)Violet (S)Tang-Marines.    │
└─────────────────────────────────────────────────────────────┘
```

Fourth Season:

```
┌─────────────────────────────────────────────────────────────┐
│     (D)Violet (D)Tang-Marine x (D)Violet (D)Tang-Marine      │
└─────────────────────────────────────────────────────────────┘
```

```
┌─────────────────────────────────────────────────────────────┐
│              all (D)Violet (D)Tang-Marines.                  │
└─────────────────────────────────────────────────────────────┘
```

Violet Factor Tang–Green (ACD+AID)

Species: *Peach-faced Lovebird.*

To illustrate the matings and expectations which show the production of this compound variety, replace Marine with **Green** throughout the entire preceding section on **Violet Factor Tang–Marine.**

148

Violet Factor Tang–Lavender (ACD+AID+AR)

Species: Peach-faced Lovebird.

To illustrate the matings and expectations which show the production of this compound variety, replace Marine with **Lavender** throughout the entire preceding section on **Violet Factor Tang–Marine**.

CINNAMON PIED

Cinnamon Pied (Recessive) White–faced (SLR+AR+AR) (& Normal) (SLR+AR)

Species: Cockatiel.

First Season; if the pairing **Cinnamon White–faced cock x Pied Normal hen** *were used, the results would be the same as those below. Cocks split for Cinnamon, Pied and White-faced are needed:*

```
Cinnamon Normal cock x Pied White-faced hen
```

```
Normal cocks/Cinnamon+Pied+White-faced, & Cinnamon Normal hens/Pied+White-faced.
```

Second Season; the split cocks could be paired to Pied hens, but would have no chance of producing Cinnamon Pied cocks – only hens, i.e.:

```
Normal cock/Cinnamon+Pied+White-faced x Pied White-faced hen
```

```
                            cocks & hens:
    Pied White-faceds, Pied Normals/White-faced, White-faceds/Pied, & Normals/Pied+White-faced.
                               hens:
        Cinnamon Pied White-faceds, Cinnamon Pied Normals/White-faced,
        Cinnamon White-faceds/Pied, & Cinnamon Normals/Pied+White-faced.
                               cocks:
        Pied White-faceds/Cinnamon, Pied Normals/Cinnamon+White-faced,
        White-faceds/Cinnamon+Pied, & Normals/Cinnamon+Pied+White-faced.
```

Use of birds bred in the first season gives chance of producing cocks and hens:

```
Normal cock/Cinnamon+Pied+White-faced x Cinnamon Normal hen/Pied+White-faced
```

```
                            cocks & hens:
    Cinnamon Pied White-faceds, Cinnamon Pied Normals/White-faced, Cinnamon Pied Normals,
    Cinnamon White-faceds/Pied, Cinnamon Normals/Pied+White-faced, Cinnamon Normals/Pied,
        Cinnamon White-faceds, Cinnamon Normals/White-faced, & Cinnamon Normals.
                               hens:
            Pied White-faceds, Pied Normals/White-faced, Pied Normals,
            White-faceds/Pied, Normals/Pied+White-faced, Normals/Pied,
                White-faceds, Normals/White-faced, & Normals.
                               cocks:
    Pied White-faceds/Cinnamon, Pied Normals/Cinnamon+White-faced, Pied Normals/Cinnamon,
    White-faceds/Cinnamon+Pied, Normals/Cinnamon+Pied+White-faced, Normals/Cinnamon+Pied,
        White-faceds/Cinnamon, Normals/Cinnamon+White-faced, & Normals/Cinnamon.
```

As can be seen from the wide array of types which can be bred, this pairing is a long shot – but the sought after compound varieties may pop up! In the third season, any **Pied White–faced cocks/Cinnamon** from the above pairing would be a useful choice to pair to the **Cinnamon Normal hens/Pied & White–faced** produced in the first season if Cinnamon Pied White-faceds were not available – e.g. pairing (a) third season.

Alternatively, the **Pied cocks** (which must all be split Cinnamon, and, if Normal, may be split White-faced) can be paired to any **Cinnamon Pied hens** (which if Normal may be split White-faced), or the **Cinnamon White–faced hens/Pied** and **Cinnamon Normal hens/Pied and White–faced** from the first pairing of the second season; e.g. pairings (b) and (c).

Third Season; three examples:

(a)

Pied White-faced cock/Cinnamon x Cinnamon Normal hen/Pied+White-faced

▮

cocks & hens:
Cinnamon Pied White-faceds, Cinnamon Pied Normals/White-faced,
Cinnamon White-faceds/Pied, & Cinnamon Normals/Pied+White-faced.
hens:
Pied White-faceds, Pied Normals/White-faced, White-faceds/Pied, & Normals/Pied+White-faced.
cocks:
Pied White-faceds/Cinnamon, Pied Normals/Cinnamon+White-faced,
White-faceds/Cinnamon+Pied, & Normals/Cinnamon+Pied+White-faced.

(b)

Pied White-faced cock/Cinnamon x Cinnamon Pied Normal hen/White-faced

▮

cocks & hens: **Cinnamon Pied White-faceds, & Cinnamon Pied Normals/White-faced.**
hens: Pied White-faceds, & Pied Normals/White-faced.
cocks: Pied White-faceds/Cinnamon, & Pied Normals/Cinnamon+White-faced.

(c)

Pied Normal cock/Cinnamon+White-faced x Cinnamon White-faced hen/Pied

▮

cocks & hens:
Cinnamon Pied White-faceds, Cinnamon Pied Normals/White-faced,
Cinnamon White-faceds/Pied, & Cinnamon Normals/Pied+White-faced.
hens:
Pied White-faceds, Pied Normals/White-faced, White-faceds/Pied, & Normals/Pied+White-faced.
cocks:
Pied White-faceds/Cinnamon, Pied Normals/Cinnamon+White-faced,
White-faceds/Cinnamon+Pied, & Normals/Cinnamon+Pied+White-faced.

Cinnamon Pied (Recessive) Pale–faced (SLR+AR+AR) (& Normal) (SLR+AR)

Species: *Cockatiel.*

To illustrate the matings and expectations which show the production of this compound variety, replace White-faced with **Pale–faced** throughout the entire preceding section on **Cinnamon Pied (Recessive) White–faced (& Normal).**

Cinnamon Pied (Recessive) Marine (SLR+AR+AR) (& Green) (SLR+AR)

Species: *Peach-faced Lovebird.*

To illustrate the matings and expectations which show the production of this compound variety, replace Normal with **Green** and White-faced with **Marine** throughout the entire preceding section on **Cinnamon Pied (Recessive) White-faced (& Normal).**

Cinnamon Pied (Recessive) Lavender (SLR+AR+AR) (& Green) (SLR+AR)

Species: *Peach-faced Lovebird.*

To illustrate the matings and expectations which show the production of this compound variety, replace Normal with **Green** and White-faced with **Lavender** throughout the entire preceding section on **Cinnamon Pied (Recessive) White-faced (& Normal).**

Cinnamon Pied (Recessive) Green (SLR+AR)

Species: *Red-fronted Kakariki.*

Firstly, cocks which are split for both Cinnamon and Pied are needed. These can be provided in several ways but it will be obvious that pairing (a) is preferable because the split cocks can be identified by eye colour or in nest feather - which is of great benefit.

Note: while breeders list the inheritance of the existing Pied variety of the Kakariki as Autosomal Recessive, a recent report on a specific British strain questions this assumption.

First Season:

(a)

Cinnamon Green cock x Pied Green hen

|

Cinnamon Green hens/Pied, & **Green cocks/Cinnamon+Pied.**

(b)

Pied Green cock x Cinnamon Green hen

|

Green hens/Pied, & **Green cocks/Cinnamon+Pied.**

(c)

Green cock/Cinnamon x Pied Green hen

|

Green hens/Pied, Cinnamon Green hens/Pied, **Green cocks/Cinnamon+Pied,** & Green cocks/Pied.

Second Season; the split cocks can be paired to Pied Green hens or Cinnamon Green hens/Pied:

(a)

```
Green cock/Cinnamon+Pied x Pied Green hen
```

▮

```
        cocks & hens: Pied Greens, & Greens/Pied.
    hens: Cinnamon Pied Greens, & Cinnamon Greens/Pied.
    cocks: Pied Greens/Cinnamon, & Greens/Cinnamon+Pied.
```

(b)

```
Green cock/Cinnamon+Pied x Cinnamon Green hen/Pied
```

▮

```
cocks & hens: Cinnamon Pied Greens, Cinnamon Greens/Pied, & Cinnamon Greens.
            hens: Pied Greens, Greens/Pied, & Greens.
    cocks: Pied Greens/Cinnamon, Greens/Cinnamon+Pied, & Greens/Cinnamon.
```

By now a wide selection of stock should be available for breeding in the third season, and a predominance of Cinnamon Pied Greens can be achieved by the following pairings – other than Cinnamon Pied Green x Cinnamon Pied Green.

Third Season; a selection of pairings:

(a)

```
Cinnamon Pied Green cock x Cinnamon Green hen/Pied
```

▮

```
cocks & hens: Cinnamon Pied Greens, & Cinnamon Greens/Pied.
```

(b)

```
Cinnamon Green cock/Pied x Cinnamon Pied Green hen
```

▮

```
cocks & hens: Cinnamon Pied Greens, & Cinnamon Greens/Pied.
```

(c)

```
Cinnamon Green cock/Pied x Cinnamon Green hen/Pied
```

▮

```
cocks & hens: Cinnamon Pied Greens, Cinnamon Greens/Pied, & Cinnamon Greens.
```

(d)

```
Pied Green cock/Cinnamon x Cinnamon Pied Green hen
```

▮

```
Cinnamon Pied Green cocks & hens, Pied Green hens, & Pied Green cocks/Cinnamon.
```

(e)

> Cinnamon Green cock/Pied x Pied Green hen

> **Cinnamon Pied Green hens**, Cinnamon Green hens/Pied,
> Pied Green cocks/Cinnamon, & Green cocks/Cinnamon+Pied.

Cinnamon Pied (Dominant) Brown (SLR+ACD)

Species: Bourke's Grass Parrakeet.

First Season:

> Cinnamon Brown cock x Pied Brown hen

> hens: **Cinnamon Pied Browns**, Cinnamon Browns,
> cocks: **Pied Browns/Cinnamon**, & Browns/Cinnamon.

Second Season:

> Pied Brown cock/Cinnamon x Cinnamon Pied Brown hen

> cocks & hens: **Cinnamon Pied Browns**, & Cinnamon Browns.
> hens: Pied Browns, & Browns.
> cocks: Pied Browns/Cinnamon, & Browns/Cinnamon.

Cinnamon Pied (Dominant) Green (SLR+ACD)

Species: Elegant Grass Parrakeet.

To illustrate the matings and expectations which show the production of this combination variety, replace Brown with **Green** throughout the entire preceding section on **Cinnamon Pied (Dominant) Brown.**

CINNAMON PEARL

Cinnamon Pearl White-faced (SLR+SLR+AR) (& Normal) (SLR+SLR)

Species: Cockatiel.

First Season; four suggested pairings; cocks which are split for Pearl, Cinnamon and White-faced are needed, and these can be produced in several ways:
(a)

> Pearl Normal cock x Cinnamon White-faced hen

153

Continued from previous page.

```
Pearl Normal hens/White-faced & Normal cocks/Pearl+Cinnamon+White-faced.
```

(b)

```
Cinnamon White-faced cock x Pearl Normal hen
```

```
Cinnamon Normal hens/White-faced, & Normal cocks/Pearl+Cinnamon+White-faced.
```

(c)

```
Pearl White-faced cock x Cinnamon Normal hen
```

```
Pearl Normal hens/White-faced, & Normal cocks/Pearl+Cinnamon+White-faced.
```

(d)

```
Cinnamon Normal cock x Pearl White-faced hen
```

```
Cinnamon Normal hens/White-faced, & Normal cocks/Pearl+Cinnamon+White-faced.
```

Second Season; the split cocks can be paired to either Pearl White-faced hens or Cinnamon White-faced hens:

```
Normal cock/Pearl+Cinnamon+White-faced x Pearl White-faced hen
```

```
                              hens:
    Cinnamon Pearl White-faceds, Cinnamon Pearl Normals/White-faced,
          Pearl White-faceds, Pearl Normals/White-faced,
      Cinnamon White-faceds, Cinnamon Normals/White-faced,
         White-faceds, & Normals/White-faced.
                             cocks:
   *Pearl White-faceds/Cinnamon, *Pearl Normals/Cinnamon+White-faced,
        *Pearl White-faceds, *Pearl Normals/White-faced,
   White-faceds/Pearl+Cinnamon, Normals/Pearl+Cinnamon+White-faced,
       *White-faceds/Pearl, & *Normals/Pearl+White-faced.
```

By using a **Cinnamon White-faced hen** in the above pairing instead of a **Pearl White-faced hen**, those cock birds marked with an asterisk (*) will be omitted from the expectations and replaced by the following:

```
   Cinnamon White-faceds/Pearl, Cinnamon Normals/Pearl+White-faced,
      Cinnamon White-faceds, Cinnamon Normals/White-faced,
      White-faceds/Cinnamon, & Normals/Cinnamon+White-faced.
```

The following cocks can be selected from both types of pairings for use with the young Cinnamon Pearl hens in the third season: **Pearl White-faceds** (hoping those chosen are split Cinnamon), **Pearl Normals** (hoping those chosen are split Cinnamon and White-faced), **Cinnamon White-faceds** (hoping those chosen are split Pearl), and

Cinnamon Normals (hoping those chosen are split Pearl and White-faced). Should this be the case a greater amount of Cinnamon Pearls (cocks and hens) is likely to be produced.

Third Season; four examples:

(a)

Pearl White-faced cock/Cinnamon x Cinnamon Pearl White-faced hen

▮

Cinnamon Pearl White-faced cocks & hens, Pearl White-faced hens, and Pearl White-faced cocks/Cinnamon.

(b)

Pearl Normal cock/Cinnamon+White-faced x Cinnamon Pearl White-faced hen

▮

cocks & hens: **Cinnamon Pearl White-faceds, & Cinnamon Pearl Normals/White-faced.** hens: Pearl White-faceds, & Pearl Normals/White-faced. cocks: Pearl White-faceds/Cinnamon, & Pearl Normals/Cinnamon+White-faced.

(c)

Cinnamon White-faced cock/Pearl x Cinnamon Pearl Normal hen/White-faced

▮

cocks & hens: **Cinnamon Pearl White-faceds, & Cinnamon Pearl Normals/White-faced.** hens: Cinnamon White-faceds, & Cinnamon Normals/White-faced. cocks: Cinnamon White-faceds/Pearl, & Cinnamon Normals/Pearl+White-faced.

(d)

Cinnamon Normal cock/Pearl+White-faced x Cinnamon Pearl White-faced hen

▮

cocks & hens: **Cinnamon Pearl White-faceds, & Cinnamon Pearl Normals/White-faced.** hens: Cinnamon White-faceds, & Cinnamon Normals/White-faced. cocks: Cinnamon White-faceds/Pearl, & Cinnamon Normals/Pearl+White-faced.

Cinnamon Pearl Pale-faced (SLR+SLR+AR) (& Normal) (SLR+SLR)

Species: Cockatiel.
   To illustrate the matings and expectations which show the production of this compound variety, replace White-faced with **Pale-faced** in the entire preceding section on **Cinnamon Pearl White-faced (& Normal).**

Cinnamon Pearl Pied (Rec.) White-faced (SLR+SLR+AR+AR) (& Normal) (SLR+SLR+AR)

Species: Cockatiel.
   The more factors needed in the creation of a compound variety, the more ways there are of producing it; here are just two suggested methods. The first produces Cinnamon Pearl Pieds in Normal split White-faced *and* White-faced, and the second in White-faced only.

155

First Method:
First Season:

Cinnamon Pearl Normal cock x Pied White-faced hen

▮

Cinnamon Pearl Normal hens/Pied+White-faced, & **Normal cocks/Cinnamon+Pearl+Pied+White-faced.**

Second Season; produces Cinnamon Pearl Pied **hens** *only:*

Normal cock/Cinnamon+Pearl+Pied+White-faced x Pied White-faced hen

▮

cocks & hens:
Pied White-faceds, White-faceds/Pied, Pied Normals/White-faced, & Normals/Pied+White-faced.
hens:
Cinnamon Pearl Pied White-faceds, Cinnamon Pearl White-faceds/Pied,
Cinnamon Pearl Pied Normals/White-faced, Cinnamon Pearl Normals/Pied+White-faced,
Cinnamon Pied White-faceds, Cinnamon White-faceds/Pied,
Cinnamon Pied Normals/White-faced, Cinnamon Normals/Pied+White-faced,
Pearl Pied White-faceds, Pearl White-faceds/Pied,
Pearl Pied Normals/White-faced, & Pearl Normals/Pied+White-faced.
cocks:
Pied White-faceds/Cinnamon+Pearl, White-faceds/Cinnamon+Pearl+Pied,
Pied Normals/Cinnamon+Pearl+White-faced, Normals/Cinnamon+Pearl+Pied+White-faced,
Pied White-faceds/Cinnamon, White-faceds/Cinnamon+Pied,
Pied Normals/Cinnamon+White-faced, Normals/Cinnamon+Pied+White-faced,
Pied White-faceds/Pearl, White-faceds/Pearl+Pied,
Pied Normals/Pearl+White-faced, & Normals/Pearl+Pied+White-faced.

Third Season; produces Cinnamon Pearl Pied hens **& cocks:**

Normal cock/Cinnamon+Pearl+Pied+White-faced x Cinnamon Pearl Pied White-faced hen

▮

cocks & hens:
Cinnamon Pearl Pied White-faceds, Cinnamon Pearl Pied Normals/White-faced,
Cinnamon Pearl White-faceds/Pied, & Cinnamon Pearl Normals/Pied+White-faced.
hens:
Cinnamon Pied White-faceds, Cinnamon Pied Normals/White-faced,
Cinnamon White-faceds/Pied, Cinnamon Normals/Pied+White-faced,
Pearl Pied White-faceds, Pearl Pied Normals/White-faced,
Pearl White-faceds/Pied, Pearl Normals/Pied+White-faced,
Pied White-faceds, Pied Normals/White-faced,
White-faceds/Pied, & Normals/Pied+White-faced.
cocks:
Cinnamon Pied White-faceds/Pearl, Cinnamon Pied Normals/Pearl+White-faced,
Cinnamon White-faceds/Pearl+Pied, Cinnamon Normals/Pearl+Pied+White-faced,
Pearl Pied White-faceds/Cinnamon, Pearl Pied Normals/Cinnamon+White-faced,
Pearl White-faceds/Cinnamon+Pied, Pearl Normals/Cinnamon+Pied+White-faced,
Pied White-faceds/Cinnamon+Pied, Pied Normals/Cinnamon+Pied+White-faced,
White-faceds/Cinnamon+Pearl+Pied, & Normals/Cinnamon+Pearl+Pied+White-faced.

Second Method:
First Season:

Cinnamon Pied White-faced cock x Pearl Pied White-faced hen

▮

Continued from previous page.

Cinnamon Pied White-faced hens, & Pied White-faceds cocks/Cinnamon+Pearl.

Second Season:

Pied White-faced cock/Cinnamon+Pearl x Cinnamon Pied White-faced hen

cocks & hens:
Cinnamon Pied White-faceds.
hens:
Cinnamon Pearl Pied White-faceds, Pearl Pied White-faceds, & Pied White-faceds.
cocks:
Cinnamon Pied White-faceds/Pearl, Pied White-faceds/Cinnamon+Pearl, & Pied White-faceds/Cinnamon.

Third Season:

Cinnamon Pied White-faced cock/Pearl x Cinnamon Pearl Pied White-faced hen

Cinnamon Pearl Pied White-faceds cocks & hens, Cinnamon Pied White-faceds hens,
& Cinnamon Pied White-faceds cocks/Pearl.

Cinnamon Pearl Pied (Rec.) Pale-faced (SLR+SLR+AR+AR) (& Normal) (SLR+SLR+AR)

Species: Cockatiel.

To illustrate the matings and expectations which show the production of this compound variety, replace White-faced with **Pale-faced** throughout the entire preceding section on **Cinnamon Pearl Pied (Recessive) White-faced (& Normal).**

PIED BLUE (& PIED WHITE-FACED)

Pied (Dominant) Blue (ACD+AR)

Species: Splendid Grass Parrakeet.

First Season:

Pied Green x Blue

Pied Greens/Blue, & Greens/Blue.

Second Season:

Pied Green/Blue x Pied Green/Blue

157

Continued from previous page.

Pied Blues, Blues, Pied Greens/Blue, Greens/Blue, Pied Greens, & Greens.

Third Season:

Pied Blue x Pied Blue

Pied Blues, & Blues.

Pied (Dominant) Marine (ACD+AR)

Species: Splendid Grass Parrakeet and Peach-faced Lovebird.
  To illustrate the matings and expectations which show the production of this combination variety, replace Blue with **Marine** throughout the entire preceding section on **Pied (Dominant) Blue.**

Pied (Dominant) Lavender (ACD+AR)

Species: Peach-faced Lovebird.
  To illustrate the matings and expectations which show the production of this combination variety, replace Blue with **Lavender** throughout the entire preceding section on **Pied (Dominant) Blue.**

Pied (Recessive) Blue (AR+AR)

Species: Indian Ringneck Parrakeet and Red-rumped Parrakeet.

First Season:

Pied Green x Blue

all **Greens/Pied+Blue**

Second Season:

Green/Pied+Blue x Green/Pied+Blue

Pied Blues, Pied Greens/Blue, Pied Greens, Blues/Pied, Greens/Pied+Blue, Greens/Pied, Blues, Greens/Blue, & Greens.

Third Season; the following examples of useful pairings can be made from the young provided in the second season:
(a)

Pied Blue x Pied Green

158

Continued from previous page.

> all Pied Greens/Blue.

(b)

> Pied Blue x Pied Green/Blue

> **Pied Blues**, & Pied Greens/Blue.

(c)

> Pied Blue x Blue/Pied

> **Pied Blues**, & Blues/Pied.

(d)

> Pied Blue x Pied Blue

> all **Pied Blues**.

Pied (Recessive) White-faced (AR+AR)

Species: *Cockatiel.*
    To illustrate the matings and expectations which show the production of this combination, replace Blue with **White-faced** in the entire preceding section on **Pied (Recessive) Blue.**

Pied (Recessive) Marine (AR+AR)

Species: *Indian Ringneck Parrakeet, Red-rumped Parrakeet, Turquoisine Grass Parrakeet and Peach-faced Lovebird.*
    To illustrate the matings and expectations which show the production of this combination, replace Blue with **Marine** in the entire preceding section on **Pied (Recessive) Blue.**

Pied (Recessive) Pale-faced (AR+AR)

Species: *Cockatiel.*
    To illustrate the matings and expectations which show the production of this combination, replace Blue with **Pale-faced** in the entire preceding section on **Pied (Recessive) Blue.**

Pied (Recessive) Lavender (AR+AR)

Species: *Peach-faced Lovebird.*

To illustrate the matings and expectations which show the production of this combination, replace Blue with **Lavender** in the entire preceding section on **Pied (Recessive) Blue**.

PIED DARK FACTOR

Pied (Recessive) Dark Factor Marine (AR+AID+AR) (& Green) (AR+AID)

Species: *Turquoisine Grass Parrakeet and Peach-faced Lovebird.*

*First Season; apart from the unconfirmed theoretical possibility of percentages of expectations being affected by crossover, if the pairing **Pied Green x Slate Marine** were used instead, the results obtained from their progeny in following seasons would be identical to those which follow - and their progeny would be identical in appearance to those in the pairing below:*

Pied Marine x Olive Green

▌

all **Dark Greens/Pied+Marine**.

Second Season:

Dark Green/Pied+Marine x Dark Green/Pied+Marine

▌

Pied Slate Marines, **Pied Dark Marines**, Pied Marines,   **Pied Olive Greens/Marine**, **Pied Dark Greens/Marine**, Pied Greens/Marine,   **Pied Olive Greens**, **Pied Dark Greens**, Pied Greens,   Slate Marines/Pied, Dark Marines/Pied, Marines/Pied,   Olive Greens/Pied+Marine, Dark Greens/Pied+Marine, Greens/Pied+Marine,   Olive Greens/Pied, Dark Greens/Pied, Greens/Pied,   Slate Marines, Dark Marines, Marines,   Olive Greens/Marine, Dark Greens/Marine, Greens/Marine,   Olive Greens, Dark Greens, & Greens.

From the above expectations, it will be seen that the likelihood of producing Pied Dark Factor *Marines* is very small, but other 'by-product' varieties can be used in future pairings to heighten the probability of their production; i.e. any **Pied Olive Greens** or **Pied Dark Greens** (in the hope that they are split Marine), and any **Slate Marines** or **Dark Greens** (in the hope that they are split Pied).

Third Season; two examples:
(a)

Pied Olive Green/Marine x Pied Dark Marine

▌

Pied Slate Marines, **Pied Dark Marines**, Pied Olive Greens/Marine, & Pied Dark Greens/Marine.

(b)

> Slate Marine/Pied x Dark Marine/Pied

I

> **Pied Slate Marines, Pied Dark Marines,**
> Slate Marines/Pied, Dark Marines/Pied, Slate Marines, & Dark Marines.

Pied (Recessive) Dark Factor Lavender (AR+AID+AR) (& Green) (AR+AID)

Species: Peach-faced Lovebird.

To illustrate the matings and expectations which show the production of this combination, replace Marine with **Lavender** in the entire preceding section on **Pied (Recessive) Dark Factor Marine (& Green)**.

Pied (Recessive) Greyblue (AR+ACD+AR) (& Greygreen) (AR+ACD)

Species: Indian Ringneck Parrakeet.

Grey: (S)= Single Factor   (D)= Double Factor

First Season:

> Pied Green x (D)Greyblue

I

> all **(S)Greygreens/Pied+Blue.**

Second Season:

(a)

> (S)Greygreen/Pied+Blue x (S)Greygreen/Pied+Blue

I

> **Pied (D)Greyblues, Pied (D)Greygreens/Blue, Pied (D)Greygreens,**
> **Pied (S)Greyblues, Pied (S)Greygreens/Blue, Pied (S)Greygreens,**
> Pied Blues, Pied Greens/Blue, Pied Greens,
> (D)Greyblues/Pied, (D)Greygreens/Pied+Blue, (D)Greygreens/Pied,
> (S)Greyblues/Pied, (S)Greygreens/Pied+Blue, (S)Greygreens/Pied,
> Blues/Pied, Greens/Pied+Blue, Greens/Pied,
> (D)Greyblues, (D)Greygreens/Blue, (D)Greygreens,
> (S)Greyblues, (S)Greygreens/Blue, (S)Greygreens,
> Blues, Greens/Blue, & Greens.

To increase the incidence of this compound variety, the following 'by-product' types which could be paired to any young Pied Greyblues include the **Pied Greygreens** (in the hope that they are Double Factor Grey and split Blue), and the **Greyblues** (in the hope that they are Double Factor Grey and split Pied). The splits from the first season continue to be useful and, failing all else, any **Pied Greygreens** (in the hope that they are split Blue) could be paired to **Pied Blues.**

161

Third Season; four suggested pairings:

(a)

Pied (D)Greygreen/Blue x Pied (D)Greyblue

I

Pied (D)Greyblues, & Pied (D)Greygreens/Blue.

(b)

(D)Greyblue/Pied x Pied (D)Greyblue

I

Pied (D)Greyblues, & (D)Greyblues/Pied.

(c)

Pied (D)Greygreen/Blue x Pied Blue

I

Pied (S)Greyblues, & Pied (S)Greygreens/Blue.

(d)

Pied (D)Greyblue x Pied (D)Greyblue

I

all **Pied (D)Greyblues.**

Pied Greymarine (AR+ACD+AR) (& Greygreen) (AR+ACD)

Species: *Indian Ringneck Parrakeet.*

To illustrate the matings and expectations which show the production of this compound variety, replace Blue with **Marine** in the preceding section on **Pied (Recessive) Greyblue (& Greygreen).**

PIED DILUTE

Pied (Recessive) Dilute (Dominant) White–faced (AR+AID+AR) (& Normal) (AR+AID)

Species: *Cockatiel.*

Dilute: (S)= Single Factor   (D)= Double Factor

First Season; if the pairing **Pied Normal x (D)Dilute White–faced** *were used, the result would be identical to the one shown below:*

Pied White-faced x (D)Dilute Normal

I

Continued from previous page.

```
all (S)Dilute Normals/Pied+White-faced.
```

Second Season:

```
(S)Dilute Normal/Pied+White-faced x (S)Dilute Normal/Pied+White-faced
```

```
        Pied (D)Dilute White-faceds, Pied (S)Dilute White-faceds, Pied White-faceds,
   Pied (D)Dilute Normals/White-faced, Pied (S)Dilute Normals/White-faced, Pied Normals/White-faced,
              Pied (D)Dilute Normals, Pied (S)Dilute Normals, Pied Normals,
          (D)Dilute White-faceds/Pied, (S)Dilute White-faceds/Pied, White-faceds/Pied,
   (D)Dilute Normals/Pied+White-faced, (S)Dilute Normals/Pied+White-faced, Normals/Pied+White-faced,
              (D)Dilute Normals/Pied, (S)Dilute Normals/Pied, Normals/Pied,
              (D)Dilute White-faceds, (S)Dilute White-faceds, White-faceds,
       (D)Dilute Normals/White-faced, (S)Dilute Normals/White-faced, Normals/White-faced,
                   (D)Dilute Normals, (S)Dilute Normals, & Normals.
```

To increase the incidence of Pied Dilutes, any that are bred should be paired to each other during the third season, or paired to the **(S)Dilute Normals split Pied (and White-faced)** which were bred in the first season.

Third Season; best example:

```
Pied (D)Dilute White-faced x (S)Dilute Normal/Pied+White-faced
```

```
          Pied (D)Dilute White-faceds, Pied (S)Dilute White-faceds,
       Pied (D)Dilute Normals/White-faced, Pied (S)Dilute Normals/White-faced,
              (D)Dilute White-faceds/Pied, (S)Dilute White-faceds/Pied,
       (D)Dilute Normals/Pied+White-faced, & (S)Dilute Normals/Pied+White-faced.
```

Pied (Recessive) Dilute (Dominant) Pale-faced (AR+AID+AR) (& Normal) (AR+AID)

Species: Cockatiel

To illustrate the matings and expectations which show the production of this compound variety, replace White-faced with **Pale-faced** in the entire preceding section on **Pied (Recessive) Dilute (Dominant) White-faced (& Normal).**

Pied (Dominant) Dilute (Recessive) Marine (ACD+AR+AR) (& Green) (ACD+AR)

Species: Peach-faced Lovebird.

*First Season; if the pairing **Pied Green x Dilute Marine** were used, the results would be identical to those shown below:*

```
Pied Marine x Dilute Green
```

```
Pied Greens/Dilute+Marine, & Greens/Dilute+Marine.
```

Second Season; two suggested pairings:
(a)

Pied Green/Dilute+Marine x Pied Green/Dilute+Marine

I

Pied Dilute Marines, Pied Dilute Greens/Marine, Pied Dilute Greens, Pied Marines/Dilute, Pied Greens/Dilute+Marine, Pied Greens/Dilute, Pied Marines, Pied Greens/Marine, Pied Greens, Dilute Marines, Dilute Greens/Marine, Dilute Greens, Marines/Dilute, Greens/Dilute+Marine, Greens/Dilute, Marines, Greens/Marine, & Greens.

(b)

Pied Green/Dilute+Marine x Dilute Marine

I

Pied Dilute Marines, Pied Dilute Greens/Marine, Pied Marines/Dilute, Pied Greens/Dilute+Marine, Dilute Marines, Dilute Greens/Marine, Marines/Dilute, & Greens/Dilute+Marine.

Third Season; two suggested pairings:
(a)

Pied Dilute Green/Marine x Pied Dilute Marine

I

Pied Dilute Marines, Pied Dilute Greens/Marine, Dilute Marines, & Dilute Greens/Marine.

(b)

Pied Dilute Marine x Pied Dilute Marine

I

Pied Dilute Marines, & Dilute Marines.

Pied (Dominant) Dilute (Recessive) Lavender (ACD+AR+AR) (& Green) (ACD+AR)

Species: Peach-faced Lovebird.

To illustrate the matings and expectations which show the production of this compound variety, replace Marine with **Lavender** in the entire preceding section on **Pied (Dominant) Dilute (Recessive) Marine (& Green).**

Pied (Dominant) Melanistic (ACD+AR)

Species: Eastern Rosella.

First Season:

Pied Normal x Melanistic

I

Continued on next page.

I

> Pied Normals/Melanistic, & Normals/Melanistic.

Second Season:

> Pied Normal/Melanistic x Pied Normal/Melanistic

I

> **Pied Melanistics**, Melanistics, Pied Normals/Melanistic, Normals/Melanistic, Pied Normals, & Normals.

Third Season:

> Pied Melanistic x Pied Melanistic

I

> **Pied Melanistics**, & Melanistics.

Pied (Dominant) Ruby (ACD+SLR)

Species: Eastern Rosella Parrakeet.

First Season:

> Ruby Normal cock x Pied Normal hen

I

> hens: **Pied Ruby Normals**, Ruby Normals,
> cocks: **Pied Normals/Ruby**, & Normals/Ruby.

Second Season:

> Pied Normal cock/Ruby x Pied Ruby Normal hen

I

> cocks & hens: **Pied Ruby Normals**, & Ruby Normals.
> hens: Pied Normals, & Normals.
> cocks: Pied Normals/Ruby, & Normals/Ruby.

GREYBLUE

Greyblue (ACD+AR)

Species: Indian Ringneck Parrakeet.

Grey: (S)= Single Factor (D)= Double Factor

First Season:

(D)Greygreen x Blue

all **(S)Greygreens/Blue.**

Second Season; two suggested pairings:

(a)

(S)Greygreen/Blue x (S)Greygreen/Blue

(D)Greyblues, (S)Greyblues, Blues, (D)Greygreens/Blue, (S)Greygreens/Blue, Greens/Blue, (D)Greygreens, (S)Greygreens, & Greens.

(b)

(S)Greygreen/Blue x Blue

(S)Greyblues, Blues, (S)Greygreens/Blue, & Greens/Blue.

In subsequent breeding seasons, the Greyblues can be paired together to increase the stock, or may be paired to the **(S)Greygreens split Blue** produced in the first season.

Third Season:

(a)

(D)Greyblue x (D)Greyblue

all **(D)Greyblues.**

(b)

(D)Greyblue x (S)Greyblue

(D)Greyblues, & (S)Greyblues.

(c)

(S)Greyblue x (S)Greyblue

(D)Greyblues, (S)Greyblues, & Blues.

(d)

(D)Greyblue x (S)Greygreen/Blue

▌

(D)Greyblues, (S)Greyblues, (D)Greygreens/Blue & (S)Greygreens/Blue.

Greymarine (ACD+AR)

Species: *Indian Ringneck Parrakeet.*

To illustrate the matings and expectations which show the production of this compound variety, replace Blue with **Marine** throughout the entire preceding section on **Greyblue.**

PEARL BLUE (& PEARL WHITE-FACED)

Pearl White-faced (SLR+AR)

Species: *Cockatiel.*

Firstly, cocks which are split for both Pearl and White-faced are needed. These can be provided in several ways but it will be obvious that pairing (a) is preferable because the split cocks can be identified in nest feather.

First Season:

(a)

Pearl Normal cock x White-faced hen

▌

Pearl Normal hens/White-faced, & **Normal cocks/Pearl+White-faced.**

(b)

White-faced cock x Pearl Normal hen

▌

Normal hens/White-faced, & **Normal cocks/Pearl+White-faced.**

(c)

Normal cock/Pearl x White-faced hen

▌

Normal hens/White-faced, Pearl Normal hens/White-faced, **Normal cocks/Pearl+White-faced,** & Normal cocks/White-faced.

Second Season; two possible pairings; the split cocks can be paired to White-faced hens or Pearl Normal hens/White-faced:

(a)

Normal cock/Pearl+White-faced x White-faced hen

I

cocks & hens: White-faceds, & Normals/White-faced. hens: **Pearl White-faceds,** & Pearl Normals/White-faced. cocks: White-faceds/Pearl, & Normals/Pearl+White-faced.

(b)

Normal cock/Pearl+White-faced x Pearl Normal hen/White-faced

I

cocks & hens: **Pearl White-faceds,** Pearl Normals/White-faced, & Pearl Normals. hens: White-faceds, Normals/White-faced, & Normals. cocks: White-faceds/Pearl, Normals/Pearl+White-faced, & Normals/Pearl.

By now a wide selection of stock should be available for breeding in the third season, and a predominance of Pearl White-faceds can be achieved by the following pairings – other than Pearl White-faced x Pearl White-faced. It should be noted that although no Pearl White-faced cocks are bred from pairing (a) there is likely to be a larger predominance of White-faced birds than would be produced from pairing (b).

Third Season; a selection of pairings:
(a)

Pearl White-faced cock x Pearl Normal hen/White-faced

I

cocks & hens: **Pearl White-faceds,** & Pearl Normals/White-faced.

(b)

Pearl Normal cock/White-faced x Pearl White-faced hen

I

cocks and hens: **Pearl White-faceds,** & Pearl Normals/White-faced.

(c)

Pearl Normal cock/White-faced x Pearl Normal hen/White-faced

I

cocks & hens: **Pearl White-faceds,** Pearl Normals/White-faced, & Pearl Normals.

(d)

White-faced cock/Pearl x Pearl White-faced hen

I

Continued from previous page.

Pearl White-faced cocks & hens, White-faced hens, & White-faced cocks/Pearl.

(e)

Pearl Normal cock/White-faced x White-faced hen

Pearl White-faced hens, Pearl Normal hens/White-faced, White-faced cocks/Pearl, & Normal cocks/Pearl+White-faced.

Pearl Pale-faced (SLR+AR)

Species: Cockatiel.

To illustrate the matings and expectations which show the production of this combination variety, replace White-faced with **Pale-faced** in the entire preceding section on **Pearl White-faceds.**

Pearl Marine (SLR+AR)

Species: Turquoisine Grass Parrakeet.

To illustrate the matings and expectations which show the production of this combination variety, replace Normal with **Green** and White-faced with **Marine** in the entire preceding section on **Pearl (Sex-linked) White-faceds.**

PEARL DARK FACTOR BLUE

Pearl Dark Factor Marine (SLR+AID+AR) (& Green) (SLR+AID)

Species: Turquoisine Grass Parrakeet.

Though Pearl Dark Factor Marines could be produced by first breeding Pearl Olive Greens and then crossing these with Pearl Marines (in which case the sex of the individuals would be irrelevant), the variety could also be produced by making a first cross of **Pearl Marine cock with Olive Green hen.**

First Method:
First Season:

Pearl Olive Green x Pearl Marine

all **Pearl Dark Green/Marines**.

Second Season:

Pearl Dark Green/Marine x Pearl Dark Green/Marine

169

Continued from previous page.

> **Pearl Slate Marines,** Pearl Dark Marines, Pearl Marines,
> **Pearl Olive Greens/Marine,** Pearl Dark Greens/Marine, Pearl Greens/Marine,
> **Pearl Olive Greens,** Pearl Dark Greens, & Pearl Greens.

Second Method:

First Season; apart from the unconfirmed theoretical possibility of percentages of expectations being affected by crossover, if the pairing **Pearl Green cock x Slate Marine hen** were used instead, their progeny would be identical in appearance to those in the pairing below, and the results obtained from their progeny in following seasons would be identical to those which follow:

> Pearl Marine cock x Olive Green hen

> **Pearl Dark Green hens/Marine,** & **Dark Green cocks/Pearl+Marine.**

Second Season; two suggested pairings:

(a)

> Dark Green cock/Pearl+Marine x Pearl Dark Green hen/Marine

> cocks & hens:
> **Pearl Slate Marines,** Pearl Dark Marines, Pearl Marines,
> **Pearl Olive Greens/Marine,** Pearl Dark Greens/Marine, Pearl Greens/Marine,
> **Pearl Olive Greens,** Pearl Dark Greens, & Pearl Greens.
> hens:
> Slate Marines, Dark Marines, Marines,
> Olive Greens/Marine, Dark Greens/Marine, Greens/Marine,
> Olive Greens, Dark Greens, & Greens.
> cocks:
> Slate Marines/Pearl, Dark Marines/Pearl, Marines/Pearl,
> Olive Greens/Pearl+Marine, Dark Greens/Pearl+Marine, Greens/Pearl+Marine,
> Olive Greens/Pearl, Dark Greens/Pearl, & Greens/Pearl.

(b)

> Dark Green cock/Pearl+Marine x Slate Marine hen

> hens:
> **Pearl Slate Marines,** Pearl Dark Marines, **Pearl Olive Greens/Marine,** Pearl Dark Greens/Marine,
> Slate Marines, Dark Marines, Olive Greens/Marine, & Dark Greens/Marine.
> cocks:
> Slate Marines/Pearl, Dark Marines/Pearl, Olive Greens/Pearl+Marine, Dark Greens/Pearl+Marine,
> Slate Marines, Dark Marines, Olive Greens/Marine, & Dark Greens/Marine.

Consolidation and increase in production of Pearl Dark Factor birds can take place in the third season by using by-products of the second season's breeding – as well as the Pearl Double Dark Factor birds. The most useful cocks would be from pairing (a):- **Slate Marines split Pearl,** and **Olive Greens split Pearl and Marine.**

Third Season; best example:

> Slate Marine cock/Pearl x Pearl Olive Green hen/Marine

❙

> cocks & hens: **Pearl Slate Marines, & Pearl Olive Greens/Marine.**
> hens: Slate Marines, & Olive Greens/Marine.
> cocks: Slate Marines/Pearl, & Olive Greens/Pearl+Marine.

PEARL LUTINO

Pearl Lutino (SLR+SLR)

Species: Cockatiel.

First Season; cocks split for Ino and Pearl are needed, and these can be provided in two ways:

(a)

> Lutino cock x Pearl Normal hen

❙

> Lutino hens, & **Normal cocks/Ino+Pearl.**

(b)

> Pearl Normal cock x Lutino hen

❙

> Pearl Normal hens, & **Normal cocks/Ino+Pearl.**

Second Season; the split cocks can be paired to Lutino hens or Pearl Normal hens:

(a)

> Normal cock/Ino+Pearl x Lutino hen

❙

> hens: **Pearl Lutinos,** Lutinos, Pearl Normals, & Normals.
> cocks: Lutinos/Pearl, Lutinos, Normals/Ino+Pearl, & Normals/Ino.

(b)

> Normal cock/Ino+Pearl x Pearl Normal hen

❙

> hens: **Pearl Lutinos,** Lutinos, Pearl Normals, & Normals.
> cocks: Pearl Normals/Ino, Pearl Normals, Normals/Ino+Pearl, & Normals/Pearl.

The following cocks can be selected from the two previous pairings for use with the young Pearl Lutino hens in the third season: **Lutinos** (hoping those chosen are split Pearl) and **Pearl Normals** (hoping those chosen are split Ino). Should this be the case a greater amount of Pearl Lutinos (cocks and hens) is likely to be produced.

Third Season; two suggested pairings:

(a)

Lutino cock/Pearl x Pearl Lutino hen

I

Pearl Lutino cocks & hens, Lutino hens, & Lutino cocks/Pearl.

(b)

Pearl Normal cock/Ino x Pearl Lutino hen

I

Pearl Lutino cocks & hens, Pearl Normal hens, & Pearl Normal cocks/Ino.

Fourth Season; Pearl Lutinos can be paired together and will breed true.

PEARL PIED

Pearl Pied (Recessive) White-faced (SLR+AR+AR) (& Normal) (SLR+AR)

Species: Cockatiel.

First Season; cocks split for Pearl, Pied and White-faced are needed:

Pearl Normal cock x Pied White-faced hen

I

Normal cocks/Pearl+Pied+White-faced, & Pearl Normal hens/Pied+White-faced.

*Second Season; the split cocks could be paired to Pied hens, but would have no chance of producing Pearl Pied cocks – only **hens**, i.e.:*

Normal cock/Pearl+Pied+White-faced x Pied White-faced hen

I

cocks & hens: Pied White-faceds, Pied Normals/White-faced, White-faceds/Pied, & Normals/Pied+White-faced. hens: **Pearl Pied White-faceds, Pearl Pied Normals/White-faced,** Pearl White-faceds/Pied, & Pearl Normals/Pied+White-faced. cocks: Pied White-faceds/Pearl, Pied Normals/Pearl+White-faced, White-faceds/Pearl+Pied, & Normals/Pearl+Pied+White-faced.

To provide a chance of breeding both cock and hen Pearl Pieds, the following pairing can be made by using the birds produced in the first season:

Normal cock/Pearl+Pied+White-faced x Pearl Normal hen/Pied+White-faced

▌

---

cocks & hens:
Pearl Pied White-faceds, Pearl Pied Normals/White-faced, Pearl Pied Normals,
Pearl White-faceds/Pied, Pearl Normals/Pied+White-faced, Pearl Normals/Pied,
Pearl White-faceds, Pearl Normals/White-faced, & Pearl Normals.
hens:
Pied White-faceds, Pied Normals/White-faced, Pied Normals,
White-faceds/Pied, Normals/Pied+White-faced, Normals/Pied,
White-faceds, Normals/White-faced, & Normals.
cocks:
Pied White-faceds/Pearl, Pied Normals/Pearl+White-faced, Pied Normals/Pearl,
White-faceds/Pearl+Pied, Normals/Pearl+Pied+White-faced, Normals/Pearl+Pied,
White-faceds/Pearl, Normals/Pearl+White-faced, & Normals/Pearl.

As can be seen from the wide array of types which can be bred, this pairing is a long shot - but the sought after compound varieties can appear. In the third season, any **Pied White-faced cocks/Pearl** from the above pairing would be a useful choice to pair to the **Pearl Normal hens/Pied & White-faced** produced in the first season if Pearl Pied White-faceds were not available - e.g. pairing (a) third season.

Alternatively, the **Pied cocks** (which must all be split Pearl, and, if Normal, may be split White-faced) can be paired to any **Pearl Pied hens** (which if Normal may be split White-faced), or the **Pearl White-faced hens/Pied** and **Pearl Normal hens/Pied and White-faced** from the first pairing of the second season; e.g. pairings (b) and (c).

Third Season; three examples:

(a)

Pied White-faced cock/Pearl x Pearl Normal hen/Pied+White-faced

▌

---

cocks & hens:
Pearl Pied White-faceds, Pearl Pied Normals/White-faced,
Pearl White-faceds/Pied, & Pearl Normals/Pied+White-faced.
hens:
Pied White-faceds, Pied Normals/White-faced,
White-faceds/Pied, & Normals/Pied+White-faced.
cocks:
Pied White-faceds/Pearl, Pied Normals/Pearl+White-faced,
White-faceds/Pearl+Pied, & Normals/Pearl+Pied+White-faced.

(b)

Pied White-faced cock/Pearl x Pearl Pied Normal hen/White-faced

▌

---

cocks & hens: **Pearl Pied White-faceds, & Pearl Pied Normals/White-faced.**
hens: Pied White-faceds, & Pied Normals/White-faced.
cocks: Pied White-faceds/Pearl, & Pied Normals/Pearl+White-faced.

173

(c)

```
┌─────────────────────────────────────────────────────────────────────────────┐
│          Pied Normal cock/Pearl+White-faced x Pearl White-faced hen/Pied      │
└─────────────────────────────────────────────────────────────────────────────┘
```

```
┌─────────────────────────────────────────────────────────────────────────────┐
│                              cocks & hens:                                    │
│       Pearl Pied White-faceds, Pearl Pied Normals/White-faced,                │
│       Pearl White-faceds/Pied, & Pearl Normals/Pied+White-faced.              │
│                                 hens:                                         │
│  Pied White-faceds, Pied Normals/White-faced, White-faceds/Pied, & Normals/Pied+White-faced. │
│                                 cocks:                                         │
│            Pied White-faceds/Pearl, Pied Normals/Pearl+White-faced,           │
│       White-faceds/Pearl+Pied, & Normals/Pearl+Pied+White-faced.              │
└─────────────────────────────────────────────────────────────────────────────┘
```

Pearl Pied (Recessive) Pale-faced (SLR+AR+AR) (& Normal) (SLR+AR)

Species: *Cockatiel.*

To illustrate the matings and expectations which show the production of this compound variety, replace White-faced with **Pale-faced** throughout the entire preceding section on **Pearl Pied (Recessive) White-faced (& Normal).**

PEARL DILUTE

Pearl Dilute (Dominant) White-faced (SLR+AID+AR) (& Normal) (SLR+AID)

Species: *Cockatiel.*
Dilute: (S): Single Factor   (D): Double Factor

First Season:

```
┌─────────────────────────────────────────────────────────────────────────────┐
│              Pearl White-faced cock x (D)Dilute Normal hen                     │
└─────────────────────────────────────────────────────────────────────────────┘
```

```
┌─────────────────────────────────────────────────────────────────────────────┐
│   Pearl (S)Dilute Normal hens/White-faced, & (S)Dilute Normal cocks/Pearl+White-faced. │
└─────────────────────────────────────────────────────────────────────────────┘
```

Second Season; three suggested pairings:
(a)

```
┌─────────────────────────────────────────────────────────────────────────────┐
│  (S)Dilute Normal cock/Pearl+White-faced x Pearl (S)Dilute Normal hen/White-faced │
└─────────────────────────────────────────────────────────────────────────────┘
```

```
┌─────────────────────────────────────────────────────────────────────────────┐
│                              cocks & hens:                                    │
│     Pearl (D)Dilute White-faceds, Pearl (S)Dilute White-faceds, Pearl White-faceds, │
│ Pearl (D)Dilute Normals/White-faced, Pearl (S)Dilute Normals/White-faced, Pearl Normals/White-faced, │
│        Pearl (D)Dilute Normals, Pearl (S)Dilute Normals, & Pearl Normals.     │
│                                 hens:                                         │
│          (D)Dilute White-faceds, (S)Dilute White-faceds, White-faceds,        │
│    (D)Dilute Normals/White-faced, (S)Dilute Normals/White-faced, Normals/White-faced, │
│           (D)Dilute Normals, (S)Dilute Normals, & Normals.                    │
│                                 cocks:                                         │
│    (D)Dilute White-faceds/Pearl, (S)Dilute White-faceds/Pearl, White-faceds/Pearl, │
│     (D)Dilute Normals/Pearl+White-faced, (S)Dilute Normals/Pearl+White-faced, │
│                  Dilute Normals/Pearl+White-faced,                            │
│      (D)Dilute Normals/Pearl, (S)Dilute Normals/Pearl, & Normals/Pearl.       │
└─────────────────────────────────────────────────────────────────────────────┘
```

(b)

```
┌──────────────────────────────────────────────────────────────────────────┐
│     (S)Dilute Normal cock/Pearl+White-faced x (D)Dilute White-faced hen    │
└──────────────────────────────────────────────────────────────────────────┘
```

▮

```
┌──────────────────────────────────────────────────────────────────────────┐
│                             cocks & hens:                                  │
│              (D)Dilute White-faceds, (S)Dilute White-faceds,               │
│          (D)Dilute Normals/White-faced, & (S)Dilute Normals/White-faced.   │
│                                 hens:                                      │
│            Pearl (D)Dilute White-faceds, Pearl (S)Dilute White-faceds,     │
│      Pearl (D)Dilute Normals/White-faced, Pearl (S)Dilute Normals/White-faced, │
│                                 cocks:                                     │
│              (D)Dilute White-faceds/Pearl, (S)Dilute White-faceds/Pearl    │
│       (D)Dilute Normals/Pearl+White-faced, (S)Dilute Normals/Pearl+White-faced, │
└──────────────────────────────────────────────────────────────────────────┘
```

(c)

```
┌──────────────────────────────────────────────────────────────────────────┐
│     (S)Dilute Normal cock/Pearl+White-faced x Pearl White-faced hen        │
└──────────────────────────────────────────────────────────────────────────┘
```

▮

```
┌──────────────────────────────────────────────────────────────────────────┐
│                             cocks & hens:                                  │
│            Pearl (S)Dilute White-faceds, Pearl White-faceds,               │
│        Pearl (S)Dilute Normals/White-faced, & Pearl Normals/White-faced.   │
│                                 hens:                                      │
│               (S)Dilute White-faceds, White-faceds,                        │
│          (S)Dilute Normals/White-faceds, & Normals/White-faced.            │
│                                 cocks:                                     │
│              (S)Dilute White-faceds/Pearl, White-faceds/Pearl,             │
│        (S)Dilute Normals/Pearl+White-faced, & Normals/Pearl+White-faced.   │
└──────────────────────────────────────────────────────────────────────────┘
```

Consolidation and increase in production of Pearl Dilutes can take place in the third season by using by-products of the second season's breeding, as well as the Pearl Dilutes. The most useful cocks would be the following: from pairing (a), **(D)Dilute White-faced split Pearl**, and **(D)Dilute Normals split Pearl and White-faced**; from pairing (c), **(S)Dilute White-faceds split Pearl** and **(S)Dilute Normal split Pearl and White-faced**.

Third Season; best example:

```
┌──────────────────────────────────────────────────────────────────────────┐
│   (D)Dilute White-faced cock/Pearl x Pearl (D)Dilute Normal hen/White-faced │
└──────────────────────────────────────────────────────────────────────────┘
```

▮

```
┌──────────────────────────────────────────────────────────────────────────┐
│  cocks & hens: Pearl (D)Dilute White-faceds, & Pearl (D)Dilute Normals/White-faced. │
│        hens: (D)Dilute White-faceds, & (D)Dilute Normals/White-faced.      │
│    cocks: (D)Dilute White-faceds/Pearl, & (D)Dilute Normals/Pearl+White-faced. │
└──────────────────────────────────────────────────────────────────────────┘
```

Pearl Dilute (Dominant) Pale-faced (SLR+AID+AR) (& Normal) (SLR+AID)

Species: Cockatiel.

To illustrate the matings and expectations which show the production of this compound variety, replace White-faced with **Pale-faced** throughout the entire preceding section on **Pearl Dilute (Dominant) White-faced (& Normal)**.

175

PEARL FALLOW

Pearl Fallow White-faced (SLR+AR+AR) (& Normal) (SLR+AR)

Species: Cockatiel.

First Season; cocks split for Pearl, Fallow and White-faced are needed:

Pearl Normal cock x Fallow White-faced hen

▌

Normal cocks/Pearl+Fallow+White-faced, & Pearl Normal hens/Fallow+White-faced.

Second Season; the split cocks could be paired to Fallow hens, but would have no chance of producing Pearl Fallow cocks - only **hens**, *i.e.:*

Normal cock/Pearl+Fallow+White-faced x Fallow White-faced hen

▌

cocks & hens: Fallow White-faceds, Fallow Normals/White-faced, White-faceds/Fallow, & Normals/Fallow+White-faced. hens: **Pearl Fallow White-faceds, Pearl Fallow Normals/White-faced,** Pearl White-faceds/Fallow, & Pearl Normals/Fallow+White-faced. cocks: Fallow White-faceds/Pearl, Fallow Normals/Pearl+White-faced, White-faceds/Pearl+Fallow, & Normals/Pearl+Fallow+White-faced.

To provide a chance of breeding both **cock and hen** Pearl Fallows, the following pairing can be made by using the birds produced in the first season:

Normal cock/Pearl+Fallow+White-faced x Pearl Normal hen/Fallow+White-faced

▌

cocks & hens: **Pearl Fallow White-faceds, Pearl Fallow Normals/White-faced, Pearl Fallow Normals,** Pearl White-faceds/Fallow, Pearl Normals/Fallow+White-faced, Pearl Normals/Fallow, Pearl White-faceds, Pearl Normals/White-faced, & Pearl Normals. hens: Fallow White-faceds, Fallow Normals/White-faced, Fallow Normals, White-faceds/Fallow, Normals/Fallow+White-faced, Normals/Fallow, White-faceds, Normals/White-faced, & Normals. cocks: Fallow White-faceds/Pearl, Fallow Normals/Pearl+White-faced, Fallow Normals/Pearl, White-faceds/Pearl+Fallow, Normals/Pearl+Fallow+White-faced, Normals/Pearl+Fallow, White-faceds/Pearl, Normals/Pearl+White-faced, & Normals/Pearl.

Even though such a wide array of types can be bred, and the pairing seems to provide only a slim chance – the sought after compound varieties can and do appear. In the third season, any **Fallow White-faced cocks/Pearl** from the above pairing would be a useful choice to pair to the **Pearl Normal hens/Fallow & White-faced** produced in the first season if Pearl Fallow White-faceds were not available – e.g. pairing (a) third season.

Alternatively, the **Fallow cocks** (which must all be split Pearl, and, if Normal, may be split White-faced) can be paired to any **Pearl Fallow hens** (which if Normal may be split White-faced), or the **Pearl White-faced hens/Fallow** and **Pearl Normal hens/Fallow and White-faced** from the first pairing of the second season; e.g. pairings (b) and (c).

Third Season; three examples:

(a)

Fallow White-faced cock/Pearl x Pearl Normal hen/Fallow+White-faced

▮

cocks & hens: **Pearl Fallow White-faceds, Pearl Fallow Normals/White-faced,** Pearl White-faceds/Fallow, & Pearl Normals/Fallow+White-faced. hens: Fallow White-faceds, Fallow Normals/White-faced, White-faceds/Fallow, & Normals/Fallow+White-faced. cocks: Fallow White-faceds/Pearl, Fallow Normals/Pearl+White-faced, White-faceds/Pearl+Fallow, & Normals/Pearl+Fallow+White-faced.

(b)

Fallow White-faced cock/Pearl x Pearl Fallow Normal hen/White-faced

▮

cocks & hens: **Pearl Fallow White-faceds, & Pearl Fallow Normals/White-faced.** hens: Fallow White-faceds, & Fallow Normals/White-faced. cocks: Fallow White-faceds/Pearl, & Fallow Normals/Pearl+White-faced.

(c)

Fallow Normal cock/Pearl+White-faced x Pearl White-faced hen/Fallow

▮

cocks & hens: **Pearl Fallow White-faceds, Pearl Fallow Normals/White-faced,** Pearl White-faceds/Fallow, & Pearl Normals/Fallow+White-faced. hens: Fallow White-faceds, Fallow Normals/White-faced, White-faceds/Fallow, & Normals/Fallow+White-faced. cocks: Fallow White-faceds/Pearl, Fallow Normals/Pearl+White-faced, White-faceds/Pearl+Fallow, & Normals/Pearl+Fallow+White-faced.

Pearl Fallow Pale-faced (SLR+AR+AR) (& Normal) (SLR+AR)

Species: Cockatiel.

To illustrate the matings and expectations which show the production of this compound variety, replace White-faced with **Pale-faced** throughout the entire preceding section on **Pearl Fallow (Recessive) White-faced (& Normal).**

Pearl Fallow Marine (SLR+AR+AR) (& Green) (SLR+AR)

Species: *Turquoisine Grass Parrakeet.*

To illustrate the matings and expectations which show the production of this compound variety, replace Normal with **Green** and White-faced with **Marine** throughout the entire preceding section on **Pearl Fallow (Recessive) White-faced (& Normal).**

DARK FACTOR BLUE

Dark Factor Blue (AID+AR)

Species: *Masked Lovebird.*

First Season:

Olive Green x Blue

|
|---|

all **Dark Greens/Blue.**

Second Season:

Dark Green/Blue x Dark Green/Blue

|
|---|

Slate Blues, Dark Blues, Blues, Olive Greens/Blue, Dark Greens/Blue, Greens/Blue, Olive Greens, Dark Greens, & Greens.

In subsequent breeding seasons, the Dark Factor Blues can be paired to each other to increase the stock, may be paired to those splits produced in the first season, to the Olive Greens produced in the second season or the Olive Greens could be paired together in the hope that they are split Blue, e.g.:

Third Season; four examples:

(a)

Slate Blue x Dark Green/Blue

|
|---|

Slate Blues, Dark Blues, Olive Greens/Blue, & Dark Greens/Blue.

(b)

Olive Green/Blue x Olive Green/Blue

|
|---|

Slate Blues, Olive Greens/Blue, & Olive Greens.

(c)

Slate Blue x Olive Green/Blue

I

Slate Blues, & Olive Greens/Blue.

(d)

Dark Blue x Dark Blue

I

Slate Blues, Dark Blues, & Blues.

(e)

Slate Blue x Slate Blue

I

all Slate Blues.

Dark Factor Marine (AID+AR)

Species: *Turquoisine Grass Parrakeet, Lineolated Parrakeet and Peach-faced Lovebird.*

To illustrate the matings and expectations which show the production of this combination variety, replace Blue with **Marine** throughout the entire preceding section on **Dark Factor Blue.**

Dark Factor Lavender (AID+AR)

Species: *Peach-faced Lovebird.*

To illustrate the matings and expectations which show the production of this combination variety, replace Blue with **Lavender** throughout the entire preceding section on **Dark Factor Blue.**

Pied (Dominant) Dark Factor Marine (ACD+AID+AR) (& Green) (ACD+AID)

Species: *Peach-faced Lovebird.*

*First Season; apart from the unconfirmed theoretical possibility of percentages of expectations being affected by crossover, if the pairing **Pied Green x Slate Marine** were used instead, their progeny would be identical in appearance to those in the pairing below, and the results obtained from their progeny in following seasons would be identical to those which follow:*

Pied Marine x Olive Green

I

Pied Dark Greens/Marine, & Dark Greens/Marine.

179

Second Season:

Pied Dark Green/Marine x Pied Dark Green/Marine

▮

Pied Slate Marines, **Pied Dark Marines,** Pied Marines, **Pied Olive Greens/Marine, Pied Dark Greens/Marine,** Pied Greens/Marine, **Pied Olive Greens, Pied Dark Greens,** Pied Greens, Slate Marines, Dark Marines, Marines, Olive Greens/Marine, Dark Greens/Marine, Greens/Marine, Olive Greens, Dark Greens, & Greens.

Third Season; in the hope that they are split Marine, the young **Pied Olive Greens** *can be chosen as partners for any* **Pied Slate Marines** *in the third season:*

Pied Slate Marine x Pied Olive Green

▮

Pied Slate Marines, Pied Olive Greens/Marine, Slate Marines, & Olive Greens/Marine.

Pied (Dominant) Dark Factor Lavender (ACD+AID+AR) (& Green) (ACD+AID)

Species: *Peach-faced Lovebird.*

To illustrate the matings and expectations which show the production of this compound variety, replace Marine with **Lavender** throughout the entire preceding section on **Pied (Dominant) Dark Factor Marine (& Green)**.

Cinnamon Dark Factor Marine (SLR+AID+AR) (& Green) (SLR+AID)

Species: *Peach-faced Lovebird.*

Though Cinnamon Dark Factor Marines could be produced by first breeding Cinnamon Olive Greens and then crossing these with Cinnamon Marines (in which case the sex of the individuals would be irrelevant), the variety could also be produced by making a first cross of **Cinnamon Marine cock with Olive Green hen.**

First Method:
First Season:

Cinnamon Olive Green x Cinnamon Marine

▮

all **Cinnamon Dark Green/Marines.**

Second Season:

Cinnamon Dark Green/Marine x Cinnamon Dark Green/Marine

▮

Cinnamon Slate Marines, Cinnamon Dark Marines, Cinnamon Marines, **Cinnamon Olive Greens/Marine,** Cinnamon Dark Greens/Marine, Cinnamon Greens/Marine, **Cinnamon Olive Greens,** Cinnamon Dark Greens, & Cinnamon Greens.

Second Method:

First Season; apart from the unconfirmed theoretical possibility of percentages of expectations being affected by crossover, if the pairing **Cinnamon Green cock x Slate Marine hen** *were used instead, their progeny would be identical in appearance to those in the pairing below, and the results obtained from their progeny in following seasons would be identical to those which follow:*

```
Cinnamon Marine cock x Olive Green hen
```

■

```
Cinnamon Dark Green hens/Marine, & Dark Green cocks/Cinnamon+Marine.
```

Second Season; two suggested pairings:

(a)

```
Dark Green cock/Cinnamon+Marine x Cinnamon Dark Green hen/Marine
```

■

```
cocks & hens:
Cinnamon Slate Marines, Cinnamon Dark Marines, Cinnamon Marines,
Cinnamon Olive Greens/Marine, Cinnamon Dark Greens/Marine, Cinnamon Greens/Marine,
Cinnamon Olive Greens, Cinnamon Dark Greens, & Cinnamon Greens.
hens:
Slate Marines, Dark Marines, Marines,
Olive Greens/Marine, Dark Greens/Marine, Greens/Marine,
Olive Greens, Dark Greens, & Greens.
cocks:
Slate Marines/Cinnamon, Dark Marines/Cinnamon, Marines/Cinnamon,
Olive Greens/Cinnamon+Marine, Dark Greens/Cinnamon+Marine, Greens/Cinnamon+Marine,
Olive Greens/Cinnamon, Dark Greens/Cinnamon, & Greens/Cinnamon.
```

(b)

```
Dark Green cock/Cinnamon+Marine x Slate Marine hen
```

■

```
hens:
Cinnamon Slate Marines, Cinnamon Dark Marines,
Cinnamon Olive Greens/Marine, Cinnamon Dark Greens/Marine,
Slate Marines, Dark Marines, Olive Greens/Marine, & Dark Greens/Marine.
cocks:
Slate Marines/Cinnamon, Dark Marines/Cinnamon
Olive Greens/Cinnamon+Marine, Dark Greens/Cinnamon+Marine,
Slate Marines, Dark Marines, Olive Greens/Marine, & Dark Greens/Marine.
```

Consolidation and increase in production of Cinnamon Dark Factor birds can take place in the third season by using by-products of the second season's breeding – as well as the Cinnamon Double Dark Factor birds. The most useful cocks would be from pairing (a): **Slate Marines split Cinnamon**, and **Olive Greens split Cinnamon and Marine.**

Third Season; best example:

```
Slate Marine cock/Cinnamon x Cinnamon Olive Green hen/Marine
```

■

Continued from previous page.

> cocks & hens: **Cinnamon Slate Marines, & Cinnamon Olive Greens/Marine.**
> hens: Slate Marines, & Olive Greens/Marine.
> cocks: Slate Marines/Cinnamon, & Olive Greens/Cinnamon+Marine.

Cinnamon Dark Factor Lavender (SLR+AID+AR) (& Green) (SLR+AID)

Species: Peach-faced Lovebird.

To illustrate the matings and expectations which show the production of this compound variety, replace Marine with **Lavender** throughout the entire preceding section on **Cinnamon Dark Factor Marine (& Green)**.

Dilute (Sex-linked) Dark Factor Marine (SLR+AID+AR) (& Green) (SLR+AID)

Species: Peach-faced Lovebird.

To illustrate the matings and expectations which show the production of this compound variety, replace Cinnamon with **Dilute** throughout the entire preceding section on **Cinnamon Dark Factor Marine (& Green)**.

Dilute (Sex-linked) Dark Factor Lavender (SLR+AID+AR) (& Green) (SLR+AID)

Species: Peach-faced Lovebird.

To illustrate the matings and expectations which show the production of this compound variety, replace Cinnamon with **Dilute** and Marine with **Lavender** throughout the entire preceding section on **Cinnamon Dark Factor Marine (& Green)**.

RED & DEEP YELLOW SUFFUSION IN COMBINATION & COMPOUND VARIETIES

*BY INCLUDING birds with these Deep Yellow Suffused and Red Suffused characteristics in the respective **Universal Breeding Programmes for Combination and Compound Varieties** as they have been laid out, and by referring back to the section on **Selective Breeding**, pairings can be made to breed such varieties as are described below.*

It is most important to remember that once these characteristics have been instilled into a strain they may be impossible to completely remove - especially where Red Suffusion is concerned. Turquoisine and Splendid Grass Parrakeets of the common wild type, with yellow underparts, could become rarities if the Red-fronted and Red-bellied types became predominant because of their popularity.

Deep Yellow Suffusion (S)

Species: Cockatiel.

By laborious selective back pairing, a deeper yellow suffusion can be introduced with benefit into the following varieties: *Lutino, Cinnamon Normal, Cinnamon (D)Dilute Normal, Cinnamon Fallow Normal, Cinnamon Lutino, Cinnamon Pearl Normal, Cinnamon Pearl Pied Normal, Cinnamon Pied Normal, (D)Dilute Normal, Fallow Normal, Fallow (D)Dilute Normal, Pearl Normal, Pearl (D)Dilute Normal, Pearl Fallow Normal, Pearl Lutino, Pearl Pied Normal, Pied Normal and Pied (D)Dilute Normal* - in fact any variety of the Normal (yellow ground colour) Series.

Red Suffusion (S)

Species: *Peach-faced Lovebird.*
Though there is contention over the nature of Red Suffusion in this species, its effect is attractive in varieties such as *Pied Green, Dilute Green* and *Lutino* – any varieties or combination/compound varieties which normally reveal yellow ground colour fully or partially. Attempts at establishing the effect through selective breeding are worth while.

Species: *Princess of Wales Parrakeet.*
The Red Suffusion shown in some rare specimens could create an attractive new combination variety if introduced via selective breeding into a strain of Lutinos; *Red Suffused Lutino (S+AR).*

Species: *Turquoisine Grass Parrakeet.*
Red Suffused breasts and bellies have been introduced through selective breeding into Dilute Green – *Red-fronted Dilute Green (S+AR)* – and could also be combined with the Dark Factor and Pearl to good effect; *Red-fronted Dark Factor Green (S+AID) Red-fronted Pearl Dark Factor Green (S+SLR+AID).*
Combined with Marine (cream ground colour), the Red Suffusion of Green series (yellow ground colour) would be changed to Salmon (orange pink) Suffusion, and this could be used to create *Salmon-fronted Marine (S+AR), Salmon-fronted Dark Factor Marine (S+AID+AR), Salmon-fronted Pearl Marine (S+SLR+AR), Salmon-fronted Dark Factor Pearl Marine (S+AID+SLR+AR)* and *Salmon-fronted Dilute Marine (S+AR+AR).*

Species: *Splendid Grass Parrakeet.*
Red-bellied characteristics have been introduced through selective breeding, and can be added by the same method with great effect to Cinnamon Dilute Green – *Red-bellied Cinnamon Dilute Green (S+SLR+SLR).* When modified by Marine (cream ground colour), the Red Suffusion is changed to Salmon (orange pink), and this can be used to create *Salmon-bellied Marine (S+AR)* and *Salmon-bellied Cinnamon Dilute Marine (S+SLR+AR).*

MARINE–LAVENDER (AR+AR: alleles, acting as :AID+AR)
– INADVISABLE COMBINATION

Species: *Peach-faced Lovebird.*
Caution is advised in making indiscriminate crosses between Marine and Lavender; the resulting young are various shades of colour which range between the two types and this means that the two varieties in their pure form could become scarce. Some breeders believe that a minute proportion of specimens which are close to a true blue are produced off **Marine–Lavender x Marine–Lavender**, but no proof can be traced to support this hypothesis.
Marine and Lavender are believed to be alleles, it is known that the first cross (a) produces birds which are roughly intermediate in colour, therefore the pairings (b), (c) and (d) follow:

(a)

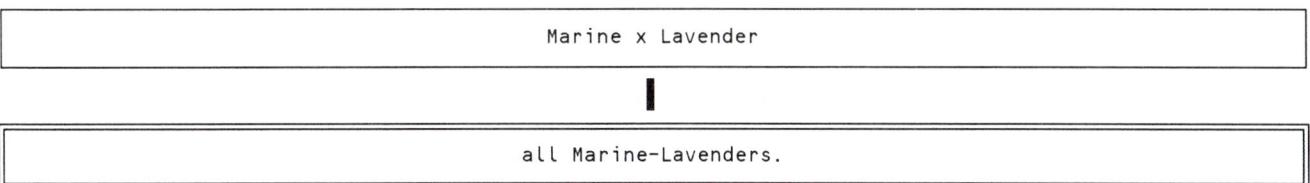

183

(b)

Marine-Lavender x Marine-Lavender

▌

Lavenders, Marines, & Marine-Lavenders.

(c)

Marine x Marine-Lavender

▌

Marines, & Marine-Lavenders.

(d)

Lavender x Marine-Lavender

▌

Lavenders, & Marine-Lavenders.

Only *pure bred* Marines or Lavenders should be used in the programmes for combination and compound varieties.

DILUTE (RECESSIVE) COCKATIELS ONLY: COMBINATION & COMPOUND VARIETIES

Dilute (Recessive) (AR+?) SPECIAL INSTRUCTIONS: *for Combination and Compound Varieties equivalent to those made with other primary varieties in conjunction with Dilute (Dominant).*

Species: *Cockatiel.*

SPECIAL INSTRUCTIONS:
1. Turn to the required programme as set out for the equivalent Combination or Compound Variety made with **Dilute (Dominant)**.
2. Read **(D)Dilute** as **visual Dilute** and **(S)Dilute** as **split Dilute** throughout all the pairing and progeny boxes.

Using pairings-expectations from **Dilute (Dominant) White-faced (AID+AR)** as an example, we can change the pairings-expectations which include Dilute (Dominant):

(D)Dilute Normal x White-faced

▌

all (S)Dilute Normals/White-faced.

to pairings-expectations which include **Dilute (Recessive) (AR+AR)**:

Dilute Normal x White-faced

▌

184

Continued from previous page.

> all **Normals/Dilute + White-faced**.

and:

> (S)Dilute Normal/White-faced x (S)Dilute Normal/White-faced

> **(D)Dilute White-faceds**, **(S)Dilute White-faceds**, White-faceds,
> (D)Dilute Normals/White-faced, (S)Dilute Normals/White-faced, Normals/White-faced,
> (D)Dilute Normals, (S)Dilute Normals, & Normals.

to:

> Normal/Dilute+White-faced x Normal/Dilute+White-faced

> **Dilute White-faceds**, White-faceds/Dilute, White-faceds,
> Dilute Normals/White-faced, Normals/Dilute+White-faced, Normals/White-faced,
> Dilute Normals, Normals/Dilute, & Normals.

and:

> (D)Dilute White-faced x (S)Dilute Normal/White-faced

> **(D)Dilute White-faceds**, **(S)Dilute White-faceds**,
> (D)Dilute Normals/White-faced, & (S)Dilute Normals/White-faced.

to:

> Dilute White-faced x Normal/Dilute+White-faced

> **Dilute White-faceds**, White-faceds/Dilute, Dilute Normals/White-faced, & Normals/Dilute+White-faced.

Note: **Dilute (Recessive) x Dilute (Dominant)** *is an inadvisable pairing; the resulting young will be Single Factor Dilutes (Dominant) split for Dilute (Recessive) - the progeny and confusion arising from the second and subsequent generations could help bring about the disappearance of the Recessive form.*

READER'S NOTES on UNIVERSAL BREEDING PROGRAMMES SELECTED for USE

Species	*Universal Breeding Programme*	*Page No*

READER'S NOTES on UNIVERSAL BREEDING PROGRAMMES SELECTED for USE

9

TECHNIQUES & DETECTIVE WORK

IMPORTANCE & USE OF THE WILD TYPE

THE VALUE AND IMPORTANCE of maintaining strains of pure bred wild type birds which carry no hidden factors for established colour varieties *must* be appreciated, especially in those psittacine species where mutant varieties are numerous and increasing. Apart from the fact that they must be bred for the sake of preserving true examples of the wild type of the species within aviculture and to provide future breeders with as wide a variety of colour forms as is possible, the normal pure wild coloured birds are the wisest choice of colour for use in establishing rare new mutant varieties.

Wherever possible a new mutation should always be paired to a strong, healthy, unrelated specimen of the pure normal type. This will help considerably in discovering the true nature of the new mutation, by eliminating the possibility of any unexpected and unwanted results arising from already established varieties in its young – time will be saved. Until a strain of the new variety is firmly established, attempts at combining it with other existing varieties should be avoided. In this way the new variety is far less likely to become adulterated and ruined by more dominant or co-dominant forms which could swamp a delicate Recessive variety so that it is lost forever. This has happened in the past with rare mutations of the Canary, Budgerigar, Cockatiel, Lovebirds and Finches.

The colour breeder should aim to increase the range of attractive varieties available to aviculturists within a chosen species. Without doubt, this increases interest in the breeding of the species and helps in the promotion of bird keeping in general. However, this increased popularity should always be accompanied by an encouragement in the culture of the wild type colour at a corresponding level of advancement.

Returning to the Wild Type

If pure bred wild type specimens are required – but only colour varieties are available – it is possible for these birds to be reconstituted, but as much time and patience will be needed as have been used in breeding the combination colours. The more factors involved, the longer it will take. Breeding programmes would again need to be planned. For instance, if there were no Green Masked Lovebirds to be found, Blues paired to Dilute Greens would produce Green young in the first season – but they would be split for both Blue and Dilute, e.g.:

First Season:

Dilute Green x Blue

all **Greens/Dilute+Blue.**

Second Season:

```
Green/Dilute+Blue x Green/Dilute+Blue
```

```
Dilute Blues, Dilute Greens/Blue, Dilute Greens,
              Blues/Dilute, Blues,
Greens/Dilute+Blue, Greens/Dilute, Greens/Blue, & Greens.
```

Third Season; laborious test pairings would need to be made to find the pure Green birds, the proof being:

```
Green x Dilute Blue
```

```
all Greens/Dilute & Blue,
with NO Dilute Blues, Dilute Greens, or Blues —
WHATSOEVER!
```

and finally:

```
Green x Green
```

```
ALL GREENS!
```

Establishing a New Mutant Variety

Every breeder with an interest in colour varieties dreams of having the good fortune of a beautiful new colour mutation arising in their own strain of birds. Very often such an incident as this happens not with a breeder of experience, but with a complete beginner who is in great need of advice – if the wrong advice is taken a once in a lifetime chance is lost.

The breeder must be prepared to enter into a long term venture which will mean holding a much larger stock of birds than may initially have been intended before the mutant cropped up. Building adequate accommodation for this stock and spending a great deal of time and money on the project is a necessary requirement. If such an undertaking is not feasible, it may be wiser to either sell the bird(s) to a specialist breeder, or to come to an agreement whereby an interest is retained in the mutation but the project is placed in experienced hands.

One of the usual mistakes the novice breeder makes is to break up the pair which has produced the mutant in order to pair it back to either its father or mother during the next possible season. This attempt at producing more of the new variety as quickly as possible is a bad move for two main reasons. Firstly, inbreeding is quite likely to produce weak substandard young which lack fertility – more likely with the larger species – which will be of no use for breeding purposes, and so time and efforts of the mutant bird will have been wasted. The same problems may occur if the young mutant is paired to its brother or sister.

Secondly, the larger the species the more difficult it is to persuade one of an established breeding pair to accept a new partner, resulting in needlessly wasted time – possibly years. If the new partner will not be accepted under any circumstances and the old pair have to be returned to each other, the time apart may have soured them so that they will not renew their previously successful partnership. Instead: the breeder should take great care of the old pair and leave them together to see if they will produce more mutants in subsequent breeding seasons, which is more likely than not - they may even produce yet another new form.

It is surprising but true that the owner often only values the new mutant and not the original breeding pair, nor any apparently normal nest mates of the valued bird. In fact, these normal looking young should all be retained, because any of them are also likely to be able to reproduce the new colour.

Initially, birds exhibiting new mutations are often weaker and more susceptible to disease than average specimens, especially Autosomal Recessive examples, not least because they are themselves frequently the results of inbreeding - whether by accident or by design. They need to be treated with extra care and attention.

The young mutant should be allowed to become fully mature before any attempts are made to breed with it, and then a strong and healthy unrelated partner selected to be its mate, as has been previously advised. This is the way to start to build a strong foundation for the strain. Even though the birds produced may not show the new variety visually, some or all should be splits, and can be saved for future use along with any nest mates of their mutant parent - so that a larger and stronger stud of birds will be the end result.

Without putting a great strain on the breeding capabilities of the mutant, as many young as possible must be produced in case the bird is lost. If the bird is a cock, and the nature of the species will allow, it could be paired to several hens over its breeding life so as to provide a selection of less related stock. It would be reasonably safe to pair half brothers to half sisters, or even to pair nieces and nephews to uncles and aunts. Detailed records of pairings and their results must be kept for future reference, and close ringing employed to identify specimens, if - and only if - the habits and strength of the species will allow this without causing desertion by the parents, or future damage to legs and feet.

Reliable Foster Pairs could be set up to help incubate eggs and raise young to increase production. If the mutant is a hen, it must not be induced to lay in a manner and at a rate which would cause it damage; for example, continued induced laying can ultimately cause prolapse of the oviduct or death through soft shelled eggs breaking inside the hen. Three clutches per breeding season are quite sufficient for the smaller species and two for the larger species. There should be a few weeks rest between each clutch.

Foster parents need not be of the same species or - in some cases - even of the same genus. Grass Parrakeets will raise each others young (Turquoisines, Splendids, etc.) and Eye-ring and Peach-faced Lovebirds will bring up each others nestlings. The hatchlings of Rosellas can be interchanged (Easterns, Pennant's, Stanleys, etc.) and Red-rumpeds will raise parrakeets much larger than themselves. Kakarikis have been used successfully to incubate and raise unrelated species, young Conures of various types can be interchanged, Pionus Parrots have been used to rear Amazons, even Cockatiels have been persuaded to foster Parrakeets on a few occasions - and so it goes on. Artificial incubation and hand rearing can also be used in emergencies.

Discovering the Type of Inheritance of New Mutants
If a new Autosomal Dominant variety appears within an aviary strain, then it must be assumed that the mutant gene has been created at parental meiosis; when paired to a normal, a mutant which is Dominant can itself produce at least some specimens showing features of the variety - and these may be of either sex.

If a new Sex-linked Recessive variety appears within an aviary strain, the visual mutant can only be a hen and it is most likely that the mutation has been created at the parental meiosis of its father or grandfather - in both instances along the male line. It is unlikely to have been carried down several generations without showing itself, because a proportion of a split cock's daughters must show the mutation in visual form. It would be possible for a Sex-linked Recessive to be created at the parental meiosis of the visual mutant.

If a new Autosomal Recessive appears within an aviary strain, the possibility of creation at meiosis is extremely remote. For a visual Recessive to be bred, both parents must be split for the variety. In this case, it is practically certain that the parent birds both share a common ancestry (paternal or maternal lines) and have inherited the gene in a split form which may have been travelling down many generations before being able to show itself. Here, the likelihood of the mutant appearing in visual form increases in ratio with the closeness in blood relationship of the breeding pair.

If a Sex-linked Dominant variety were ever to appear within an aviary strain (as far as is known none exist), it must be assumed that the mutant gene would be created at parental meiosis.

The initial detective work as to the possible pattern of inheritance of a new mutation should take the previous examples into account. If its parents can be proved to have come from totally unrelated sources, then an *Autosomal Recessive variety* would be extremely unlikely; the chances for two splits of the same new mutation to meet and produce a visual mutant after evolving along parallel unrelated strains must be non-existent.

Determination of the sex of the mutant will help very little in providing clues without other information being available; if it is a hen, any type of inheritance is possible, but if it proves to be a cock, *Sex-linked Recessive* is ruled out.

Breeding results, when the mutant itself is paired to a Normal will give further indication:

Should the mutant be a cock: if some of its young are of its own colour, *Autosomal Recessive* is ruled out but not *Autosomal Dominant;* if the mutant young prove to be of both sexes, *Sex-linked Recessive* is ruled out but not *Autosomal Dominant;* if only hens of the new colour are produced, chances are that the mutation is *Sex-linked Recessive* - and the prospect of this is increased with the number of nests raised which produce only hen mutants.

Should the mutant be a hen and paired to a Normal cock: if any young of the mutant colour are produced, *Autosomal Recessive* and *Sex-linked Recessive* can be ruled out, and chances are that an *Autosomal Dominant* mutation is involved - if only cocks of the new colour are continually produced a suspicion exists that the first known *Sex-linked Dominant* psittacine may have arisen.

As an indication as to which birds can be sold off in reasonable safety where space is limited: if the mutation is proved to be *Sex-linked Recessive,* the Normal hens produced cannot be split and can be sold; if proved to be an *Autosomal Recessive,* any of the Normal birds from this first pairing will be split and must be kept; if proved to be straightforward *Autosomal Dominant* (or *Sex-linked Dominant*) none of the Normal birds can be split for the variety, and can be sold.

Discovering the Source of Known Established Varieties

When unexpected and established known colour varieties crop up amongst the young of apparently Normal parents: if young of an *Autosomal Recessive* type appear, both parents *must* be split for the variety; if young of a *Sex-linked Recessive* type appear, these will be hens and the parent cock *must* be split for the colour variety; where young of a combination of *two Autosomal Recessives* pop up, both parents *must* be split for both varieties.

Should youngsters of a combination of *two Sex-linked Recessives* be produced, these will be hens and the parent cock must be split for *both* varieties. If young of a combination of an *Autosomal Recessive* and a *Sex-linked Recessive* appear, these will be hens, *both* parents must be split for the *Autosomal Recessive* type and the cock will be split for the *Sex-linked Recessive.*

With the exception of some recorded occurrences with Dominant Pied varieties, it is not possible for a young *Dominant* type to appear unless at least one of the parents exhibits the features of the variety to some degree.

Inbreeding and Line-breeding

No two writers on bird breeding seem to provide the same definitions of *inbreeding* and *line-breeding*, both of which describe ways of breeding selectively with related birds in order to 'fix' certain desirable characteristics. These characteristics may not relate solely to colour, but to size, shape, stamina, fertility, resistance to disease, prolific nature, intelligence, and so on. Reasons have already been given for avoiding inbreeding during the establishing of a new mutant variety, and a warning must again be given that – without the skill and knowledge that comes with experience – close inbreeding and line-breeding can be hazardous.

Desirable traits are obvious from their appearance and usually of Dominant inheritance, but unwanted Recessive traits may be lurking beneath the surface and these can be reinforced by inbreeding. Such characteristics might include stunted growth, susceptibility to certain diseases, feather problems, lack of parental instinct, production of malformed eggs, infertility, etc.; *good* features can be magnified, but so can *bad* features.

Inbreeding is generally accepted as meaning the pairing together of closely related individuals such as brother and sister, mother and son, or father and daughter. Line-breeding is sometimes described as controlled breeding with more distantly related specimens such as nephew to aunt, uncle to niece, cousin to cousin and further and further distantly related stock. It is true that long established specialist breeders find a stock of distantly related birds – carefully built up over many years – produces more consistent results and shows a greater degree of compatibility than does a hotchpotch of totally unrelated specimens which has a greater genetic diversity. Yet, most psittacine breeders purchasing stock with which to found a new strain always seek out totally unrelated birds, and are generally advised to do so by the most experienced aviculturists.

In some large well planned stocks which are advanced in their domestication, there may be several separate *lines* of more closely related strains, and this method of production illustrates another definition of line-breeding. This type of breeding involves *backcrossing* of progeny to parents in a strict regime which completely ignores all the taboos about inbreeding. At the head of the line the original *key bird* is the most outstanding and perfect cock bird available, and he is paired to an equally outstanding hen. From amongst this pair's young is selected a hen of better quality than her mother and the key bird is then paired to this – his daughter.

If possible, from amongst their young is selected an even better hen and the key bird is then paired to his grand daughter. So it goes, on down the *line* of generations until finally a cock is produced which is better than its father; to this is paired the best hen available from stock (usually slightly related), and the process is repeated with another line. Due to the physical strains of egg production, hens have a shorter breeding life than cocks, hence a cock being chosen as key bird.

When this method works according to plan, the birds begin to look like clones, peas in a pod. Where several controlled strains of close relatives exist within a stock of slightly related specimens, superior individuals can be taken from one strain and paired with the superior birds from another – so providing the first key bird and its partner to head *another* strain. This system produces its own *outcrosses* which need be only distantly related. Long term pedigree breeding projects lead to strains of birds in which each individual carries the *stamp* of those characteristics most favoured by their master breeder.

The master breeder is always looking for that rare specimen which has *prepotence*; it is possessed of numerous superior characteristics and whichever way it is paired, its young always seem to inherit these sought after characteristics because they are Dominant in their inheritance.

Smaller species of psittacine lend themselves to such methods of reproduction far more than do the larger species; degeneration through inbreeding has found to be far more likely in the latter.

191

KEY BIRD   MOTHER   KEY BIRD   MOTHER

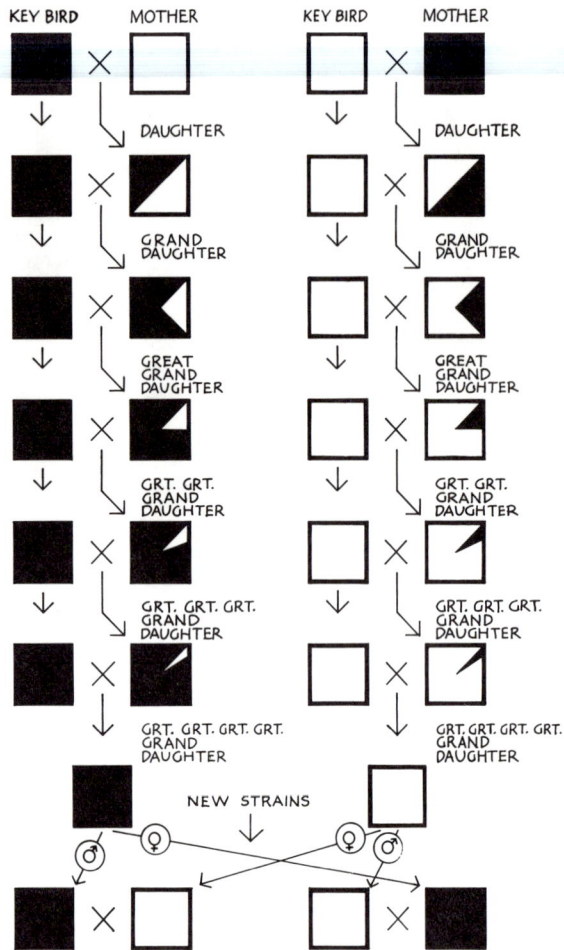

Continued linebreeding between parent and progeny.

DAUGHTER

GRAND DAUGHTER

GREAT GRAND DAUGHTER

GRT. GRT. GRAND DAUGHTER

GRT. GRT. GRT. GRAND DAUGHTER

GRT. GRT. GRT. GRT. GRAND DAUGHTER

NEW STRAINS

Building a strain which provides birds sharing family characteristics.

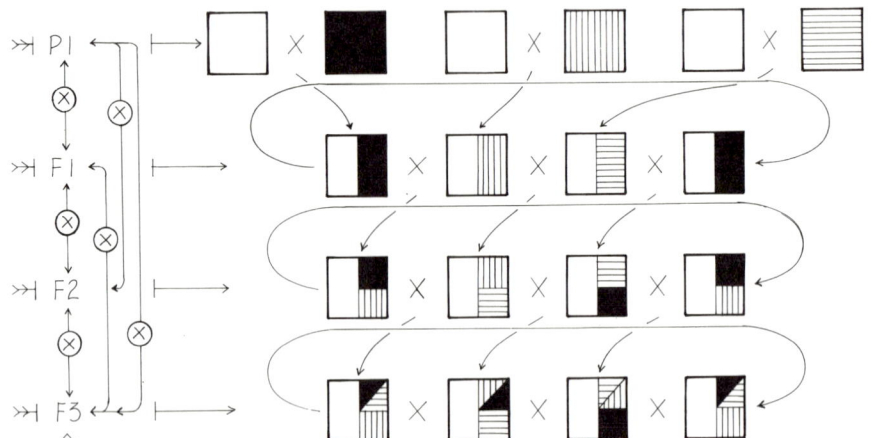

Numerous genetic permutations are provided with planned pairings between P1, F1, F2 and F3 generations.

Diagram 20: Line-breeding

10

USING the INHERITANCE CODES

METHOD of ALTERING the UNIVERSAL BREEDING PROGRAMMES

IN THIS MANUAL, the inheritance of each variety (factor) is denoted by (AR) for Autosomal Recessive, (SLR) for Sex-linked Recessive, (AID) for Autosomal Incomplete Dominant, (ACD) for Autosomal Complete Dominant, and (S) for Selective Breeding. The Inheritance Code that identifies each factor which makes up a combination or compound variety, follows the name and any further clarification of that variety – e.g. (SLR+AR), (SLR+ACD+AR), etc..

Within a specified pattern of inheritance or combination and compound Breeding Programme, new primary varieties of those species listed (or even new primary varieties of species not shown) can be exchanged with examples sharing the same type of inheritance. This makes the Breeding Programmes contained in this book *truly* Universal.

As far as can be envisaged, the patterns of inheritance of the psittacines identified herein can be applied to any new primary variety which might occur in the future. Where an exact parallel cannot be found in phenotype and genotype – or even just genotype – the Universal Breeding Programmes can be modified to accommodate the new variety. To do this complete the following instructions:

(a) Check through the Index of **Universal Breeding Programme Inheritance Codes for Combination & Compound Varieties** to find one which includes the mix of inheritance types you require.
(b) Turn to the most suitable of the Universal Breeding Programmes which the Code represents.
(c) Presuming it is necessary to alter only *one* of the primary varieties in the programme; select the *existing* primary variety which represents the inheritance type of the *new* primary variety, and exchange the *existing* for the *new* throughout the programme.

More than one new primary variety can be inserted into a Universal Breeding Programme in this way. In fact a whole string of primary varieties in a programme can be replaced with primary varieties of totally different colour effects – provided they are slotted into the correct inheritance type positions throughout that programme.

For example: with a combination which has an Inheritance Code of (SLR+AID+AR), *any* Sex-linked Recessive variety of *any* species could replace the variety shown in the actual Breeding Programme, *any* Autosomal Incomplete Dominant could replace the existing example, and likewise *any* Autosomal Recessive variety could replace *its* equivalent inheritance type. Of course, it may be necessary to rearrange the names which result; e.g. in the case of programmes containing the Ino factor.

When two primary varieties included in the *same* Breeding Programme are to be replaced, but also share the *same* type of inheritance, extra care is needed in mapping out their individual routes throughout the programme so as to prevent errors. Another provision to be allowed for is the modification required in the unlikely event of any of the interacting varieties being allelomorphic.

Can be Used with non-Psittacine Species

There is no reason why the above method of using the Inheritance Codes to insert new primary varieties into the patterns of inheritance and Breeding Programmes should not also be applied to Budgerigars and even non-psittacine species such as: *Canaries, Zebra Finches, Bengalese, Gouldians, Parrot Finches, all other Grass Finches, Diamond Doves, Pigeons, Quail, Waterfowl, British Finches and Softbills, and even Game birds, Bantams and larger Poultry – in fact, any avian species which has – or develops – a selection of primary colour varieties.*

For example: a programme which shows how to breed *Cinnamon Dilute (Recessive) Marine Peach-faced Lovebirds* can be changed to one which shows how to breed *Opaline Clearwing Skyblue Budgerigars:*

sample pairing:

Cinnamon Green cock x Dilute Marine hen

Green cocks/Cinnamon+Dilute+Marine, & Cinnamon Green hens/Dilute+Marine.

changes to:

Opaline Light Green cock x Clearwing Skyblue hen

Light Green cocks/Opaline+Clearwing+Blue, & Opaline Light Green hens/Clearwing+Blue.

Another showing how to produce *Dilute Rosa Bourke's Grass Parrakeets* can illustrate how to produce *Recessive Dilute Fawn Zebra Finches;* a programme for breeding *Albino Princess of Wales Parrakeets* can be modified to one which shows how to breed *White-breasted Blue-backed Gouldian Finches:*

sample pairing:

Green/Ino+Blue x Green/Ino+Blue

Albinos, Lutinos/Blue, Lutinos, Blues/Ino, Greens/Ino+Blue, Greens/Ino, Blues, Greens/Blue, & Greens.

changes to:

Normal/White-breasted+Blue-backed x Normal/White-breasted+Blue-backed

White-breasted Blue-backeds, White-breasted Normals/Blue-backed, White-breasted Normals, Blue-backeds/White-breasted, Normals/White-breasted+Blue-backed, Normals/White-breasted, Blue-backeds, Normals/Blue-backed, & Normals.

(As can now be seen, where Lutino and Albino occur, names need rearrangement.)

With this manual, the bird breeder has to hand a vast array of Combination and Compound Breeding Programmes which can be modified for use with practically *any* species within aviculture.

194

11

INDICES

USING THE INDICES to find Universal Breeding Programmes for Combination & Compound Varieties:

*1. Check in **section 6, Glossary of Equivalent Names of Varieties**, to confirm that the names used are correct.*

*2. When searching for species first, followed by variety, check the Index for **section 5, Known Primary Varieties (this index also includes the Combination & Compound Varieties from** section 8).*

*3. When searching for variety first, check the Index for **section 8, Universal Breeding Programmes for Combination & Compound Varieties.***

INDICES of SECTIONS

UNIVERSAL BREEDING PROGRAMME INHERITANCE CODES for COMBINATION & COMPOUND VARIETIES

DIAGRAMS

Index

1
COLOUR in PARROTS

Index

2
MUTATED COLOUR

Index

3
RELEVANT GENETIC THEORY

Index

4
PATTERNS of INHERITANCE

Index

5
KNOWN PRIMARY VARIETIES

Index
(Species & Primary Varieties; also Combination & Compound Varieties from *section 8*.)

Lineolated Parrakeet (Bolborhynchus lineola) 57

Primary Varieties

Combination Varieties

Masked Lovebird (Agapornis personata) 57

Primary Varieties

Combination & Compound Varieties

Nyasa Lovebird (Agapornis lilianae) 57

Primary Variety

Peach-faced Lovebird (Agapornis roseicollis) 58

Primary Varieties

Combination & Compound Varieties

6
GLOSSARY of EQUIVALENT NAMES of VARIETIES

No Index

7
INHERITANCE of KNOWN PRIMARY VARIETIES

Index

8
UNIVERSAL BREEDING PROGRAMMES for COMBINATION & COMPOUND VARIETIES

Index

Note: *all programmes relating to combination and compound varieties which contain two Sex-linked Factors (SLR+SLR) are subject to the Crossover Theory, but this does not need to be considered where percentages of young are not quoted - as with these Universal Breeding Programmes.*

9
TECHNIQUES & DETECTIVE WORK

Index

10
USING the INHERITANCE CODES

Index

UNIVERSAL BREEDING PROGRAMME INHERITANCE CODES for COMBINATION & COMPOUND VARIETIES

Index

Note: *all programmes relating to combination and compound varieties which contain two Sex-linked Factors (SLR+SLR) are subject to the Crossover Theory, but this does not need to be considered where percentages of young are not quoted - as with these Universal Breeding Programmes.*

READER'S NOTES

Subject	Reference	Page No